The English Musical Renaissance and the Press
1850–1914: Watchmen of Music

For My Mother

# The English Musical Renaissance and the Press 1850–1914: Watchmen of Music

MEIRION HUGHES

**Ashgate**

Published by
Ashgate Publishing Limited
Gower House
Croft Road
Aldershot
Hants GU11 3HR
England

Ashgate Publishing Company
131 Main Street
Burlington
Vermont, 05401–5600
USA

Ashgate website: http://www.ashgate.com

British Library Cataloguing in Publication Data

Hughes, Meirion, 1949–
The English Musical Renaissance and the Press 1850–1914: Watchmen of Music
(Music in Nineteenth-Century Britain)
  1. Mass media—England—History.  2. Music—England—19th century.  3. Music—England—20th century. I. Title.
  780.9'42'09034

US Library of Congress Cataloging in Publication Data

Hughes, Meirion, 1949–
  The English Musical Renaissance and the Press 1850–1914: Watchmen of Music /
  Meirion Hughes.
     p.  cm. (Music in Nineteenth-Century Britain)
  Originally presented as the author's thesis (Ph.D., University of Wales, 1998) under
  the title: The Watchmen of Music: The Reception of English Music in the Press,
  1850–1914.
  Includes bibliographical references.
  1. Musical criticism—England —History—19th century.  2. Musical criticism—
  England —History—20th century.  3. Music critics—England.  4. Music—
  England—19th century—History and criticism.  I. Title: Watchmen of Music.
  II. Series.
  ML3880.H84 2002
  070.4'4978'094209034–dc21                                              2001046138

ISBN 0 7546 0588 4

This book is printed on acid free paper.

Typeset in Sabon by Manton Typesetters, Louth, Lincolnshire, UK and printed in Great Britain by MPG Books Ltd, Bodmin, Cornwall.

# Contents

# Acknowledgements

My thanks first go to Susan, mate and muse, for her love and for all our days on the high hill of summer. My thanks also to Professor Rob Stradling, friend and mentor, for his brotherly encouragement and support over the years.

A number of fellow-scholars and librarians have assisted me in the preparation of this book. I am particularly grateful to Professor Cyril Ehrlich (Goldsmith's College, University of London) and Dr Bennett Zon (University of Durham) for their boundless enthusiasm for the watchmen. At the Royal College of Music, I thank Dr Peter Horton and the library staff, while Paul Collen and Oliver Davies, curators of the Department of Portraits and Performance History, deserve special mention for their help with the illustrations. I also thank Rachel Lynch and Kirsten Weissenberg at Ashgate for the efficient and good-humoured way in which the watchmen have finally been put to bed.

Several friends and colleagues have given their backing to this project and my gratitude goes to them: Liz Bird, for her myriad insights; Ben Martin-Hoogewerf, for his life-enhancing wit and our countless convivial evenings; Margaret Rutherford and Byron Williams, for enabling me to combine full-time teaching and research; and Walter Storey, for being ever the kind physician.

Last, but not least, I would like to thank my son, Tom, and my family for their love and patient commitment to my work. This book is dedicated to my mother who first brought music into my life.

# List of Illustrations

# General Editor's Preface

There are few scholars who can write with such authority on the English Musical Renaissance as Meirion Hughes. This book takes up, in essence, where Hughes and Stradling's *The English Musical Renaissance 1840–1940* (1993/2001) left off. It does so by expanding on the nature of the musical press and its influence on the Renaissance during the later-nineteenth and early-twentieth, centuries. The title of Hughes' book is, of course, indicative of this focus, but it is only in the colourful subtitle, 'watchmen of music', that the author hints at his approach to reception history.

Indeed, it is subtitle of the book which effectively gives this study its shape for Hughes divides his history in two: the watchmen and their towers (critics and publications); and the watched (composers). This division not only informs the structure of Hughes' book, but also provides the framework of his methodology. Implicit in his subtitle is the acknowledgement that any musicological text is simultaneously 'the watchman' and 'the watched'. Hughes stresses the absence of objectivity in the watchmen he studies; as he says, their work was rarely value-free.

Like the watchmen of his book, Hughes speaks his own mind. He embraces the inability of musicological language to express a de-politicised discourse and invests his writing with frequently controversial ideas. At the same time, he is himself aware of the need for circumspection and grounds his ideas in an extensive bibliographical and historical erudition. The result is a work of impressive scope and import yet of concentrated detail. His reading of the press provides musicologists with an extended discussions of the nineteenth and early twentieth-century musical press which encompasses the full breadth of bibliographical diversity. His work on Sullivan, Parry and Elgar reveals the differing relationships between individual composers and the press, specifically: Sullivan's failure to convince critics of his artistic integrity; the watchmen's construction of Parry's Englishness; and Elgar's productive affinity for the press. In each instance Hughes deftly untangles the myriad relationships and connections of the time while managing to portray the watched and the watchmen as individuals. This is a study which goes to the heart of nineteenth-century British music studies.

Bennett Zon
*University of Durham 2002*

# Glossary of Acronymns and Abbreviations

| | |
|---|---|
| *Ath* | The *Athenaeum* |
| BL | British Library |
| *DTel* | The *Daily Telegraph* |
| HWRO | Hereford and Worcester Record Office, Worcester |
| *MR* | The *Monthly Musical Record* |
| *MP* | The *Morning Post* |
| *MT* | The *Musical Times* |
| *MW* | The *Musical World* |
| Oxf. Bod. | Bodleian Library, Oxford |
| RAM | The Royal Academy of Music |
| RCM | The Royal College of Music |
| *T* | *The Times* |

Meirion Hughes, a freelance historian, co-authored with R. A. Stradling *The English Musical Renaissance 1860–1940: Construction and Deconstruction* (1993), a volume which appeared in a revised edition as *The English Musical Renaissance 1840–1940: Constructing a National Music* (MUP 2001). He contributed essays on Elgar to *Music and the Politics of Culture* (1989), on Rossini to *Conflict and Coexistence* (1997), and has written and presented several broadcasts for BBC Radio 3. He is currently working on a new edition of Liszt's *Life of Chopin*.

# Introduction

> Those whose duty it is to stand like watchmen on the walls of
> music, have special advantages for noting the pace and manner of
> approach in those who would fain to enter the citadel.[1]

Thus did John A. Fuller Maitland, music critic, acknowledge the power
of music journalism. Although scholars have long accepted the importance of nineteenth century writing about culture, Art-Music (hereafter
music) criticism has attracted relatively little attention. Victorian music
criticism in particular has been an area of scholarly neglect. The only
music critic of this era with a major profile in our own time is the
*playwright*, George Bernard Shaw. Yet the sheer quantity of music
journalism in the Victorian and Edwardian press was vast, with much
of it displaying a richness and diversity of critical perspectives. The aim
of this book is to examine the reception history of new English music in
the Victorian and Edwardian press and to attempt an assessment of its
cultural and political importance.

This study will argue that the revival of English music in the second
half of the nineteenth century could not have taken place without the
support of journalists. It will argue that it was no accident that the
'renaissance' in national music occurred at that same time when the
press experienced unprecedented expansion. It will also analyse the
processes by which the majority of music writers and critics supported
and projected the cause of English music.

The phrase, 'watchmen on the walls of music', cited above, was first
coined by Fuller Maitland to describe the role of the critic. Although he
did not expand the idea into a fully-fledged metaphor, in this study I
have extended it to provide a powerful trope for the crucial role that
music journalists played in creating an 'English Musical Renaissance'.
The 'renaissance' construct was itself invented by one of the most
eminent music journalists of the day, Joseph Bennett, chief critic of the
*Daily Telegraph*.[2] Throughout the book the term 'English', rather than
'British', music is preferred because the Victorians and Edwardians
tended not to use the 'British' adjective in cultural matters and the
watchmen themselves almost never used the term 'British music'.

---

[1] Fuller Maitland, *Musician's Pilgrimage*, p. x. The short title reference system is
followed throughout this volume. Appendix A provides summaries of the biographical
and career details of many music critics of the period, including all those featured in this
study.

[2] *DTel* 4 Sept. 1882. See also Chapter 2 below.

In the promotion and projection of English music, the critics self-consciously followed their German contemporaries. Carl Maria von Weber (1786–1826) was among the first to grasp the power and potential of music criticism. As early as 1810, Weber had founded the *Harmonischer Verein*, a society of musicians and literary men committed to 'the elevation of musical criticism by musicians themselves', a goal which Weber consistently pursued in his music journalism.[3] Where Weber led, so Robert Schumann (1810–56) followed; most importantly with *die Neue Zeitschrift für Musik* (founded 1834), a radical journal which challenged the musical status quo by exploiting the power of the critic-journalist. *Die Neue Zeitschrift* changed music journalism as both radicals and conservatives in Germany began to grapple with the weapon which Schumann had forged. Several key figures of the Romantic movement in music were critics as well as composers; most notably Wagner, Berlioz and Liszt, all of whom used journalism to promote their musical ideologies. It should be remembered that both Schumann and Wagner were themselves involved in the revolutionary upheavals of 1848 in Germany, because they viewed music as a means to social, political and cultural transformation.[4]

By the 1850s, several convergent elements were working to transform the place of music journalism in British national life. These factors were: the changing perspectives on high culture and the place of music within that culture; the rapid transformation in the role of the national press and the concomitant rise in the socio-cultural status of journalists; and an intensifying climate of self-confident patriotism and pride.

Victorians by the mid-nineteenth century viewed culture in a more positive light. It was no longer something which was the preserve of an aristocratic elite, but a force which could benefit society as a whole. Thomas Carlyle, the 'voice and conscience' of the 1840s generation, led the way in elevating the artist as a worthy hero for a society which he felt was in desperate need of moral and spiritual regeneration.[5] Carlyle, with his enthusiasm for German Romanticism, emphasised the beneficial effects of the arts, philosophy and the study of history in creating a 'healthy society' which was both just and stable.[6] John Ruskin, a disci-

---

[3] Weber, q. in Spitta, entry on 'Carl Maria von Weber' in *Grove 1*, vol. iv pp. 387–429. I have adopted this abbreviation for ease of reference to the successive editions of *Grove's Dictionary of Music and Musicians*.

[4] Composers were made and unmade by the power of the critics, the conservative Rossini being one of the first victims of the new music journalism. See Hughes, 'Lucifer of Music'.

[5] Le Quesne, 'Carlyle', p. 35.

[6] Ibid., pp. 16–17.

ple of Carlyle, added his voice to the debate about the nature and importance of culture by stressing the seriousness and the relevance of art for a society dominated by the 'philistinism' of its educated classes. Ruskin held that the appreciation of art was a 'moral and religious act' and that the role of the critic was to strengthen the intellectual and spiritual mainsprings of society by spreading the gospel of good art.[7] The notion that art and the 'cultural critic' were at the heart of things was reinforced by Matthew Arnold, in his *Essays in Criticism* (1865) and *Culture and Anarchy* (1869), in which he argued that the English middle-classes had a 'bad civilisation' that was so parochial, complacent and materialistic, that it was detrimental to the social stability of Britain.[8] Although neither Carlyle, Ruskin nor Arnold regarded music as a co-equal with the other arts, they nevertheless contributed to a profound shift in attitudes which had the effect of enhancing the place and value of music in the cultural life of the nation. All three, too, can be seen as transforming the status of cultural criticism itself to the extent that the 'Critic' mutated into a priest-like figure whose primary role was to connect the masses with the godhead of art.

Within this broad re-assessment of the role and importance of culture, the revival of English music, the first stirrings of what later became known as the Musical Renaissance, can be detected around the mid-century. One reason was that, alongside the other arts, music was increasingly seen as having a social role, in helping to 'improve' the masses and assist in stabilising a society in the throes of industrial change. Some contemporary commentators went further and hoped that music would perform a quasi-political function, in helping to bind the nation closer together especially after the Chartist upheavals of the 1840s. Alongside these socio-political factors there was a more personal and charismatic element at work – the sensational success of Mendelssohn in England in the late-1830s and 1840s. After all, had not Prince Albert himself, on the occasion of the premiere of *Elijah* at the Birmingham Festival of 1846, hailed Mendelssohn as the 'Elijah of the New Music' (*der Elias der neuen Kunst*) and prophet of the new romantic style?

Mendelssohn was, for many middle-class Victorians, an irresistible composer-hero. Rich and attractive, his Jewishness was made acceptable by his conversion to Christianity and the patronage of the young queen and her prince consort. Mendelssohn's popularity in England rested on the impact of his two oratorios, *St Paul* and *Elijah*, works that transformed contemporary music in England. Thereby the oratorio form,

[7] Landow, 'Ruskin' p. 116.
[8] Collini, 'Arnold', p. 285.

which for generations had drawn heavily on the Handel-Haydn repertoire, gained a new lease of life in England, nurtured by the conventional
piety and innate conservatism of the choral festival circuit. It was no
coincidence that the years of Mendelssohn's personal success in England
also witnessed the first flowering of the musical press.[9]

The press in the nineteenth century was the single most important
medium for the communication of ideas. Yet in 1850 there were still
only five national daily newspapers, four of which had been founded in
the previous century. These were the *Morning Chronicle*, *Morning Post*,
*Morning Herald*, *The Times* and the *Daily News*, the last having been
established in 1846. All five were priced at either 4d or 5d and could
only be afforded by middle and upper class readers. In 1855, this
situation changed dramatically when the Newspaper Act liberalised the
market for newspapers and initiated a news and information revolution. Before the decade was out, three new national dailies had been
established all priced at an unprecedented 1d. These were the *Morning
Star*, the *Morning News* and, most importantly in terms of its eventual
market domination, the *Daily Telegraph*. By 1859, the newspaper had
become a symbol of civilisation, a 'mighty Mind-Engine', a 'Giant
which now awes potentates', and a social force which wielded 'tremendous moral power'.[10] The advent of this 'penny press' led to an 'eruption
of newspapers' which was to characterise the remainder of the century.[11]

The condition and status of professional journalists was also changing by the 1850s. The literary and gentlemanly amateurism of an earlier
age had already given way to a more professional approach. This
process was assisted by the pioneering reports of *The Times* correspondent, William Howard Russell, from the Crimean War, which did
much to secure an enhanced importance and a new glamorous image
for journalists.

By 1850, music criticism had established a secure place in journalistic
culture. All the national newspapers covered important musical events
as a matter of course. As the newspaper market spectacularly expanded
after 1855, so too did the sheer quantity of music criticism. The coverage of music in the literary journals was however patchy, with the
*Athenaeum* being for many years the only publication of its type with a

---

[9] For a fuller discussion of Mendelssohn's impact on English music and its Renaissance, see Hughes and Stradling, *The English Musical Renaissance 1840–1940:
Constructing a National Music*, pp. 8–19.

[10] Andrews, *The History of British Journalism* (1859), q. in Lee, *The Origins of the
Popular Press in England*, p. 21.

[11] Williams, *English Newspaper*, p. 61.

regular music column.[12] Furthermore, by 1850, a viable music press as such had been established, with the foundation of two important journals, the *Musical World* (in 1836) and the *Musical Times* (in 1844).[13]

The taste of the public and that of the music journalists were basically convergent in the 1850s. Critics and consumers alike were largely agreed that the classical romanticism epitomised by Mendelssohn was a suitable tradition with which to move into the future. This was, in the context of the changes already happening on the continent, a conservative agenda which represented a comfortable blend of the past with what was deemed to be the best of the present. Complaisantly, the Victorian music public accepted that England was a 'land without music' and was content to educate itself in the Mendelssohnian spirit. The critics of the mid-century were anxious to divert public taste away from Schumann and the politico-artistic agenda of Wagner, and it was many years before 'progressive' German music made an impact in England. Mendelssohn-worship long held sway, so that even in 1889, George Bernard Shaw, an arch-Wagnerian, who was a music critic before he became a playwright, still felt the need to attack Mendelssohn for 'his kid glove gentility, his conventional sentimentality, and his despicable oratorio mongering'.[14]

Another element that tended to assist the development of music was the rising tide of national self-confidence and pride. This trend was especially marked in the period after the huge success of the Great Exhibition of 1851. Within the context of Victorian nationalism, many felt that England should be able to compete with other nations in all things. Music too became a site of nationalist struggle, most especially with a newly-unified Germany, which was keen to stress its 'great power' status in the musical world. In short, in the years after 1850, and particularly after 1870, music was increasingly regarded as an integral part of nationhood and of a viable national identity. There were many watchmen who were not prepared to accept that England was a minor power in music, still less a 'land without music'. The convergence of several disparate elements: the changing value accorded to music; the cult of the critic within the expanded importance of the press; and the climate of patriotism and international competition – all worked to ensure that the relationship between English composers and critics had an influential dynamic in the second half of the nineteenth century.

The watchmen, almost without exception, vigorously supported the idea of promoting and projecting English music throughout the period

---

[12] See Chapter 3 below.
[13] See Chapter 4 below.
[14] Shaw, The *Star*, 23 Feb. 1889.

surveyed. By the 1850s European music had already entered a period of turmoil which was characterised by clashing ideologies: conservatives versus 'progressives'; 'pure' (or 'abstract') music versus programme-music; the defenders of 'melody' versus those who advocated advanced Wagnerian harmonic techniques. The majority of English music critics found this internecine bitterness profoundly troubling and unhelpful, serving not only to encourage the enemies of music at home, but also to alienate a public whose musical education had left it ill-equipped to cope with controversy. Yet, over time, there appeared a small but increasing number of English critics who were prepared to espouse the 'progressive' in continental music, and were willing to promote the new in their columns. Music criticism thereby became a site of struggle for England's musical future.

One outcome of the watchmen's determination that native composers should strive for the greater glory of the national music was that a parallel set of quests became characteristic of the music reception of the period. The search for a 'great' English oratorio composer was already evident in the 1850s as the watchmen avidly sought an English 'Mendelssohn'. In parallel there was a quest for an English operatic masterpiece which would provide the foundation for a national school of opera production, an 'English Freischütz' no less. After all, Weber, Verdi and Wagner had illustrated how important and powerful a weapon opera could be in inspiring patriotism and forging national unity and cultural identity.[15] The failure to construct a national opera tradition was a source of unending frustration and disappointment to the watchmen in the decades after 1850. Last, but by no means least, a quest for a great English symphony, the highest prize of abstract music, characterised the period from 1860 onwards.

Critics promoted composers for a number of reasons apart from musical patriotism. Some had a genuine liking for a composer's work or celebrated a personal link or friendship in their notices. Musical 'ideology' too played its part, as with the controversies surrounding Wagner's *Zukunftsmusik* ('music of the future') and its impact on English music. Several critics also supported composers in the hope of gain: money, expensive knick-knacks (cuff-links, tie-pins), hospitality, libretto commissions, all were traded from time to time. Conversely, critics savaged composers in their columns for personal and ideological reasons. Yet despite the complexity of the critic-composer relationship, there was an almost unanimous desire amongst the watchmen for English music to

---

[15] See Hughes, 'Lucifer of Music' for a discussion on Rossini, Wagner and German music nationalism.

prosper. If the project itself was rarely in question, the nature and direction of the nation's musical destiny was much disputed.

Without anticipating the arguments set out below, it might be useful to point to the generational shifts which characterised the press reception of English music in the publications selected over the period surveyed. In 1850, a generation of conservative critics and editors was already in place which wanted English music to develop along Mendelssohnian lines. The leading lights among them were: Henry Chorley (*Athenaeum*), James W. Davison (*The Times* and *Musical World*), Charles Gruneisen (*Morning Post* and later *Athenaeum*), Campbell Clarke (*Daily Telegraph*) and Alfred J. Novello (*Musical Times*). As old age and death took their toll in the 1870s, this group was followed by a second generation of Mendelssohn conservatives who were by and large prepared to accept the music of Schumann. This cohort, which included Henry Lunn (*Musical Times*), Joseph Bennett (*Daily Telegraph*), William A. Barrett (*Morning Post* and *Musical Times*), was united by its fear and loathing of Wagner and the impact of his 'music of the future' in England. It was only around 1880, with the arrival of Francis Hueffer at *The Times*, that other more 'progressive' voices began to be heard among the watchmen. Hueffer was the first of a younger generation of critics who embraced Wagner and urged English composers to look to developments on the continent for inspiration. This third generation of critics later came to include G. B. Shaw (the *World* and various other papers), Ebenezer Prout (*Athenaeum*), and Arthur Johnstone (*Manchester Guardian*). There were naturally a number of critics, most notably Frederick G. Edwards of the *Musical Times*, whose musical affiliations are not so neatly categorised and whose careers straddle this (oversimplified) generational pattern.

It is hoped that this study will take forward the reception history of English music of this period in several respects. It will attempt to bring some of the most influential critics out of the shadows and place them and their writings in the context of the publications for which they wrote. It will re-assess and re-evaluate the importance of music criticism in British cultural history, and most especially in the construction of what came to be called the English Musical Renaissance. This book will, above all, explore aspects of the symbiotic relationship between the watchmen and the English composers which they promoted (and rebuffed) in their columns. Finally, the book will seek to show how the watchmen sought to give leadership both in terms of the formation of composers' reputations and in moulding the taste of the musical public.

In terms of the reception history of new English music, this study concentrates on four publications and their respective critics. They are: *The Times*, as the most powerful paper of the age; the *Daily Telegraph*, as the most commercially successful and widely-read newspaper; the *Athenaeum*, for its position as the most eminent literary-cultural journal; and the *Musical Times*, as the leading music periodical. By piecing together evidence from contemporary (or near-contemporary) biographies, autobiographies, obituary-notices and archival material, it has been possible to identify most (if not all) of the critics who worked for the publications chosen. In Part One, 'Watchmen and Watchtowers', the emphasis will fall on the critics themselves set in the context of the publications for which they wrote. In Part Two, 'Watched', the stress will be on the relationship between key English composers and the music press. The research phase of the book identified three composers who were of particular importance to the watchmen: Arthur Sullivan, Hubert Parry and Edward Elgar. The choice of these three arose out of reading the source material and was not pre-imposed. In terms of sources, Part One will draw mainly on the four publications named above, while Part Two will call upon a wider range of material. The influence of aesthetic and philosophical movements on English music criticism is not investigated.

By its very nature reception history relies primarily on contemporary printed reviews which make up the core of original material. This study concentrates on such reviews, with respect to a range of composers, the selection of whom has been determined by the watchmen. If a composer was important to the critics, then he has found his way into the survey. Similarly, within a composer's oeuvre, if a contemporary source (or sources) held a composition important, then its reception history is examined in terms of the publications selected. Clearly the choice of works cannot be either definitive or exhaustive, but it is hoped that from an analysis of the reception history of approximately 150 individual compositions, some general conclusions can be drawn about the projection and promotion of English music at the hands of the critics. Throughout the emphasis is to allow the watchmen to speak for themselves, their notices being foregrounded and extensively quoted in the text. Appendix B provides a list of the compositions examined, with the date and venue of first performance, together with the review date for each of the publications selected.[16]

The book will concern itself *passim* with the discourse of music criticism. Accordingly, in appropriate places, I have commented on the

---

[16] The question of the attribution of music reviews is a tricky one. Although in newspapers and journals, critics rarely signed their notices, we know from contemporary sources that full-time critics attached to the newspapers and journals surveyed provided most of the review copy for most of the time. Internal stylistic evidence and the opinions expressed can also, of course, be useful if the attribution of a notice is in doubt.

critics' use of allegorical preferences. The language used in reviews is not, of course, neutral, but represents the interests and values of the watchmen themselves. The discourses found in the press coverage of music in this period draw, for example, on the vocabulary of religion, warfare, sport, business and trade. When terms such as 'major', 'significant' and 'important' are used, these are based on contemporary estimations and are not pre-imposed. The watchmen rarely felt that they were engaged in objective value-free reporting of musical events. On the contrary, the majority wrote copy that was subjective and reflective of their own individual music ideologies.

This book, first and foremost, sets out to provide an overview of the reception history of English music in the Victorian and Edwardian periods. It is above all interested in the politics of music criticism, as well as the impact of the press on the canon-formation and on the creation of an English Musical Renaissance. This study was never intended to be definitive, rather it was conceived as a platform on which other researchers and scholars could build. Originally researched and written as a PhD thesis, the work has been lightly revised for publication.

PART ONE

# Watchmen and Watchtowers

# CHAPTER ONE

# The Times

> Just reflect on how colossal and universal is the paper of which I am speaking.[1]

As Richard Wagner acknowledged, in the 1850s *The Times* was the most widely-read and influential newspaper in the country, its daily sale totalling more than its five main rivals combined.[2] Although this dominance was undermined by the passing of the Newspaper Act of 1855 and ensuing revolutionary expansion of the press, *The Times* retained its intellectual authority in the teeth of the new competition – especially from the formidable *Daily Telegraph*.[3] In terms of its readership profile, it was accepted by contemporaries that *The Times* spoke with a unique authority to the political and commercial elites of Victorian Britain. Yet despite its prestige, it was not a very profitable newspaper coming under price and cost pressure from more efficiently managed papers – especially the *Daily Telegraph* and the *Daily News*. In terms of its editorial line, *The Times*, justified its 'Thunderer' epithet by taking a strong line on the great issues of the day, such as Irish Home Rule (which it opposed) and 'the Empire and its mission in the world' (which it supported).[4] *The Times* 'thundered' too in its promotion and projection of English music during the period surveyed, with the paper's coverage being dominated by three outspoken, if ideologically very different, chief critics: James W. Davison (critic 1846–78), Francis Hueffer (1878–89) and John A. Fuller Maitland (1889–1911).

*The Times* was generous in its coverage of music throughout this period. Under James Davison (1813–85) and his successors, *The Times* hardly ever missed a major concert, festival or opera performance, with most reviews, as far as communications allowed, being printed the following day.[5] Music was regarded as an intrinsic part of the paper's format and the column space allocated to music reviews was generous,

---

[1] Wagner q. in Davison, *Music during the Victorian Era* p. 65.

[2] Fox Bourne *English Newspapers* p. 224.

[3] *The Times*'s daily circulation held steady at around 60,000–70,000 copies per day from the 1850s until the new century.

[4] *History of The Times*, vol. iii p. viii.

[5] There were very few occasions when *The* Times did not cover a major premiere, one of those being the first performance of Vaughan Williams's *A London Symphony* in March 1914.

with individual works sometimes being given lengthy treatment. *The Times*'s music critics seem generally to have operated without excessive interference from editorial authority. Even so, Davison's biographer noted that the critic 'was occasionally expected to subordinate his own opinions and even the style of his writing to those of persons in authority'.[6] Despite being given broad scope to cover music events in their own way, *The Times*'s critics were not well paid, with Davison starting on a salary of £200 pa in 1846 – a sum which had only risen to £250 pa by his retirement thirty years later. In comparison, the editor's salary in the 1870s was £5,000 pa, roughly equivalent to that of a barrister.[7] Notwithstanding the poor remuneration, the history of music criticism in the 'Thunderer' is the tale of how its critics, each in his own distinctive way, tried to galvanise opinion in the cause of England's national music.

## 1.   J. W. Davison: Musical Politician.

> In art a thorough conservative, Davison was also in a certain sense a protectionist [...] he looked for the diffusion amongst all artists of a spirit of fellowship [...] leading to culture, higher effort and more successful expression of England's musical power.[8]

James W. Davison joined *The Times* as critic in 1846 and, in a career spanning over thirty years, elevated the craft of music journalism.[9] Davison was the most influential music journalist of his generation, his position on *The Times* ensuring a wide circulation for his views. His gregarious, even Rabelaisian personality mostly gave him the affection of his peers; and his prolific pen informed and entertained his readers as few others could. Davison was a seminal figure in evolving and legitimising his craft. At *The Times*, he transformed the position of music critic, ensuring that performance reviews ranged further afield than the fashionable London opera season and the social landmarks of the provincial festival circuit. Yet ultimately his was an unsteady talent which often succumbed to conservative prejudices and inconsistencies.

Davison venerated the German 'masters' from Handel to Mendelssohn and despised most developments in music after 1850. As a journalist,

---

[6] Davison, *Music during the Victorian Era* pp. 73–5.

[7] Joseph Bennett, chief critic on the *Daily Telegraph*, in 1884 signed a ten-year contract with the newspaper at £700 pa. The Daily Telegraph Archives. See also Chapter 2 below.

[8] Davison, pp. 71–2.

[9] Davison's connection with *The Times* began when he was invited to cover the premiere of Mendelssohn's *Elijah* at the Birmingham Festival in place of the paper's ailing critic, Charles Kenney. See Reid, *Music Monster* p. 103.

Davison was a music-patriot who passionately advocated the development of a 'native school' cast in the Mendelssohn mould. According to his memoirs, such a classical-romantic school was a distinct possibility in the 1840s, with the critic's friend, William Sterndale Bennett (1816–75), at its head.[10] The fact that such a development never took place, Davison blamed on the growing influence of Schumann and, especially of Wagner, after 1850. As a result, Davison spent most of his career railing against the new music, judging composers on their adherence to, or apostasy from, Mendelssohnian classicism. When Wagner arrived in London in 1855, Davison was overheard by the composer's friend Ferdinand Praeger to vow, 'so long as I hold the sceptre of music criticism, I'll not let him have any chance here'.[11] Davison duly accorded Wagner's concerts a dreadful press, confirming the composer's own estimate of the power of the critic's 'sceptre'. Wagner was well aware of Davison's threat, both in terms of reputation and hard cash, to his London visit.[12] The critic's importance lay in the imperious manner with which he used his 'sceptre' to profile music in the 'Thunderer'. Paradoxically, for all the irreverent radicalism of his journalism, Davison's conservative legacy proved a barrier that the Musical Renaissance eventually had to overcome.

Davison's reception and projection of English music in *The Times* reflected his strong prejudices against the 'progressive' in music. Among native composers, he favoured Sterndale Bennett whom, after a gilded youth in which Mendelssohn and Schumann favoured him, composed little after 1850. Consequently, on the rare occasions when Bennett ventured to premiere a new work, Davison was effusive, as with the oratorio *The Woman of Samaria* which he dubbed a 'fresh start' before going on to comment that it brought back 'the Sterndale Bennett of old times, with all his graceful finish, his pure and flowing melody'.[13] Another of Davison's friends favoured in his column was George A. Macfarren (1813–87), who shared his reverence for Handel and Mendelssohn. When, at the age of sixty-three, Macfarren received his first major choral commission, Davison was there as *The Times*'s 'own reporter' to draw a direct parallel with Mendelssohn and his *Elijah*: 'in *The Resurrection* another masterpiece has been added to the catalogue of works which the Birmingham Festival may claim the credit of having

---

[10] Davison, p. 24.

[11] Reid, p. 37.

[12] Ibid. pp. 39–41. Wagner wrote to Otto Wesendonck from London (5 Apr. 1855) fulminating against the 'worthlessness, insolence, venality and vulgarity of the local press', q. in Ehrlich, *First Philharmonic* p. 89.

[13] *T* 29 Aug. 1867.

brought into existence'.[14] Davison was a critic who ceaselessly looked back to a perceived golden age that was brutally cut short by Mendelssohn's death.

As far as younger English talent was concerned, Davison was very supportive so long as the music conformed to his conservative musical agenda. In the 1850s, *The Times* promoted and projected the music of three promising newcomers: Henry Leslie (1822–96), William Bexfield (1824–53) and Charles Horsley (1822–76), all of whom contributed to the quest for a 'great' English oratorio in the Mendelssohn tradition. Although he gave both Leslie and Bexfield generous column-space when they brought forward new choral works, his notices were encouraging rather than effusive. Bexfield was the least favoured, so that when his *Israel Restored*, was premiered, Davison could not conceal his disappointment, finding it to be 'a long oratorio, but not a great one'.[15] As for Leslie's *Immanuel*, although deemed to have music which was 'not on a level with the subject', Davison still thought it to be:

> if not a work of imagination and strong originality, [then] one of excellent tendency and unquestionable talent, an honour to its composer, and a valuable addition to the English school of sacred music.[16]

For Davison, Horsley was the composer to watch in the 1850s, and when his oratorio *David* was given its London premier it was powerfully endorsed in the *Musical World* where Davison declared:

> When will Englishmen be Englishmen to one another? When will they make common cause, not against the world – that would be silly and unjust – but against their enemies and detractors? [...] Why, then, should English talent alone be disregarded, simply because it is English [...] Englishmen are not behind the rest of Europe in musical science and acquirement.[17]

There is no more emphatic statement of Davison's musical patriotism than this editorial. Conservative he certainly was, but he was also an advocate of the renewal of national music. Davison's review of Horsley's work reveals how much he loathed entrenched upper and middle class prejudices towards music. For him, the battle for English music was as much about an enemy within as about any foreign foe, first and foremost the crusade was a domestic one.

Davison was as free with his vitriol as he was with his balm. Hugo Henry Pierson (1815–73) was a composer who might have given direc-

---

[14] *T* 31 Aug. 1876.
[15] *T* 23 Sept. 1852.
[16] *T* 6 Mar. 1854.
[17] *MW* 1 Mar. 1851. *David* was not reviewed in *The Times*.

tion to the nation's musical development. Pierson, briefly the Reid Professor of Music at the University of Edinburgh in the 1840s, was a passionate Schumannite and became a target of Davison's disapproval when he premiered his oratorio *Jerusalem* in 1852. The critic used his review of this work to launch a diatribe against the progressivism that had come to the fore in German musical life:

> Mr Pierson belongs to the 'word-painting' school, or the 'aes-thetic', as the admirers of Richard Wagner, Robert Schumann, etc. have dubbed it. We much regret, however, to find a man who evidently thinks seriously and writes *con amore* giving himself to a false idol, which if worshipped universally, music would cease to be an art. It is the barrenness of the age that has created this school – an attempt to hide poverty of invention and insufficient knowl-edge with the deceptive veil of mystery which, lifted up, discloses nothing but the hollow outlines of a skeleton.[18]

Davison here refers to music as a religion, a 'true faith' threatened by the worship of false gods. However, on the following day, the critic hoped that Pierson would see the error of his ways and return to the 'true and unchangeable principles'.[19] In the event, Pierson returned to Germany (his adopted home), and it was to be many years before he again premiered a major new choral work in his native land. When the unrepentant composer finally brought extracts of his *Hezekiah* to the Norwich Festival of 1869, Davison simply brushed the new work aside:

> As Mr Pierson is an Englishman, it would be more agreeable to us to speak of him in a very different tone; but as an oratorio is a formidable matter, alike for the composer to compose, and for the hearer to hear; [...] we have no inclination to break butterflies on wheels.[20]

Davison needed to do no more; seventeen years earlier he had, after all, destroyed any lasting influence that Pierson might have on the future of English music.

The young hopefuls of the 1850s however did not live up to Davison's expectations, and it was not until the arrival of Arthur Sullivan (1842–1900) that he again found an English musical talent worthy enough to promote in his columns. No watchman supported Sullivan so loyally and for so long as did the chief critic of *The Times*. For Davison, Sullivan had all the attributes of a future hero of the nation's music having, most of all, been trained at Mendelssohn's own Leipzig Conservatorium. The com-poser's '*Irish' Symphony* was especially welcomed in *The Times*:

---

[18] *T* 24 Sept. 1852.
[19] *T* 25 Sept. 1852.
[20] *T* 2 Sept. 1869.

> [The symphony] is not only by far the most noticeable composition
> that has proceeded from Mr Sullivan's pen, but it is the best musi-
> cal work for a long time produced by any English composer.[21]

*The Times*'s management was not always happy with its chief music
critic. Despite patchy evidence, it appears that Davison's tenure at the
paper was characterised by 'day-to-day differences, managerial re-
bukes, even snubs'.[22] In the early 1850s, for example, the critic received
complaints from the newspaper's manager, Mowbray Morris, about
reviews that were thought to be either too blatantly biased or too
condemnatory.[23] Davison also incurred the disfavour of the newspaper's
long-serving editor John T. Delane, for pandering to selected theatre
managers, with the implication of possible impropriety.[24] Although
Davison's biographer, Charles Reid, emphasises that the critic was never
compromised by bribery or corruption, the situation seems more complex than he allows. There is no doubt that Davison, like other Victorian
music critics, received gifts from artists and impresarios as a matter of
routine, which could be valuable (cigar-cases, snuff-boxes) but whether
such items influenced Davison's reviews it is impossible to tell. More
serious though were the allegations that ultimately precipitated his
retirement from the paper. These charges which appeared in *Truth* in
1877, concerning his relationship with his house-mate, the musical
agent Henry Jarrett.[25] While Davison successfully challenged *Truth*'s
assertions that he favoured Jarrett's clients in his *Times*'s column, the
case was messy and involved the newspaper's legal team. Some of the
mud undoubtedly stuck so that within a year Davison had been removed from his post – albeit on full salary for life.[26] Although Davison
had uniquely raised the profile of music in *The Times*, his was nonethe-
less the voice of reaction and a barrier to progress.

Davison always had other strings to his fiddle and no discussion of
his career would be complete without a survey of his long tenure as
editor of the *Musical World*. It is no exaggeration to say that Davison,

---

[21] *T* 12 Mar. 1866. Davison's reception of Sullivan is discussed in more detail in
Chapter 6 below.

[22] Reid, p. 103.

[23] Ibid. pp. 103–5. Morris's surveillance of Davison's reviews continued from the late-
1840s to the 1870s.

[24] Ibid. pp. 106–10.

[25] Ibid. pp. 121–7.

[26] It seems that *The Times* thought that Davison had 'lost his old powers'. Ibid. p. 127.
During Davison's last years at the newspaper, *The Times*'s management appointed Francis
Hueffer as second critic, see Hatton, *Journalistic London* p. 78. Joseph Bennett asserts
that Davison was supplanted at *The Times* through the editor's intervention in Hueffer's
favour, see Bennett, *Forty Years of Music* Chapter 14.

with his success at the *Musical World*, made an enormous contribution to the development of a dedicated musical press.[27] Until well into the 1860s, the journal overshadowed its (few) rivals both in its range and depth of coverage, as well as in its bold and controversial style. That said, it was a conservative journal which first and foremost reflected its editor's opinions and prejudices. For example, on the death of Mendelssohn the *Musical World* bewailed:

> that great and good man whose death, a lamentable catastrophe, has plunged intellectual Europe into despair. Mendelssohn dead! let music put on a suit of mourning, let the sons and daughters of music weep. [...] Alone upon his shoulders, Atlas-like, he sustained the burden of high-art.[28]

Davison also used the *Musical World* to take on some of the most powerful figures in the nation's musical life. For example, the popular Italian-born composer-conductor, Michael Costa (1808–84), whom Davison despised for his 'operatic' approach to sacred texts, was a particular target, as when his oratorio *Eli* was premiered: 'He displays neither imagination nor originality; he is wanting in elevation of style; even when he soars, he cannot sustain himself'.[29] This notice was written of a performance where female members of the Birmingham Festival choir asked for Costa's gloves so that they could be torn into strips and cherished as souvenirs. As for the reception, projection and promotion of new native music, Davison had the widest scope in the *Musical World*. Alongside his support for his favoured composers, Davison wrote scores of articles and editorials championing the reform of English musical life. In 1851, for example, the *Musical World* published a series of three articles on 'A National Opera', intended to beat the drum for a co-ordinated campaign to bring English opera up to the standard of 'foreign establishments'.[30] Later that same year Davison complained of the low morale of English musicians in the celebrations surrounding the Great Exhibition:

> The year 1851 appears likely to benefit all the world, one solitary class of individuals excepted – the English musicians [who] want self-esteem, pride of country, and a pure love of art [and who] allow themselves to be sneered at, or coughed out of their proper places.[31]

---

[27] Davison remained as editor of the *Musical World* for over forty years (1844–85). See also Chapter 4 below.

[28] Davison q. in Reid, p. 26.

[29] *MW* 1 Sept. 1855.

[30] *MW* 22 Mar. 1851.

[31] *MW* 29 Mar. 1851.

No musician or musical institution was safe from Davison's wrath in the *Musical World*. The Philharmonic Society, the National Training School of Music, the Sacred Harmonic Society, even the Anglican Church – all in turn came in for criticism.

Davison's forced retirement from *The Times* marked the effective end of his career as a critic. Although he continued to edit the *Musical World* until his death, Davison cannot be said to have helped shape the reception history of the Musical Renaissance in the 1880s which was, by then, centred on the new Royal College of Music.[32] Accordingly, when Hubert Parry's *Prometheus Unbound* was given its first perform-ance the *Musical World* covered the concert by lamely reprinting a review from the *Daily Telegraph*.[33] Yet even in his final years, Davison could still occasionally voice his support for new English music; as with the premiere of Frederic Cowen's first festival commission, the cantata *The Corsair*: 'young as he is, this gentlemen has earned an enviable place in the rank of English composers whose progress is watched with interest amongst us'.[34] For all his faults, Davison was a major figure; dubbed a 'musical politician' by his son, he wielded his unprecedented power in the cause of an English national music.[35] As his friend and fellow-critic, Joseph Bennett, expressed it:

> Few, perhaps none, of the critics who have arisen since [...] can form any adequate idea of the power exercised by that remarkable man. It was often said that in respect of music he held the London press in the hollow of his hand.[36]

## 2.   Francis Hueffer: Stranger as Sentinel

With the appointment of German-born Dr Franz [Francis] Hueffer (1843–89) as chief music critic in 1878, *The Times* signalled a clean break with the Davison era. Whereas Davison believed that England's musical destiny lay in the Mendelssohnian past, Hueffer wanted English music to evolve on progressive lines and to embrace Wagner and his 'music of the future'. In appointing Hueffer, *The Times* clearly intended to bring intellectual *élan* and a contemporary spirit to its music cover-age. The paper's management knew their man since Hueffer had already revealed his progressive views in essays on Wagner in the *Fortnightly*

---

[32] See Hughes and Stradling, pp. 19–51.
[33] *MW* 11 Sept. 1880.
[34] *MW* 9 Sept. 1876.
[35] Davison, p. 70.
[36] Bennett, q. in Reid, p. 101.

*Review.*[37] In these pieces Hueffer proclaimed that while Beethoven had given music its 'spiritual or poetical liberation', among living composers it was Wagner who was crushing 'the hard fetters of petrified formalities'.[38] Hueffer was committed to the ideal that modern music should be spiritual, poetic and 'philosophical'. As a post-1848 radical, his discourse – with its references to struggle, 'reform' and 'liberation' – revealed a very different perspective on music from that of his predecessor at *The Times*. Hueffer believed that the modern artist should be a polemicist and a man of action, ever seeking the new in a bid for artistic reform. Hueffer proclaimed himself to be a critic of the future and his journalistic career was founded on that conviction.[39] His was a new and revolutionary voice among the watchmen.

Hueffer used *The Times* in an attempt to channel English music in a progressive, Wagnerite direction. In this endeavour Hueffer was an ardent champion of national music. He saw the renewal of English music primarily as a domestic crusade in which the main task was to recruit the middle and upper classes to the struggle. Hueffer looked to opera (or 'music drama') as the vehicle for the revival of English national music. In common with other German intellectuals, he believed that Germany had renewed its musical fortunes by creating a national opera tradition of its own.[40] Hueffer was convinced that the social and political power of opera had assisted the drive towards German national unity and self-confidence; on his reading, Weber's *Der Freischütz* (1821) and Wagner's *Lohengrin* (1850), were truly revolutionary works.[41] Hueffer hoped that England could emulate Germany by rebuilding its national music with opera as a popular and socially inclusive focus.

In the event, Hueffer first settled on Scottish-born Alexander Mackenzie (1847–1935), a friend and protégé of Franz Liszt, as the composer most likely to provide the lead that England needed. For Hueffer, Mackenzie was a composer of real potential whose German musical training and admiration of Wagner would enable him to lay the foundations for a progressive opera tradition. Hueffer set out to help Mackenzie in two ways: by providing him with opera libretti (*Columba* and *The Troubadour*), and by rigorously promoting and projecting his music in *The Times*. The premiere of *Columba* in 1883 was seen at the time as a major

---

[37] Hueffer, *Richard Wagner and the Music of the Future*.

[38] Ibid. p. 255 and p. 78.

[39] Hueffer wrote the Wagner volume in the 'Great Musicians' series. He was also the general editor of this influential series of music monographs.

[40] Hughes, 'Lucifer of Music' pp. 21–4.

[41] Ibid. pp. 24–40.

occasion in the history of English Opera, the event being staged at Covent Garden by the Carl Rosa forces with all the glamour that the house could muster. Of the premiere, *The Times*, in a massive review, observed:

> Mackenzie has a style of his own, he owes allegiance to no other composer, although he has studied the recent developments of music with care and intelligence. [*Columba* marks] the birth of a remarkable work and one which is likely to place English dramatic music on a different level from that which it has hitherto attained.[42]

Hueffer added that Prime Minister W. E. Gladstone had voiced his support for the work and would attend *Columba*'s second performance. Despite the enormous press interest in *Columba*, the work was not a success and the relationship between critic and composer entered a difficult phase. Hueffer began to have doubts about Mackenzie's commitment to the progressive cause, reservations which surfaced in his reviews of the composer's choral festival commissions of this period. For example, when Mackenzie's first oratorio *The Rose of Sharon* was premiered in 1884, *The Times* was unenthusiastic:

> the music may be called a compromise between the conventional and the poetic, the old and the new. It contains passages of the highest beauty; it contains music to which one is astonished to find the name of a modern composer of reputation and serious aim attached [... *The Rose of Sharon*] is not likely to increase one's belief in Mr Mackenzie as a composer of settled purpose and individual genius.[43]

Nevertheless Hueffer, undeterred by his misgivings about Mackenzie's 'individual genius', embarked on a second opera collaboration with the Scottish composer. Once again the intention was to create a ground breaking English opera in the Wagnerian tradition. The result was *The Troubadour*, with a libretto based on the lurid adventures of the Provencal minstrel, Guillem de Cabestanh. When the new opera was premiered by the Carl Rosa Company at Covent Garden, *The Times* printed an enthusiastic review. In particular, Act IV was described in glowing terms:

> the music is most intimately wedded to the dramatic action [...] Mr Mackenzie rises fully to the height of the situation, and it may without exaggeration be said that outside the pages of the very greatest composers his final scene would be difficult indeed to match.[44]

---

[42] *T* 11 Apr. 1883.
[43] *T* 17 Oct. 1884. Mackenzie stated in his memoirs that Hueffer's reaction stemmed from the fact that he had not been asked to write the libretto for *The Rose of Sharon*. Mackenzie, *Musician's Narrative* p. 122.
[44] *T* 9 Jun. 1886.

Yet once again, despite the best efforts of the 'Thunderer' Mackenzie's *Troubadour* failed to make a mark with the public, a setback which resulted in Hueffer and Mackenzie's permanent withdrawal from the quest for an English breakthrough in opera.

Frederic Cowen (1852–1935) was another young English composer who enjoyed special favour in *The Times*. Where Hueffer had looked to Mackenzie for the first modern English opera, he chose Cowen as the native composer most likely to write a 'great' symphony in the Austro-German tradition. By so doing he believed Cowen would provide the foundation for an English school of symphonic writing. Accordingly, when Cowen introduced his first mature symphonic essay to the public in 1880, *Symphony No. 3 'Scandinavian'*, Hueffer greeted the occasion as one of historic importance:

> here we see fancy deepened into imagination, the grace into breadth and earnestness of thought which belong to art in its most elevated forms. [...] we once more call to the attention of all lovers of music what is certainly the most important symphony by an English composer produced for many years.[45]

In the same review Hueffer was careful to point out that Hans Richter had accepted the new work for its continental debut in Vienna. As a result of this (and other favourable reviews) Cowen's new symphony went on to enjoy considerable success for the rest of the decade.[46] It would of course be useful to know how the public reacted to the opinions of the critics, but there is no methodology to estimate the effect of critic on public, critic on composer, (or indeed composer on composer). It is surely an index of the close connection between Cowen and Hueffer that the composer dedicated his *'Scandinavian' Symphony* to Hueffer. This inscription provides powerful confirmation that the English Musical Renaissance was a joint project between the watchmen and the nation's composers. Hueffer's promotion of Cowen's music continued when his *Symphony No. 4 'Cambrian'* was premiered, a work which was given its s*obriquet* in *The Times* notice:

> we should be much surprised, if the new work [...] does not go forth into the world as the "Welsh Symphony". By that name it will no doubt be heard of both at home and abroad. It is an honour to English art.[47]

And it was the same story three years later with Cowen's *Symphony No. 5*, when Hueffer took the opportunity to place Cowen's symphonic ef-

---

[45] *T* 21 Dec. 1880.

[46] The *'Scandinavian' Symphony* was the most frequently performed symphony by an Englishman until the premiere of Elgar's *Symphony No. 1* in 1908. See Chapter 7 below.

[47] *T* 29 May 1884.

forts above those of the RCM's professors: 'among the living English composers who have cultivated this highest form of orchestral music, Mr Cowen undoubtedly takes first place'.[48] Hueffer continued to promote Cowen into the late 1880s, hailing the new oratorio *Ruth* as a 'work of distinguished merit', and its composer as the 'musical hero of the hour'.[49]

Any analysis of Hueffer's favourable projection of English music would be incomplete without mentioning his support for Sullivan's work. Although the reception of Sullivan's music is the subject of a later chapter, suffice it to say that while Hueffer generally reviewed the Savoy Operas with disdain, he was quick to welcome any new Art-Music from Sullivan. For example, on the occasion of the premiere of *The Golden Legend* when *The Times* declared that:

> Popularity in the true meaning of the word, which is very different from vulgarity [...] is this composer's birthright [...] His muse does not affect [...] tragic passion, but she always moves with perfect grace and elegance and, what is more, has the accurate knowledge of her power and of its limits.[50]

Unlike a number of the other watchmen, Hueffer was prepared to acknowledge that Sullivan had his own (albeit limited) contribution to make to the revival of national music. For him, Sullivan's real strength was his popularity and his 'accurate knowledge' of the tastes of his public.

Hueffer only briefly promoted the music of Hubert Parry (1848–1918). In 1880 Hueffer was prepared to congratulate him for looking to 'future developments', and when his *Piano Concerto in F sharp major* was premiered, it was made the subject of a feature article identifying him as one of England's most progressive composers:

> the intelligent foreigner [...] would find it difficult to point to a single national or typical feature of modern English music, especially of the instrumental kind, excepting the universal leaning towards Mendelssohnian sentiment clad in Mendelssohnian form [Parry is ...] all but entirely free from such a tendency, [his] taste leading unmistakenly in the direction of the latest phase of German music.[51]

Later that year, Hueffer responded to the premiere of Parry's *Prometheus Unbound* with a long and generally favourable review which stressed that the composer was 'a disciple of the Wagner school'.[52] However, as

---

[48] *T* 14 Jun. 1887. See also *MW* 14 May 1887 and 18 Jun. 1887.
[49] *T* 9 Sept. 1887 and *MW* 17 Sept. 1887.
[50] *T* 18 Oct. 1886. See also 'portrait' of Sullivan in *MW* 23 Oct. 1886.
[51] *T* 6 Apr. 1880.
[52] *T* 8 Sept. 1880.

Parry moved away from Wagnerian influences, so Hueffer's reviews tended to berate his music as stylistically muddled and lacking in coherence. For example, on the premiere of the (revised) *Symphony No. 2 'Cambridge'* in 1887, Hueffer was particularly scathing about the work's programme: 'a subject of this kind might perhaps serve as an adequate basis for an operetta, but it is scarcely fit for embodiment in one of the most ideal of arts'.[53] Such censure, and in such terms, did not go down well at the RCM and Hueffer's uneasy relationship with George Grove and his men continued to deteriorate.

Charles Stanford (1852–1924) , Parry's colleague at the RCM, fared only a little better in *The Times*. Although Hueffer respected the technical merits of his music, he felt that its lack of expressive and dramatic power consigned it to the second-rate. For example, in his long and detailed review of the premiere of the *Elegiac Ode*, Hueffer was diplomatic:

> [it] reflects high credit on the composer and on the school to which he belongs. Its most striking merits are, perhaps its earnestness of aim and that quality which, for want of a better name, one may call 'style".[54]

Although the notice went on to praise the ode for being 'so heartfelt and so true', there is a reserve here which was characteristic of Hueffer's appraisal of Stanford's music. Stanford was a Brahmsian and Hueffer's coolness probably stemmed from the fact that he was not, in his terms, a true 'progressive'. In review after review, and despite the fact that Hueffer admired Stanford's structural competence, he denied him the highest praise; of the oratorio *The Three Holy Children*, he wrote: 'Mr Stanford does not rely for his effect upon any kind of dramatic interest'.[55] Hueffer was also unimpressed with Stanford's two major operas of the 1880s. While he condescended to accept *The Canterbury Pilgrims* as a 'welcome addition to the repertoire of our lyric stage' even though it failed to touch 'the deeper springs of dramatic passion'; he castigated *Savonarola* for its 'almost total absence of dramatic properties so-called'.[56] Reviews like these show that Hueffer held out few hopes that South Kensington could provide the foundation for a national opera revival.

Hueffer was committed to the projection of new English talent, even when he regarded it as not of a high order. Arthur Goring Thomas

---

[53] *T* 10 Jun. 1887. See also *MW* 11 Jun. 1887 and Chapter 6 below.
[54] *T* 16 Oct. 1884.
[55] *T* 29 Aug. 1885.
[56] *T* 29 Apr. 1884 and 11 Jul. 1884.

(1850–92) enjoyed critical acclaim in *The Times* for his two operas
which scored genuine popular and commercial success: *Esmeralda* (1883)
and *Nadeshda* (1885). Despite his passionate commitment to the national opera project, the critic had to admit that Goring Thomas was
unlikely to feature in the development of English 'music-drama'; even
so, he could still write of *Esmeralda*: 'if an English school of opera is to
be established, composers of this type will find a distinguished place in
it'.[57] In the cause of national music Hueffer was prepared to embrace
others who could not compose at the highest levels. In this regard
Frederick Corder (1852–1932) attracted the critic's praise. Corder's
suite *Im Schwarzwald* (1880) was celebrated in *The Times* with a
feature-article;[58] while years later, after Corder had abandoned all pre-
tence of Wagnerian inspiration in his opera *Nordisa*, Hueffer still offered
qualified approval:

> [*Nordisa*] shows no flights of musical genius, but it is, nevertheless,
> characterised by musical skill and tact. [Corder] has endeavoured,
> and with a considerable amount of success, to combine true art
> with popularity.[59]

Hueffer clearly held on to some hopes that Corder might yet eschew
commercial imperatives and return to the true faith.

Hueffer was totally uncompromising towards that generation of English composers who had survived from the first half of the century. For
example, when Macfarren's new oratorio, *King David*, was premiered
in 1883, he could not have been more scathing, declaring that '[*King
David*] is a determined severance from the living forces of artistic
progress [ ... It lacks] a single passage to prove that the composer is
acquainted with anything that has been done in music since 1847'.[60]

Hueffer's responsibilities at *The Times* did not preclude him from
writing books on music. Shortly into his period as chief critic, he
produced a volume of previously published articles, two of which reveal
his role in the construction of the English Musical Renaissance.[61] In
'The Chances of English Opera', he re-opened the issue of the 'permanent establishment of English opera' in London, being careful to make
his case in patriotic terms. He argued that while the 'national development of music' was progressing in other lands (even in backward Russia),
England still awaited its own 'national art-revival' in which opera had a

---

[57] *T* 27 Mar. 1883.
[58] *T* 6 Apr. 1880.
[59] *T* 27 Jan. 1887. When the opera was brought to London a few months later
however, Hueffer was scathing in the *Musical World* (14 May 1887).
[60] *T* 13 Oct. 1883.
[61] Hueffer, *Musical Studies*.

leading role; 'are we to accept *Pinafore* as the ultimate acme of English art?', he rhetorically opined.[62] In his article on 'Foreign Schools of Music (first published in *The Times* in 1879), Hueffer stressed the need for a new state-funded national conservatory of music, arguing that 'to have a national school of composers, we want, first of all, a great national centre of music tuition'.[63] He emphasised that such a national conservatorium must be built from scratch with government money and cited the Conservatoire de Musique in Paris as a model. The critic thereby placed himself (and *The Times*) at the centre of the debate about the future (and future funding) of advanced musical study in this country.

In the last years of his life Hueffer was engaged in writing the first history of Victorian music, a volume which was intended to mark the Queen-Empress's Golden Jubilee in 1887.[64] The importance of this volume lay not only in the fact that it was the first serious history of music in late nineteenth-century England, but also because it argued that the Renaissance still had to produce 'a genius in the proper sense of that much-abused term'.[65] Hueffer stressed that, despite the progress made, the achievements of the Renaissance were limited and that 'the greater portion of the musical work in England during the last half-century has been done by foreigners'.[66] England's musical honour, rested not on 'younger men', but on the shoulders of Sir Arthur Sullivan, a composer whom he hoped would 'rise to still higher things'.[67] Throughout his *Half a Century of Music in England* Hueffer is sceptical of the Musical Renaissance which he had promoted in his *Times* journalism. It was not until the beginning of the new century that J. A. Fuller Maitland, his successor at *The Times*, provided a more optimistic account of the revival of English national music.[68]

Any assessment of Hueffer's importance in the projection and promotion of English music has to take into account his brief editorship of the *Musical World* (1886–88). After years of drift under Davison, the journal opted for a radical change of direction with Hueffer's appointment and the new editor took up his post with zeal. In the first issue of 1886,

---

[62] Ibid. p. 235 and p. 251.

[63] Ibid. p. 69.

[64] Hueffer, *Half a Century of Music in England*. Hueffer dedicated this study (by permission) 'To Her Majesty the Queen, the Friend of Mendelssohn, and the first Englishwoman to recognise the Genius of Wagner'.

[65] Ibid. p. 27.

[66] Ibid. p. viii. Hueffer was at pains to stress the role of the royal family in promoting music, and especially the 'exertions' of the Prince of Wales in the establishment of the RCM, ibid. p. 22.

[67] Ibid. pp. 24–6.

[68] Fuller Maitland, *English Music in the Nineteenth-Century*.

he set out a new path, pointing out to his readers that the journal had been enlarged and its price reduced 'so as to bring it within reach of all classes of musical readers'.[69] Hueffer transformed the *Musical World* with a far greater emphasis on concert and festival reviews coupled with a much sharper and more extensive editorial input. The era of recycled notices and tired reprints was gone; instead the editor dragged the *Musical World* into the 1880s with a commitment to modern music so that 'due reverence for the great masters of the past will be combined with a genuine and genial appreciation of contemporary work'.[70] English music was promoted in Hueffer's *Musical World* although with Grove's men being generally out of favour. Beyond the reception history of English music in the *Musical World*, consideration must be given to the many articles and editorials which he wrote to encourage and promote native music. For example, in 1886, he wrote an editorial on 'Provincial Festivals' asserting:

> The English musician is no longer a prophet despised in his own country [...] the English Beethoven, if he ever should arise, is not likely to be weighted down by the neglect of his countrymen [...] We have not yet produced a Beethoven, but we have a rising school of able musicians [...].[71]

Under his strong editorial lead the fortunes of the *Musical World* improved and its circulation grew by 'several hundreds per cent' with Queen Victoria heading the list of subscribers.[72] Yet illness and death intervened. In the summer of 1888, Hueffer fell ill and died of cancer the following year.[73]

Hueffer's journalistic discourse was a complex one. Above all, it drew on the language of politics in which 'reform', 'renewal' and 'revolution' were at the forefront of his legitimising values.[74] His discourse borrowed from several different sources, particularly from religion and history. He also drew several tropes from sport, the military and the commercial world, with which he reinforced Victorian notions of success. Whether nations or individuals, Hueffer espoused champions, winners and favourites. For him, a nation's music was an index of its vitality, its musical achievements synonymous with national prowess. As a critic, his was a contemporary presence who looked to the past

---

[69] *MW*, 2 Jan. 1886.

[70] Ibid.

[71] *MW* 23 Oct. 1886.

[72] *MW* 1 Jan. 1887.

[73] *The Musical World* survived but another two years under new owner-editor, E. F. Jacques. It later re-appeared at the end of the 1890s surviving a decade.

[74] Hueffer, *Richard Wagner and the Music of the Future*, pp. 24–5.

only to identify the future. Hueffer well understood the power of the critic to shape the musical destiny of a nation. It was a power he used with a skill and determination rarely seen among his peers.

Hueffer's career at the pinnacle of music journalism lasted only a decade. His was a radical voice which had tirelessly supported the hope that England, like Germany, would one day experience 'a day of artistic as well as of social reformation'.[75] For all his enthusiasm for the Renaissance, by the end of his life he was clearly disillusioned with its achievements. For him, the English 'Beethoven', still less the English 'Wagner', had yet to arrive. Although his death was a blow to the cause of English music, there were some who did not mourn his passing. Most importantly, his breach with Grove and his team was never healed.[76] Despite Hueffer's generous support for the cause of national music, there were no representatives from the RCM at his funeral and no floral tributes from South Kensington to follow him to the grave.[77]

### 3. J. A. Fuller Maitland: 'Doorkeeper of Music'.[78]

John Alexander Fuller Maitland (1856–1936) was a music zealot, a critic who dedicated his professional life to building a national music revival of which England could be proud. Born into a wealthy London family, Fuller Maitland (hereafter Maitland) inherited links with the evangelical Clapham Sect (from his father), as well as connections with the capital's literary life (from his mother). The family's social status and affluence was based on a banking fortune which enabled them to live in the splendour of Park Place, a Georgian mansion in Essex famous for its Old Masters. Educated at Westminster School and Cambridge University, Maitland was an elitist who saw himself as a gentleman-critic. He brought to his vocation a high-minded morality, patrician arrogance and snobbery which permeated, and sometimes suffocated, his journalism.

As critic Maitland cast himself both as 'watchman' and 'doorkeeper' of music, tropes linked in their scrutiniser-defender function and drawn from a pre-modern, even biblical, context. He saw English music as

---

[75] *MW* 5 Feb. 1887.

[76] Grove's dislike for Hueffer was evident as early as 1880, when he commented of his coverage of the Leeds Festival: 'I am very much disgusted with Hueffer: there was never a better illustration of a beggar on horseback'. Letter from Grove to Sullivan, q. Jacobs, *Arthur Sullivan* p. 146. In the same letter Grove urged Sir Arthur to lobby Hueffer on behalf of the proposed RCM!

[77] *T* 25 Jan. 1889.

[78] Fuller Maitland entitled his 1929 autobiography, *A Doorkeeper of Music*.

citadel, tower, threatened city, and music critics as protectors and watchmen. Maitland had a specific vision of music, as a site of siege-warfare and of heroic defence. His world was one of stern exclusivity, a place of insiders and outsiders, of included and excluded, perhaps even of the 'saved' and the 'damned'. No other critic ever matched Maitland's determination to help build and then defend the walls of English music.

Maitland served the English Musical Renaissance in three crucial respects: as chief music critic of *The Times*; as Grove's successor on the *Dictionary of Music and Musicians*; and as an eminent music historian. As a student, he became attracted to the Schumann-Brahms tradition and that 'classical' strand in German music came to represent for him 'artistic aims and tenets [which] were of the purest and the highest'.[79] Conversely, he completely rejected Wagner and his vision of the 'music of the future'. These views remained fixed and unyielding throughout his long writing career.

Sir George Grove (1820–1900) launched Maitland on his career as a writer on music. Grove put him to work on his *Dictionary* and secured for him his first job as music critic on the *Pall Mall Gazette* where he rapidly made a name for himself (1882–84). At this time he also worked as London critic for the *Manchester Guardian* (1884–89). In the columns of both these papers Maitland championed the cause of the Musical Renaissance. A good example of his early notices is a review of Mackenzie's *Columba*, which he welcomed as a work to 'bear comparison with the operatic productions of contemporary France and Germany'.[80] His advocacy of the Renaissance did not go unrewarded since his application for Hueffer's job on *The Times* was 'warmly encouraged' by Grove who also provided him with 'valuable support' in a reference.[81] Maitland's appointment can be read as a 'safe' move by *The Times*, a step back from the progressive polemics of the Hueffer era. As far as the Renaissance was concerned the RCM had (at last) a watchman it could trust at the 'Thunderer'.

Alongside his burgeoning career as a journalist, Maitland was keen to establish his credentials as a music historian. In 1884–85, he brought out an English translation of Spitta's *Life of J. S. Bach*, a labour of love since Bach was always to have a special place in his *Weltanschauung*.[82] Also in 1884, Maitland published the first study of Robert Schumann by an English biographer and dedicated it to the composer's widow, Clara. In this landmark monograph, Maitland celebrated Schumann as

[79] Fuller Maitland, *Schumann* p. 102.
[80] *Pall Mall Gazette* 13 Apr. 1883.
[81] Fuller Maitland, *Doorkeeper of Music*, p. 124.
[82] Fuller Maitland, *Life of J. S. Bach* (3 vols, Novello 1884–85).

a critic-warrior and poet-musician who sent 'light into the depth of the human heart'.[83] Schumann's career as a watchman-hero of German national music was an endless source of inspiration to him.

Yet it was as chief critic of *The Times* that Maitland was to make the greatest mark on the English Musical Renaissance. From his commanding position at Printing-House Square, Maitland used *The Times* to support the quest for a national music and, to help him do so he needed reliable and talented lieutenants who shared his musical ideology. Accordingly, he appointed Robin Legge as assistant critic (1891–1906), to be followed by H. C. Colles (1906–11), the latter eventually succeeding him as chief critic.[84] Although music reviews in *The Times* were unsigned, on stylistic grounds it is most probable that Maitland undertook most of the reviewing, leaving minor musical occasions (and the uncongenial ones) to his assistants.

Maitland used *The Times* overtly to champion the Renaissance. In particular, the music of Parry and Stanford, the latter being one of Maitland's oldest friends, came in for the most extravagant praise. A good example of his reception of Parry's music is the occasion of the premiere of the oratorio *Job* in 1892 when he wrote:

> The impression produced by the work was very great and it must be said deliberately that recent years have not seen a composition more free from flaw or weak point of any kind, or one which conclusively proves that the oratorio form can still inspire works of the highest genius.[85]

This comment came from a critic who knew Parry well enough to realise that, as a radical humanist, he loathed writing sacred works for the (largely) High Anglican choral festival circuit.[86] As far as Stanford's music was concerned, Maitland's two reviews of the oratorio *Eden* reveal the intensity of his partisanship.[87] Stanford's operas were given a eulogistic reception, especially when *The Veiled Prophet of Khorassan*, was given its first outing at Covent Garden in 1893. This premiere was important on two counts: first, to Stanford's long-term aspirations as an opera composer; second, to the quest for a breakthrough in English national opera. Maitland gave *The Veiled Prophet* an enthusiastic review (despite being sung in Italian) being especially welcomed at a time when the operas of the 'sick' Wagner were already re-inventing the genre:

---

[83] Schumann q. by Fuller Maitland, *Schumann*, p. 103.

[84] Laurence Haward is mentioned as being on the music staff (1909–14). *The Times* Archive.

[85] *T* 9 Sept. 1892.

[86] See Chapter 6 below.

[87] *T* 8 Oct. 1891.

> After a succession of operas of the hysterical and incoherent school
> to listen to such music [...] is like letting a rush of fresh air into a
> sick room. [...] The composer's masterly treatment of his materials,
> vocal and instrumental, the ceaseless flow of really spontaneous
> and melodious music, the logical and organic construction of the
> whole work, and the propriety of the dramatic expression are the
> most striking characteristics of the opera [...].[88]

The critic loyally plugged Stanford's music in *The Times* well into the
new century, as evidenced by his review of the *Symphony No. 6*, of
which he wrote: 'the symphony is not only masterly in construction,
infinitely dextrous in treatment, and earnest in artistic aim, but it also
has genuine inspiration'.[89] The music of Alexander Mackenzie, Principal of the Royal Academy of Music and an important ally of South
Kensington, was also given generous coverage in *The Times*. For example, the '*Scottish' Piano Concerto*, premiered by the eminent Polish
virtuoso Ignaz Paderewski (1860–1941) at the Philharmonic Society,
was judged 'beautiful' and 'brilliant', and 'of all the compositions of the
kind which Sir Alexander has given us this is the most successful in the
best sense'.[90]

It was however a different story as far as Cowen was concerned. The
reason for this antipathy is unclear: was the composer too fond of
material success and the trappings of fame?; or could it be that the anti-
Semitic Maitland let his prejudice influence his reception of Cowen's
music? Whatever the reason, Cowen was given a rough ride in *The
Times*. For example, when *Thorgrim* was premiered at Covent Garden
in 1890, Maitland commented that the composer had:

> neither dramatic force nor breadth of treatment to enable him to
> import vitality to the characters [and] in situations demanding any
> depth of passion his music seems wanting in grip and dramatic
> significance.[91]

In a similar vein, Cowen's oratorio *The Transfiguration*, specially commissioned for the Three Choirs (Gloucester) Festival of 1895, was
judged to be an 'unconvincing', 'unequal' and 'unimpressive' work.
And when his *Coronation Ode* for Edward VII was premiered at the
Norwich Festival, Maitland (in a paltry notice) witheringly commented:
'there is no very great cause to regret the improbability that this work
will be often heard in the future'.[92]

---

[88] *T* 27 Jul. 1893. The libretto of *The Veiled Prophet* was written by William Barclay
Squire, Fuller Maitland's brother-in-law.
[89] *T* 19 Jan. 1906.
[90] *T* 25 Mar. 1897.
[91] *T* 23 Apr. 1890.
[92] *T* 13 Sept. 1895 and 23 Oct. 1902.

Maitland showered praise on the new generation of composers nurtured by the Grove-Parry Renaissance. The music of Henry Walford Davies (1869–1941), an ex-student of Parry and Stanford and a member of the RCM staff, received ample recognition in *The Times*'s music columns; as when the paper gave his cantata *Everyman* an excellent launch-review remarking that it 'easily surpassed all that the composer has hitherto achieved'.[93] The music of several other RCM alumni was similarly favoured; for instance, *Ballade for Orchestra*, the first important festival work by Samuel Coleridge-Taylor (1875–1912), was accorded a superb notice:

> The chief honours of the evening fell to a new composer – Mr S. Coleridge-Taylor, a young man whose student compositions have for some time been watched with eager expectation by those who have the true interests of English music at heart.[94]

The music of another student of the RCM (and of Stanford at Cambridge University), Arthur Somervell (1863–1937), was welcomed. When the latter's *Ode to the Sea* was premiered in 1897, it was judged to be 'so distinctively English that it cannot but recall some of Parry's choral odes'. On the basis of this recommendation, and of other favourable notices, Somervell went on to secure a solid reputation in the immediate pre-Great War period.[95] Edward German (1862–1936), a product of the RAM, was also among Maitland's favoured ones, his *Symphony No. 2 'Norwich'* (1893) being singled out as an example of how the English Musical Renaissance was gaining strength:

> A work of very decided merit and beauty, marked by much breadth of style, ingenuity of treatment, originality, and [...] distinction [ ... which took] very high rank among the symphonies of the younger generation of the modern English school.[96]

These notices provide ample confirmation of the extent to which Maitland's nationalism suffused his music journalism. His favourable reception of new English works largely depended on how far they reflected the dominant values of the two London academies.

In contrast, Maitland's reception of Sir Arthur Sullivan's music in *The Times* was almost always negative, the reviews being tinged with a half-suppressed loathing and contempt.[97] Maitland's true estimate of the composer's career was finally and witheringly revealed in his *English*

---

[93] *T* 10 Oct. 1904.

[94] *T* 15 Sep. 1898.

[95] *T* 8 Oct. 1897.

[96] *T* 5 Oct. 1893. This review was probably written by the second critic Robin Legge – given his Norwich Festival connections.

[97] See Chapter 5 below.

*Music of the Nineteenth Century*, where the composer was castigated as a peddler in 'light music' who merely satisfied the taste of the masses 'and took no part whatever in the work of the renaissance itself'.[98]

Maitland performed one last service to the Renaissance as *Times* critic in his reception of the 'Pastoral School'. This advocacy is hardly surprising since he had long-since been involved in the folk song revival. No composer benefited more from Maitland's favourable reception of the new 'pastoralism' than Ralph Vaughan Williams (1872–1958) – yet another 'old boy' of the RCM.[99] When his first major festival commission, *Toward the Unknown Region* (1907), was premiered, Maitland was almost certainly there in person to give the work his Brahmsian seal of approval:

> The composition is easily ahead of anything that the young composer has yet given us, and here we see the perfect maturity of his genius, the art that conceals art most effectually, and a nobility and earnestness of invention which mark the composer as the foremost of the younger generation. [...] in musical power, the little cantata is a worthy counterpart of the *Schicksalslied* of Brahms.[100]

Further confirmation of *The Times*'s commitment to Vaughan Williams is found in its review of the *Tallis Fantasia*, that core text of the Folk-Tudor revival, premiered at the Three Choirs (Gloucester) Festival:

> the work is wonderful because it seems to lift one into some unknown region of musical thought and feeling. Throughout its course one is never quite sure whether one is listening to something very old or very new [...] it cannot be assigned to a time or a school but it is full of the visions which have haunted the seers of all times.[101]

The intensity of Maitland's prose here reflects his strong response to and absorption in Vaughan Williams's music. It is surely significant that the construction, 'something very old or very new', is still regularly recycled on BBC Radio 3 a century later, further proof of the enduring influence of Edwardian music criticism. The third major Vaughan Williams work reviewed in *The Times* in the twilight years of Maitland's tenure as critic was *A Sea Symphony*, premiered in 1910. This notice too reflects his rapt response to the composer's contemporaneity:

> The first impression we receive from the work is that the poet and musician are marvellously akin. In both there is a distaste for the

---

[98] Fuller Maitland, *English Music of the Nineteenth Century* pp. 165–170.
[99] Hughes and Stradling, pp. 79–82.
[100] *T* 12 Oct. 1907.
[101] *T* 7 Sept. 1910.

old-established forms, both are striving for the newer poetic life.
[...] It will not be surprising if the Festival of 1910 is remembered
in the future as 'the Festival of the *Sea Symphony*'.[102]

Maitland's reviews of Vaughan Williams's early premieres are suffused
with an almost neurotic concern, even obsession, with the future direction of the national music. It is easy to understand the attraction of
Vaughan Williams's music for him, with its blend of folk and 'Tudor'
elements combined with an ethical seriousness, which for him defied a
*Zeitgeist* redolent with modern pessimism and 'decadence'.

Maitland used *The Times* too as a weapon against composers whom
he deemed unworthy of admission to the citadel of English music. In
Maitland's demonology this meant anyone tainted with 'progressive'
influences, such as the disciples of Wagner and Richard Strauss and the
admirers of contemporary Russian or French music.

There are no more striking instances of Maitland's bias than his
reception of the music of Edward Elgar (1857–1934) and Frederick
Delius (1862–1934). As far as Elgar was concerned, the composer's
progressivism, his lack of formal music training, together with his Catho-
lic faith and lower middle-class background, compromised him in the
critic's eyes. Even as late as 1906, Maitland felt able to pillory Elgar for
his adherence to 'Wagnerian doctrines', as when he denigrated *The
Kingdom* for melodic progressions and thematic transitions which gave
it 'an inevitable effect of monotony and restlessness at the same time.'[103]
As for Delius, Maitland not only objected to his lack of concern for the
fate of English music, but also for his unconventional and immoral
private life. In fact, Maitland decided early on that Delius was not to be
considered 'English' at all; so that when his first London concert took
place, the composer's German family-roots were disingenuously emphasised in *The Times* notice:

> The elaborate concert given in St James's Hall last night for the
> purpose of exploiting the music of Fritz Delius was a somewhat
> melancholy affair, for a settled melancholy pervades the music,
> [...] the exceedingly unmelodious character of much of the music
> and its prevailing gloom mark it out for the admiration of the few
> who profess a preference for ugly music.[104]

When Delius's music re-appeared in England years later – *In a Summer
Garden* was premiered at the Philharmonic Society – it fared no better
in Maitland's column:

---

[102] *T* 14.Oct. 1910.
[103] *T* 4 Oct. 1906.
[104] *T* 31 May 1899.

> There is no organic idea in the piece, no thematic germ of any
> consequence, it is a little like a play in which there should be
> nothing but scenery and limelight [...] Brahms's second symphony
> came like a breath of sweet country air in the second part of the
> concert, after the exotics of the first part.[105]

Delius's music then, in contrast to that of Brahms, gave off a foul stench
(even in a summer garden!). In reviews like these *The Times* presented
Delius as a thoroughly unhealthy influence, an un-English exotic who
had no place within the walls of the Renaissance. In his reception of
both these composers' music, Maitland allowed himself to be influenced
by extra-musical factors. The irony was that Delius and Elgar were, by
1908, the only two English composers to have made any serious impression beyond their native land.

Maitland's antipathy to most trends in contemporary music ensured
that the music of Granville Bantock (1868–1946) and Rutland Boughton
(1878–1960) was also negatively received in his columns. Yet Maitland
had to recognise that audiences were increasingly receptive to the rapid
changes occurring in modern music; and so, when 'uncongenial' concerts came up, from stylistic evidence, it seems that the reviewing was
delegated to the assistant critic.[106]

During his tenure at *The Times*, Maitland continued to write works
of music history. His most important effort in this field was *English
Music of the Nineteenth Century* (1902). This volume had two overlap-
ping objectives: first, to project and celebrate the RCM's contribution
to the national music revival; and second, to rally future support for the
Renaissance. In Book One ('Before the Renaissance') Maitland concentrated on the pre-Victorian history of English music, a dark time of
'national humiliation' and 'foreign domination', when obscure musicians 'in their organ-lofts' alone preserved 'the pure traditions' of English
music.[107] Maitland's discourse here is that of foreign occupation and
heroic resistance reminiscent of the 'Norman yoke' legends of Robin
Hood and Hereward the Wake so popular with Edwardians. In Book
Two ('The Renaissance'), Maitland focused on the national music revival of the mid-nineteenth century, that time of 'liberation' when a
'transformation of national character' ensured that 'ladies and gentlemen' took a new and serious interest in music.[108] For him social class

---

[105] *T* 12 Dec. 1908.
[106] A concert of 'progressive' music at the Three Choirs Festival of 1902, in which
Bantock's orchestral poem *The Witch of Atlas* was premiered was given a good review –
probably written by Legge. *T* 11 Sept. 1902.
[107] Fuller Maitland, *English Music of the Nineteenth Century* p. 84.
[108] Ibid. p. 126 and p. 135.

was crucial. The revival, as he saw it, was the work of a social and intellectual elite, of a new musical intelligentsia, with the 'average man' taking 'no part whatever in the work of the renaissance itself'.[109] Maitland identified Parry, Stanford, Mackenzie, Goring Thomas and Cowen, as the core-group of the Renaissance in the 1880s, each man drawn from 'a class that had before their time been seldom represented in the musical profession'.[110] Of the five, he declared Parry to be the most 'representative English master', a composer whose *Prometheus Unbound* marked the beginning of the Renaissance proper.[111] Maitland thereby at a stroke consigned to oblivion those English composers who had contributed to the revival of national music earlier in the century.

Other volumes flowed from Maitland's pen during his time at the 'Thunderer'. In 1902, he published *The Age of Bach and Handel* in the 'Oxford History of Music' series; a history which presented Bach as a musician of the future, and which denigrated Handel as a musical dead-end, a squalid composer-businessman wedded to a decadent age.[112] English composers, he hoped, would follow the ethical and spiritual path of Bach. Maitland also published several monographs on German music, all of which reflected, in one way or another, his hopes for the English Musical Renaissance. Perhaps the most important was his *Masters of German Music* (1894) in which he eulogised Brahms while speculating that, since the ageing composer had no German successor, England might then finally rule the staves:

> If [...] Germany is to become a second-rate power in art, it will be interesting to see which of the nations will succeed her in the supremacy. [ ... Especially since] a wave of music has lately been passing over England which may bring about a condition of things only to be compared with the glorious days when England was chief among musical nations.[113]

Alongside his work on *The Times* Maitland's most signal contribution to the Renaissance lay in his role of editor of *Grove 2*, a role which clearly expressed his determination to act as the arch-watchman and 'doorkeeper of music'. From the start of his editorship Maitland brought in a fresh young team of contributors so that *protégés* like Henry Walford Davies, W. H. Hadow (1859–1937) and Robin Legge (1862–1933) rubbed shoulders with more established scholars. So far as English music was

---

[109] Ibid. p. 170.

[110] Ibid. p. 187.

[111] Ibid. p. 201.

[112] Fuller Maitland, *Age of Bach and Handel*.

[113] Fuller Maitland, *Masters of German Music* pp. 4–5. Maitland also wrote the first English monographs of Joseph Joachim (1905) and Brahms (1911).

concerned *Grove 2*, like *Grove 1*, had an intensely Anglo-centric perspective. In particular, Maitland used his editorial position shamelessly to project Parry and Stanford, who were both accorded expanded entries written by the editor himself.[114] In this way Maitland constructed in *Grove 2* the notion of 'Parry and Stanford' as the twin pillars of the English Musical Renaissance. In contrast, the entry on Elgar (also written by the editor) revealed his antipathy towards the composer both in its choice of detail and tone. Maitland, like his friend and mentor George Grove before him, cast the *Dictionary* in his own image.

When Maitland retired from *The Times* he chose, perhaps appropriately, to live in a castle, Borwick Hall in Lancashire. From this new vantage point he continued to promote the English Musical Renaissance in a stream of books. In his *The Spell of Music* (1926), Maitland sought to direct the flappers and music-lovers of the 'Jazz Age' towards the paths of musical 'righteousness'; while in his last work, *The Music of Parry and Stanford* (1933), he provided a re-hash of all that he had said elsewhere.[115]

More importantly however, in 1929, he published his autobiography, aptly entitled *A Doorkeeper of Music*, a curious blend of name-dropping, prejudice and polemic.[116] In this fascinating memoir Maitland explores his past in loving detail: the Clapham Sect evangelicalism; the family Botticellis; the conversion to Brahms at Cambridge; the social links with two prime ministers (Gladstone and Balfour); and always the trials and tribulations of writing up a very personal 'renaissance'. In this volume Maitland aptly referred to *The Times* as the 'big door' and summed up his mission: to encourage English composers to take on the 'Agamemnons' of Germany. Only then would the Renaissance be complete and England have a truly 'great' national music.[116]

In this way Maitland remained at his post until the end. As 'doorkeeper of music', he saw his vocation as clearly as any of his Puritan ancestors. His was a sectarian vision of composers as 'pure' and 'impure'; for him, among the arts, music had the greatest power for good and evil. In his role as watchman, Maitland's commitment to the safety and integrity of the citadel was absolute. The impact of his zeal on England's music history is hard to overestimate.[117]

---

[114] In his entry on Parry Maitland stressed that the composer's *Prometheus Unbound* marked 'an epoch in the history of English music [and had] had great consequences in the development of our national art'. *Grove 2*, vol. iii p. 625. See also Chapter 6 below.

[115] Fuller Maitland, *Spell of Music* and *Music of Parry and Stanford*.

[116] Fuller Maitland, *A Doorkeeper of Music*.

[117] Fuller Maitland also published pioneering studies in early music and folk music. They included: the *Fitzwilliam Museum's Catalogue of Music* (1893); *English Carols of the 15th Century* (1893); and the *Fitzwilliam Virginal Book* (1899).

## 4. H. C. Colles

Henry C. Colles (1879–1943) succeeded Maitland as chief critic of *The Times* in 1911. From the stylistic evidence it is probable that Colles had undertaken much of Maitland's reviewing responsibilities before then, the older critic being burdened with bringing *Grove 2* to publication. At any event, Colles brought a safe conservatism to the music columns of the 'Thunderer'. Vaughan Williams and the 'Pastoral School' were positively received and projected, while more experimental composers, like Gustav Holst (1874–1934) and Arnold Bax (1883–1953), were given a more mixed reception. Although Holst's *Beni Mora* suite was deemed to display 'extraordinary skill', his *The Cloud Messenger* was dismissed as a failure: 'One admired the sincerity and the big aim of the work, though one felt that Mr von Holst had not enough strength to carry it out'.[118] Bax's tone-poem *Christmas Eve on the Mountain* (1913) was given short shrift from Colles, who commented that the composer must have 'returned from his wandering on the mountains and got to his music-paper before his thought was sufficiently cleared'.[119] Under Colles, Elgar remained *persona non grata* in *The Times*, so that when *The Music Makers* was premiered, he was yet again charged with vulgar populism:

> the weak point of Elgar's work is that, while he proclaims the detachment of the artist from the multitude, he skilfully takes the most direct means of securing the suffrages of the people.[120]

*Falstaff* too was castigated as a work 'rich in fuss and flurry' but in which 'nothing particular happens'.[121] *Plus ça change*? Maitland had, in Colles, found the perfect clone: not only did they share the same Oxbridge background (and the best address in clubland, the Athenaeum), but they also shared the same elitist and academic approach to music criticism, as well as absolute loyalty to the RCM branch of the Renaissance. Colles remained faithfully on watch unto death: as critic on *The Times*; editor of *Grove 3* and *Grove 4*; and as Professor of Music History at the RCM.

The history of the reception and projection of English music in *The Times* was characterised by a tension (real and potential) between the needs of the newspaper and the ideological imperatives of successive critics. During the period surveyed, the paper's music coverage was a

---

[118] *T* 2 Mar. 1912 and 5 Mar. 1913.
[119] *T* 5 Mar. 1913.
[120] *T* 3 Oct. 1912.
[121] *T* 3 Oct. 1913.

site of struggle for the future direction English music. Although the 'Thunderer's' priority was to keep its readers informed of the most important musical events, its critics had agendas of their own which went far beyond reporting music 'news'. In Davison, *The Times* had a passionate Mendelssohnian, at a time when the future direction of music in England seemed to rest in the hands of *der Elias der neuen Kunst*. In Hueffer, the paper employed a distinguished Wagnerian, who would keep its readers up to date with contemporary developments. And when, in 1889, the newspaper appointed Maitland as chief critic, it played safe, moving its music coverage in a conservative, 'classical' and Brahmsian direction, a line to which Colles, in turn, adhered. These four watchmen used their position on the newspaper to promote their own visions of the future of the national music. To that extent each one promoted his own, very personal, English Musical Renaissance.

# CHAPTER TWO

# The *Daily Telegraph*

> Mr Parry's *Symphony in G* ... is a capital proof that English music
> has arrived at a renaissance period.[1]

Thus did Joseph Bennett, chief critic of *The Daily Telegraph*, christen the
English Musical Renaissance. In the term 'renaissance', with its powerful
connotations of 'rebirth' and 'resurrection', Bennett reached for a brilliant matrix metaphorical tool, a wonderful presentational ploy, with
which he placed Parry's *First Symphony* at the forefront of English music.
It also ensured that the project to provide England with a national music
was understood in the context of larger movements in contemporary
culture, primarily the work of Jakob Burkhardt (1818–97) and Walter
Pater (1839–94).[2] It is a measure of Bennett's journalistic invention and
the power of the press that the 'renaissance' became a self-fulfilling
prophecy, to the extent that the English Musical Renaissance remains a
dominant construction in musicological discourse at the start of the new
millennium.

   The importance of the *Daily Telegraph* (henceforth the *Telegraph*) in
the formation of the Musical Renaissance lay in the fact that it was the
largest-selling quality daily for the period surveyed, with a coverage of
the nation's musical life that was both serious and exhaustive. Over the
years, the *Telegraph*'s critics hardly missed a concert, festival or opera
performance and, given the size of its readership, this ensured that the
paper's projection of English music was of supreme importance in the
development of the Renaissance.

   The first edition of the *Telegraph* appeared in June 1855, its advent
marking the beginnings of the 'penny press' and a revolution in the
British newspaper industry. One leading contemporary authority on the
press, Henry Sell, believed that 'English journalism entered on the modern stage of its history in 1855'. He gave two reasons: the abolition of
Stamp Duty on newspapers, and the arrival of the *Telegraph*.[3] From the
start it set out to identify a new newspaper audience, a mass readership

---

[1] Joseph Bennett on the premiere of Hubert Parry's *Symphony No. 1* at the Birmingham Festival, *DTel* 4 Sept. 1882.

[2] For a discussion of the origins of the term 'English musical renaissance' see Hughes
and Stradling, pp. 42–5.

[3] Sell, *Sell's Dictionary* (1900), 'The World's Press and its Development' p. 18. See also
Introduction above.

for a popular and readable daily. Priced at only one penny in broadsheet format, the *Telegraph* sold on both price and quality pioneering what Matthew Arnold called the 'new journalism' – a phenomenon which rejected the notion that newspapers should be written 'by and for the middle-classes'.[4]

By the 1860s, the paper had developed its own journalistic housestyle known as 'Telegraphese', with an emphasis on 'human interest' and a commitment to 'lively and varied' coverage.[5] The *Telegraph*, with its 'sparkle and vigour of its style', soon 'distinguished itself from all its contemporaries, especially *The Times*, and ensured itself a dominant position in the marketplace'.[6] By 1889, with a daily circulation of 241,000 copies, it totally overshadowed the 'Thunderer' (at around 60,000) and the *Morning Post* – the latter being too embarrassed to publish its circulation figures.[7] Furthermore, it was turning in large profits (£120,000 in 1882), a return which none of its rivals could hope to match. The success and profitability of the *Telegraph* brought a new commercial edge and a more dynamic journalistic culture into the newspaper industry.

In its early years, the *Telegraph* appeared in an eight-page format and, although the paper increased in bulk over the years, its design changed little. An issue of the 1850s would have had: two pages of advertisements; two pages given to money markets, sport and 'naval and military' matters; two pages allocated to domestic, foreign and colonial news. One page was largely devoted to legal news; and one page was made over to music, theatre and the royal court. By 1900, the size of the *Telegraph* had increased to sixteen pages with music holding its own in the expanded newspaper. Music notices and reviews throughout held a regular place in the *Telegraph*, with musical news being carried on most days and with major festivals commanding lengthy reports – some of which could cover up to 20% of a page.[8]

The *Telegraph*'s coverage of musical events in its earliest years is not easily documented. The stylistic evidence suggests that the paper may not have had a full-time critic on its staff, and reports from the provincial festivals tended to be reprints from local newspapers.[9] In any event,

---

[4] Lee, *Origins of the Popular Press*, p. 38.

[5] Wiener, *Papers for the Millions*, p. 53. See also Sell, *Sell's Dictionary* (1889), p. 170.

[6] Peabody, *English Journalism*, p. 145.

[7] Sell, *Sell's Dictionary* (1889), p. 170.

[8] See *DTel* 30 Aug. 1876 for an example of typical coverage of the Birmingham Festival.

[9] For example, coverage of the 1858 Leeds Festival was reprinted from the *Leeds Mercury*.

the only identifiable critic of this period is Campbell Clarke, the newspaper's erstwhile Paris correspondent and son-in-law of the paper's proprietor, J. M. Levy.[10] Whoever they were, these journalists were erratic in their coverage of the premieres of English music.

When new English works were reviewed in the *Telegraph* in the 1850s and 1860s, the music of more established composers was promoted at the expense of that of the younger generation. Among older composers, Sterndale Bennett, still regarded by many as a contemporary voice of English music, was given precedence, this despite the fact that he had composed little since the 1840s. When a new piece did emanate from his pen, the *Telegraph* invariably urged him to return to full-time composition. For example, when the *Symphony in G minor* was premiered at the Philharmonic Society in 1864, the paper welcomed its 'exquisite instrumentation' and declared that it marked 'a reawakening of the bright inventive genius which for so many years was suffered to lie dormant'.[11] Three years later, the *Telegraph* was even more delighted when Sterndale Bennett's first extended festival work, the cantata, *The Woman of Samaria*, was premiered. This piece, which secured a major review covering nearly one-third of a page, was greeted as a 'most masterly work' from 'one of the very few Englishmen who have been successful in the very highest and purest styles of musical composition [... even though] for many long years his muse was silent'.[12]

Younger English talents were given a more mixed reception in the *Telegraph*. Arthur Sullivan was most favoured, as with *The Tempest Music*, his first composition after his return from the Leipzig Conservatorium, a work which was generously hailed as by one who had already 'attained a European reputation'.[13] Yet even the promising young Sullivan could not rely on the paper's reviewers, as when the premiere of his '*Irish*' *Symphony* was completely ignored. When another newcomer, Henry Leslie, premiered his oratorio *Judith*, the *Telegraph*, whilst giving the work generous column space, ultimately judged it merely 'pleasing and pretty' rather than genuinely 'great or grand'.[14] Alongside its patchy and unreliable projection of English music, the *Telegraph* admonished any hint of the 'avant-garde' in new English music. So that when Hugo Pierson brought extracts of his new *Hezekiah* to the Nor-

---

[10] See Bennett, *Forty Years* Chapter 3 for vignettes of the chief music critics of the 1860s.

[11] *DTel* 29 Jun. 1864.

[12] *DTel* 29 Aug. 1867.

[13] *DTel* 7 Apr. 1862. See also Chapter 5 below.

[14] *DTel* 4 Sept. 1858.

wich Festival the paper ignored the music completely, confining its notice to details of the libretto and reporting that only a 'meagre' 550 people attended the performance.[15]

This pattern of uneven coverage of new English music came to an abrupt end in 1870 when the *Telegraph* appointed Joseph Bennett (1831–1911) as its chief critic. Bennett was a man of strong and unchanging opinions and a journalist who regarded his profession more as a calling than a craft. Above all, he was a music patriot, a passionate champion of England's past glories and a determined advocate of the nation's musical potential. Although Bennett was a Schumannite, which placed him (for a while) on the progressive wing of musical opinion, he was at heart a self-confessed 'musical conservative' implacably opposed to most of the developments in European music after 1850.[16] From 1870 onwards, Bennett monopolised the music column of the *Telegraph* remaining as the paper's chief (and only) music critic until his retirement in 1906.

## 1.   Joseph Bennett: 'Patriarch and Head of the Profession'.[17]

> [Bennett] was invaluable as a commercial asset [and] had great influence. [...] People read him. Even in my own time, when an important new work was produced we used to question each other: 'What does Old Joe say'?. [...] If he damned a work – well, that work was damned. [...] He was the public: the people: the common people.[18]

Born in Gloucestershire in 1831, Joseph Bennett came from a modest nonconformist background and entered journalism with neither a formal musical education nor contacts in the musical world. Having toyed with the idea of becoming a Nonconformist minister, he spent many years as a chapel organist and schoolmaster before joining the *Sunday Times* as an occasional reviewer in 1865. Thereafter, his rise in the ranks of the watchmen was rapid, culminating in his appointment on the *Telegraph* in 1870. In his autobiography written years later, Bennett wrote of the 'strange condition' of music journalism in London in the 1860s, in which a small world of hacks was characterised by cliques and feuds, at the centre of which was *The Times*'s critic, James Davison.[19] Although he

---

[15] *DTel* 2 Sept. 1869.
[16] Bennett, 'Victorian Music' *MT* 1 Jan. 1897.
[17] Sir Edward Elgar's flattering description of Bennett in 1905. See below p. 57.
[18] Cumberland, *Set Down in Malice* pp. 143–4.
[19] Bennett, *Forty Years* p. 9.

claimed to represent a younger 'new generation of musical critics' unconcerned by the disputes of the older men, the industrious and ambitious Bennett relied on Davison, whom he referred to as 'captain of the host', for patronage in his early years as a critic.[20] The result was that by the time he joined the *Telegraph*, Bennett had built up an impressive network of contacts in the world of music and music journalism, a circle which included Sterndale Bennett, Sullivan, Carl Rosa, and August Manns, resident conductor at the Crystal Palace. The last wrote of Bennett (in 1906) that he 'greatly assisted me in my efforts in making Crystal Palace music a healthful nursery of musical art in England'.[21] The clearest indication of Bennett's musical ideology in his early career is gained from a hagiographic article which he wrote on Schumann for the *Pall Mall Gazette*, in which he described the composer as 'the prophet of a new artistic faith' to whose vision the world had not yet been 'converted'.[22] It was this piece which first brought him to the attention of George Grove, who thought the article marked 'an epoch in English musical criticism'.[23] The two men soon became very close friends.

In 1870, the year that Bennett was appointed *Telegraph* critic, the recognised standard-bearers of English music in the compositional field were Sullivan and, to a lesser degree, Macfarren.[24] The former consistently enjoyed Bennett's support, the critic regarding him as a pivotal figure in the future revival of English music. As we shall see, even when Sullivan's music flopped with other watchmen, Bennett promoted and projected the composer's operettas and Art-Music. For example, in his review of *The Mikado* (1885), he defended Sullivan as a genuine 'humorist in music' and for keeping 'the sacred lamp alight' in his stage works.[25] It was the same story when *The Gondoliers* (1889) was premiered, an occasion when Bennett broke ranks with many of his fellow-critics to defend Sullivan's theatre works in ringing terms:

> Connoisseurs of the divine art may listen to it with half contemptuous toleration [but ...] It is much less difficult to compose music that nobody understands – many people do it – than to give forth strains on which no shadow of doubt ever falls. [...] *The Gondoliers* music is as fully a work of art as anything of higher import from the same accomplished pen.[26]

---

[20] Ibid. p. 27. and p. 21.

[21] Manns q. in ibid. p. 122.

[22] Bennett, 'Robert Schumann'.

[23] Grove q. in Young, *Grove* p. 104.

[24] Sterndale Bennett finally ceased to compose around 1870 and died in 1875.

[25] *DTel* 16 Mar. 1885. Bennett's reception of Sullivan is discussed in detail in Chapter 5 below.

[26] *DTel* 9 Dec. 1889.

This review reveals Bennett's evident relish in portraying himself as the people's critic, a journalist free of elitism and snobbery who had his finger on the pulse of the musical public. In Sullivan, Bennett saw a champion of time-honoured musical ideals – melody, formal structure, wit and sentiment – in an age which had abjured these values. Bennett and Sullivan eventually celebrated their friendship and shared musical ideals in their collaboration on *The Golden Legend* (1886), the premier of which Bennett declared to be a turning-point in the struggle against Wagnerism in England. In his notice, Bennett criticised Wagner by implication when he celebrated Sullivan's 'trust in the power of tune' in an age of musical 'confusion and incoherence':

> [Sullivan] dares in all things to be simple. It is very odd that among those who pretend to lead the van of musical progress, simplicity should have come to be looked upon as an offence. [... *The Golden Legend* reflects] through the medium of beautiful and well-ordered art the very spirit of incident, utterance and situation.[27]

Although the tone here is defensive the meaning is clear: English music should look to Sullivan as its hero, even its saviour, in a decadent age. Years earlier, Bennett had declared that Sullivan was 'the most promising of young English composers' and never stopped believing that he had a vital part to play in the Musical Renaissance.[28]

In contrast, Bennett had little time for the music of Macfarren and did not support the composer's attempts to enhance his reputation in the 1870s and 1880s. As a result, Macfarren's new festival works were given a cool reception in the *Telegraph*, as with the oratorio, *The Resurrection*, of which it reported, 'it appeals more to the intellect than the emotions [and] therefore fails in its aim'.[29] Still, Macfarren was at the time a force to be reckoned with, and his last major festival work, the oratorio *King David* (1883), was given full coverage in the *Telegraph*. Bennett's notice wearily made the most of a bad job stressing that the new work was free of (Wagnerian) 'new-fangled devices' and 'crude ideas born of a reckless age'.[30]

Although Bennett's professional life was centred on the *Telegraph*, his music journalism was much in demand elsewhere. Most especially, he penned articles for the *Musical Times* and helped the ailing Davison to bring out the *Musical World*. However, perhaps the most demanding of

---

[27] *DTel* 18 Oct. 1886.

[28] *DTel* 28 Aug. 1873.

[29] *DTel* 31 Aug. 1876. Macfarren's *Violin Concerto*, premiered at the Philharmonic Society three years earlier, failed to secure a notice.

[30] *DTel* 13 Oct. 1883. Macfarren was Professor of Music at Cambridge University (1875–87), Principal of the RAM (1876–87), and a close friend of J. W. Davison.

Bennett's sidelines was his period as editor of Novello's short-lived music weekly *Concordia*. This journal ran for only a year (1875–6) and marked Novello's attempt to break into the weekly market in direct competition with the *Musical World*. *Concordia*, wide-ranging in its content, set out to place music in the context of all the arts and become a journal for 'all shades of opinion in art matters to communicate to the world'.[31] It was an ambitious project, and Bennett, who clearly relished his editorial role, was bitter when Novello's closed the journal after a year.[32]

Away from the *Telegraph* Bennett wrote some of his most important journalism for the *Musical Times*. It was for this journal that, in 1883, he produced a revealing article, 'English Music in 1884', in which he set out his vision of the future of European music. In this piece, he argued that music on the continent was in crisis: the Germans had 'no-one younger than Brahms'; the Italians could only look to the 'extinct volcano', Verdi; the French remained 'eccentric and extravagant'; while the Slavs threatened the continent with music that would 'precede the race itself into Western Europe'.[33] In this apocalyptic scenario, English music would come into its own and rescue European musical culture from the Slavic hordes. In Bennett's vision, native music, having finally entered a renaissance period would flourish because of a 'new direction of national energies'. Empire, he argued, had reached its 'limit of development' and only music could replace the outworn imperial project.[34] Bennett named five young composers – Parry, Cowen, Stanford, Mackenzie and Goring Thomas – who, with Sullivan, had 'the immediate future of English Music in their hands', and the responsibility to 'conserve everything distinctly English [and] reject modern and unproven theories'.[35] There is no clearer statement of the critic's reception strategy for English music. Bennett, a Christian moralist and patriot, was a ruthless power-broker who tried to shape the future of national music in his journalism.

Within the Renaissance Bennett had for some years the highest hopes of Frederic Cowen. Bennett his first reviewed Cowen's music in 1876 when the cantata *The Corsair* and the opera *Pauline* were premiered. Bennett liked *The Corsair* holding it to be 'a work full of imagination and skill, and one upon Mr Cowen can be fitly congratulated, and a

---

[31] Bennett's editorial in the first issue of *Concordia*, 1 May 1875.

[32] Bennett, *Forty Years* p. 229. Bennett briefly became the founder-editor of another new journal, *The Lute*, for the Patey & Willis company in 1883–4.

[33] Bennett, 'English Music in 1884'.

[34] Ibid. Bennett's patriotism extended to serving as captain in an army reserve unit. See 'Examination in Tactics' (18 Mar. 1884) in J. Bennett Letters. RCM Archive.

[35] Ibid.

distinct addition to the resources of English art'.[36] With *Pauline* however, it was a different story, with the critic berating the composer for failing to kick-start the longed-for revival of English opera:

> [Cowen] knows, as we all know, that English opera is an utterly discredited thing with the public, and could not float a loan of sixpence on its own merits if it tried. [... He] must have been touched by the thought that upon him had fallen the honour and responsibility of leading English opera in another struggle for success. [... Yet] *Pauline* wants the vitality and force which alone can make it spiritually as well as sensually felt. [...] much more than this is necessary to ensure the revival, in any degree, of English opera.[37]

This notice reveals Bennett's 'carrot and stick' approach to English composers: on the one hand he urged them on to put nation before inspiration, duty before creative imagination; on the other, he castigated their efforts if they fell short of his narrow conservative criteria. Either way, he usually proffered future support should the composer justify himself anew. For Bennett, an English musical work was to be judged on two simple criteria: on whether it rejected Wagnerite 'progressivism'; and on its value to the national music. That is, on its patriotic merits. In any case, Bennett's 'good opinion' of Cowen survived the disappointment of *Pauline*, since in 1880, he was happy to project Cowen's *'Scandinavian' Symphony* in a review which contained harsh words about English attitudes to music:

> look what obstacles an English musician who regards his vocation as something higher than a means of living has to contend [...] lofty aims are frowned upon [...] A composer may put forth the tender leaves of hope today, but there is little encouragement for tomorrow's blossoms. [...] our plain duty is to assign [the Scandinavian] a high place among kindred works [... which comes] within 'a measurable distance' of greatness.[38]

Even after he had fixed on Parry as the new best hope for the Renaissance, Bennett still gave both Cowen's *Symphony No. 4 'Cambrian'* (1884) and *Symphony No. 5* (1887) a positive reception. Of the latter, he wrote that it explored 'the limitless field of abstract music [in which ...] the greatest musical success has been made, and ever will be made though a weak-kneed generation may be unable to appreciate it'.[39] The critic's support to Cowen's cause is seen at its most extravagant in his reception of the oratorio *The Transfiguration* (1895), of which he de-

---

[36] *DTel* 30 Aug. 1876.
[37] *DTel* 25 Nov. 1876.
[38] *DTel* 20 Dec. 1880.
[39] *DTel* 15 Jun. 1887.

clared: 'no living composer has such individuality. I recognise him on the summit of the Mount of Transfiguration'.[40]

Meanwhile, Bennett had an uneasy relationship with Grove's team at the new RCM. Parry he initially regarded as too Wagnerian in his sympathies, whilst Stanford he always held to be coldly academic and lacking emotion. The egalitarian Bennett also distrusted the privilege and power that their RCM professorships conferred on the two men. Despite these reservations, he eventually saw Parry as a potential leader of the Renaissance – as long as the composer would turn his back on Wagnerite 'decadence'.[41] Accordingly, in the 1880s, Bennett's projection of Parry's music in the *Telegraph* varied depending on the 'progressivism' or 'classical' conservatism of the work premiered. On the occasion of the premiere of Parry's *Prometheus Unbound*, Bennett coldly observed that Parry was merely a 'disciple of the modern German school [and] something less at present than a master, even in the eccentric school of his adoption'.[42]

As Parry shed his Wagnerite skin so Bennett's opinion of him changed. When his *Symphony No. 3* was premiered, Bennett was delighted to draw attention to the work's perceived 'Englishness' in the programme-note for the concert.[43] It was from this reference that the symphony took its *sobriquet*. Bennett ensured that the epithet stuck by repeating the idea of the symphony being quintessentially 'English' in his *Telegraph* review the next day. This notice also proclaimed Parry as 'one of our strongest composers, in the full vigour of his manhood, disdaining the mystic and the sensational [for] simplicity and directness'.[44] For Bennett, the *'English' Symphony* marked the defining moment when Hubert Parry became the leader of the Musical Renaissance.

Bennett remained a staunch Parry supporter for the rest of his career. Even in the early 1900s, when the composer's music had lost much of its lustre for other watchmen, Bennett stayed loyal to his cause. For example, when *The Soul's Ransom* was premiered in 1906, the *Telegraph* sympathetically remarked – in the language of scripture which Bennett was so fond – that no-one could 'refuse to see the sermon which, enforced by the power of music, may bring comfort to the poor and to those who are cast down'.[45] Two years later at the end of his

---

[40] *DTel* 13 Sept. 1895.

[41] See Chapter 6 below.

[42] *DTel* 8 Sept. 1880.

[43] Bennett wrote the Philharmonic Society's programme-notes for many years (1885–1903).

[44] *DTel* 25 May 1889. See also Chapter 6 below.

[45] *DTel* 13 Sept. 1906.

career, Bennett affirmed the central importance of Parry and his *Third Symphony* to the Renaissance in a *Telegraph* feature-article when he asked: 'have we English any music properly so-called?'[46] He answered the question in the affirmative, judging the *'English' Symphony* as a ground-breaking work which inspired 'other musicians [...] towards a definite English style'.[47]

Stanford's music too had a mixed reception in the *Telegraph*, with the composer's attempts to establish himself as a major composer of opera proving particularly vexatious. Even so, Stanford's first opera, *The Canterbury Pilgrims*, was well received, Bennett declaring it an 'important opera' for its 'English flavour' and for keeping 'abreast of the musical age'.[48] Yet it was to be a very different story when Stanford's second opera, *Savonarola*, was given its English premiere (in German and with the German cast) at Covent Garden that same summer of 1884. Despite the illustrious venue and the direction of Hans Richter, *Savonarola* proved a one-performance disaster to which Bennett's notice undoubtedly contributed:

> a more depressing evening has seldom been spent in a first-class opera house, and we may assume, with perfect confidence, that those who endured it will get it out of their memory as quickly as they would a bad dream.[49]

Not surprisingly perhaps, it was to be nearly a decade before Stanford risked another 'bad dream' by bringing forward another new opera. And when he eventually did, with *The Veiled Prophet of Khorassan*, Bennett was again unimpressed; so that while admiring its 'musical scholarship', he judged it 'lacking in those higher qualities which lift an opera from the scholarly to the inspirational plane'.[50] It was only with the arrival of *Shamus O'Brien* in 1896 that Bennett was prepared to concede that Stanford had any talent for writing for the stage. The critic liked *Shamus* for two reasons: first, being based on a subject drawn from the 'annals of the poor', it sought to bring Irish peasant folk to comic life; and second, he saw in the opera a celebration of nationality in music coupled with a rejection of the 'decadent' internationalism against which he had railed for so long:

> Nationality in art is our safeguard from the cosmopolitan culture which would make all art as unattractive and narrow as cosmo-

---

[46] Bennett, 'English Music'.
[47] Ibid.
[48] *DTel* 29 Apr. 1884.
[49] *DTel* 10 Jul. 1884.
[50] *DTel* 27 Jul. 1893.

politan society. Let us, then, have Irish operas, Scottish operas, Welsh operas, as well as English – anything racy of the soil, instinct with the ideas and emotions of the people expressed through their own verbal and tonal speech.[51]

By this time, Bennett had clearly given up on his long-cherished objective, an indigenous national grand opera tradition. Instead, the best he hoped for was a proliferation of 'Shamuses' (or perhaps even of 'Gondoliers') that might do the trick in reinvigorating English opera. *Shamus O'Brien* briefly persuaded Bennett that Stanford might become an Anglo-Irish 'Dvořák', the latter being for him a composer whose music was 'new and not mischievous', and capable of capturing 'the spirit of the time present [while]guided by the wisdom of the past'.[52]

Apart from *Shamus* Bennett was equivocal about most of Stanford's music. Deep down he felt that the Irish composer was too academic and lacking in poetic feeling. Consequently, Stanford never enjoyed consistent support in the *Telegraph*. When the oratorio *Eden* was first given in 1891, Bennett cuttingly described it as a 'test of pluck of endurance' and a work in which 'beauty was designedly absent'.[53] Despite his aversion to Stanford's music, Bennett occasionally found a reason to project him more favourably. For example, the choral ballad *The Revenge*, he praised as a turning-point in English orchestral music for the way it tried to bridge 'the gulf between the 'million' and the cultured few in the matter of a common musical sympathy'.[54] As Bennett increasingly became dismayed with contemporary trends in music, he learned to ignore Stanford's academicism and appreciate the solid conservative (Schumann-Brahms) values enshrined in his work. When the composer premiered his *Requiem* at the 1897 Birmingham Festival, the critic welcomed it as his best ever effort since it had the 'breath of inspiration' and a vitality that exercised 'power over men'.[55] It was the same story a decade later, when Stanford premiered his *Symphony No. 6*, the critic plaintively remarked that it was 'pleasant to meet with a modern composition so sane as this'.[56]

During the 1880s, that decade which Bennett held to be crucial to the evolution of national music, he keenly supported the operas of Arthur Goring Thomas. Although one has the impression that the critic sus-

---

[51] *DTel* 3 Mar. 1896.
[52] Bennett, 'Anton Dvořák'.
[53] *DTel* 8 Oct. 1891.
[54] *DTel* 15 Oct. 1886.
[55] *DTel* 7 Oct. 1897.
[56] *DTel* 19 Jan. 1906.

pected that Goring Thomas was not a major talent, the composer's perceived determination to swim against the Wagnerian tide secured generous support. Accordingly, when *Esmeralda* was premiered by Rosa at Drury Lane, the *Telegraph* gave it a big review which declared it to be a 'very clever and pleasing work'. Even so the meat of the review was devoted to what the opera was not:

> So many young composers reflect the turgid tendencies of Germany that it is quite a relief to see one in love with the grace and piquancy that characterise our nearest neighbours [...] We do not know whether *Esmeralda* will keep the stage at a time when public taste demands loud noises and the concomitants of sensationalism.[57]

The 'turgid' sensationalist influences of Germany were still (as far as the critic was concerned) out of bounds two years later when Goring Thomas's *Nadeshda* was premiered by the same company:

> Those who witnessed the birth of this novelty and gave themselves time for reflection upon it, saw another proof that the long eclipse of English music is ending [...] Such success lets in light, and helps to take away a reproach to which accidental circumstances alone, and not inherent causes, have given an appearance of justice.[58]

Once again, Bennett's favourite birth metaphor is at work here; *Nadeshda* is new life brought into the world to confound those who proclaimed the barrenness of musical England. It should be remembered that childbirth in Victorian times was often fatal; birth and death were often simultaneous events. This tension is frequently present in Bennett's reception of English music.

As far as the reception of Mackenzie's music was concerned, Bennett viewed him as a fifth column of progressivism which could corrupt (and possibly destroy) the citadel of English music. It should be remembered that, in the early-1880s, the Scottish composer was seen by many watchmen as one of the brightest hopes of the Renaissance, most especially in the quest for a national opera. When therefore in 1883, Mackenzie brought forward his first opera, *Columba*, a Wagnerinspired production based on a libretto by Francis Hueffer, Bennett was ready. He gave his feelings full rein in a long review which poured scorn on Hueffer for his arrogance in thinking that he could 'perfect our lyric drama all at once'.[59] As for Mackenzie's music, Bennett had contemptuously little to say except, affecting sadness rather than anger, he admonished the composer for using the leitmotiv, that 'arbitrary

---

[57] *DTel* 29 Mar. 1883.
[58] *DTel* 17 Apr. 1885.
[59] *DTel* 11 Apr. 1883.

device' which was a 'baleful influence on dramatic music'. Despite the vitriol, Bennett still hoped that Mackenzie would yet shine and even rise to the 'highest position'.[60] Years later the composer recalled *Columba*'s dreadful press reception, ruefully observing that not even Prime Minister Gladstone's much publicised support for the work – attendance on the second night, receiving Mackenzie in his box, breakfast at No. 10 Downing Street – could save the work from ultimate oblivion.[61]

Mackenzie however, defying Bennett's bullying, did not turn away from the 'music of the future'. As already mentioned, three years later he and Hueffer tried again to launch a revival of English opera along Wagnerian lines with *The Troubadour*. In his notice of the first night, Bennett took the opportunity to launch a diatribe against Wagnerism astonishing for its violence:

> Every effect has a cause, and there must be a reason why the modern operatic stage, especially that of a certain school, is stained with filth and crime [...] The Bayreuth master – another form of Bunyan's Man with a Muckrake – never sought to disguise that garbage that he found in the Newgate Calendar of mythland, or set his imagination to invent. It suited his daring character, and furthered his personal ambition, to defy the world.[62]

This review shows Bennett, the Nonconformist chapel-organist and would-be minister, at his ranting moralising best. *The Troubadour*, he insisted had to be viewed as an opera founded on the same 'filth' and 'crime' with its priapic minstrel, adulterous wife and a 'wronged husband' portrayed as 'villain'. Of the music he had virtually nothing to say. The critic concluded his review by declaring the new work 'repellent in root and branch' while giving Hueffer and Mackenzie a short sermon on what opera should be:

> Every such work should have a moral purport, especially when it represents vice and crime [...] Human passion is strong enough and men and women are sufficiently masters of the casuistry which encourages its exercise not to need stimulating by counterfeit presentment.[63]

Bennett was clearly finding it hard to remain in touch with an age dominated by Pateresque aestheticism, Wildean decadence and Wagne-

---

[60] Ibid.

[61] Mackenzie, *Musician's Narrative*, p. 111. Despite *Columba*'s reception the work was taken on a brief tour of the provinces before being performed in Hamburg and Berlin.

[62] *DTel* 10 Jun. 1886.

[63] Ibid.

rian 'garbage'. Despite his profound disagreements with Mackenzie, Bennett never lost sight of the fact that the Scotsman was still an essential member of the core group upon which the Musical Renaissance depended. As a result, Mackenzie's new (albeit mostly orchestral) works of the 1890s had a more positive reception in the *Telegraph*.[64]

By the end of the 1880s, Bennett was at the pinnacle of his career. In January 1884, he signed a new ten-year contract with the *Telegraph* which gave him a salary of £700 pa (plus expenses) so long as he agreed to write exclusively for the paper 'save and except for occasional contributions to monthly magazines or serials not being newspapers'.[65] The *Telegraph* was clearly prepared to pay handsomely for Bennett's services, despite (or perhaps because of) the deeply conservative values he brought to his journalism. Bennett lived very well by his pen: a stylish Hampstead flat (109 Finchley Road); a wide circle of illustrious friends and contacts; free travel to musical events at home and abroad (he attended the first Bayreuth season in 1876); and, of course, real influence in national musical life. Bennett's new *Telegraph* contract was eloquent testimony to his position (in Elgar's memorable phrase) as 'patriarch and head of the profession'.

It is fascinating to ponder on how the music pages of the *Telegraph* and *The Times* reflected the two polarities of musical opinion and debate in the 1880s. There could hardly be a more striking contrast between the two papers' critics. Hueffer, the highly educated, radical, Wagnerian Rhinelander with a mission to change the face of English music. Bennett, the Gloucester Congregationalist, equally determined to protect and preserve English music from the godless decadence and immorality of Bayreuth's influence. In the same way that Hueffer promoted and projected the 'music of the future', Bennett sought to thwart this future, using his column almost as a prophylactic to prevent the deadly virus from infecting all that was good and pure in the English Musical Renaissance. A case of Hueffer *contra* Bennett?

Despite Bennett's opposition to many modern trends in music, a perceptible softening of attitude can be detected in his reviews around 1890. Especially striking is the toning down of the usual harsh, uncompromising condemnation of Wagnerism and other 'turgid tendencies of Germany'. Instead a new, more tolerant attitude towards contemporary trends in music is evident. It could be, of course, that the elderly critic

---

[64] For example, when Mackenzie's *'Scottish' Piano Concerto*, commissioned by Paderewski, was premiered at the Philharmonic Society, Bennett wanly commented that it gave him 'decided pleasure', *DTel* 25 Mar. 1897.

[65] Bennett's contract in the *Daily Telegraph* Archives.

had a genuine conversion to the music of Bayreuth. Far more likely though is that Bennett realised that he could no longer swim against the tide without drowning in his own musical prejudices. Although Bennett was a family man (married, one daughter) he clearly loved his work and his journalism was, one suspects, his life. Could it be that the only way for him to stay at the *Telegraph* in the long-term was to make some accommodation with the changing musical times?

Evidence of the fact that Bennett's more tolerant approach to Wagnerism was more pragmatic than authentic may be found in a series of articles on Wagner which he wrote for the *Musical Times* in 1890–91.[66] In this series, which drew heavily on Wagner's relationship with Liszt, Bennett sought not only to chart the composer's life, but also to assassinate his character. At turns Wagner is presented as an exploiter of friends, an arch-materialist, and an artist corrupted by arrogance and self-love. Bennett also condemned the composer for his anti-Semitism and political radicalism, suggesting that his politics stemmed more from petty grievance than any genuine revolutionary ideal. Of Wagner's famed involvement in the Dresden Revolt (1849), Bennett wrote: 'from bitter discontent to treason was but a short step and Wagner took it [...] faithless to the bread he had eaten, he joined the mob musket in hand'.[67] Even worse the composer, an embittered 'revolutionist', had plunged music into a state of 'warfare', an up-heaval which threatened the fabric of the world of music.[68] Throughout, Bennett had almost nothing to say about Wagner's music, confining himself to bald performance dates and details. The *Musical Times* series is a remarkable and extended piece of character assassination, clearly designed as a counter-blast to the Wagner cult already power-fully under way in England.

Even so Bennett understood that he had to compromise with *der Meister's* influence on new English music. The first significant sign of his more tolerant approach can be detected in his reception of Elgar. Despite the composer's avowed admiration for Wagner and Richard Strauss, Bennett was drawn to Elgar for many reasons. First, he was keen to support a native composer who palpably lacked the support of any clique or faction. Second, he empathised with Elgar's lower middle-class background in 'trade' and self-taught musical talent. Third, the compos-er's Severnside roots struck a chord with the critic's own regional pride and loyalty. Fourth, Bennett also warmed to Elgar's Christian faith and

---

[66] In all, the *MT* series consisted of twenty-three articles which appeared over a period of two years (Jan. 1890–Dec. 1891).

[67] *MT* Jun. 1890.

[68] *MT* Dec. 1891.

his willingness to write within the oratorio tradition so cherished by the critic. Finally, Bennett was flattered by the fact that Elgar kept him up to date on his plans and projects.

Bennett's reception of Elgar played a vital part in the Worcester composer's rise to national fame. His notice of the premiere of *Caractacus* (1898) conveyed the rapture with which he promoted his favourite's talents:

> For Mr Elgar, however, the freedom of modern workmanship is the breath of life [...] his choral writing is always virile, fluent and emphatic [... his] great gifts can be denied by no musician, whatever his personal faith may be [...].[69]

The same tone can be detected in a review of *The Apostles*, premiered five years later, when Bennett commented that the new oratorio was:

> not the work of a mere trafficker in musical goods. Its sincerity is unquestionable, the loftiness of its aim cannot be denied [...] whatever may be thought of its methods.[70]

More was to come. In 1904, the Worcester composer's pre-eminence in the Musical Renaissance was sealed with a three-day Elgar Festival at Covent Garden and Bennett was there to record the event in glowing terms. Of the new overture *In the South*, he gushed:

> We account *In the South* to be a really great and beautiful creation. [...] The fresh feeling of gladness; the gentle musing melancholy [... but] best of all is the artistic restraint that controlled the musician's thick-coming fancies, and made his whole powers minister to the beauty without which music is no better than the tinkling of a cymbal.[71]

In Bennett's reception of Elgar there is a genuine and deeply-felt admiration for a composer who, though contemporary, still adhered to the ideal of 'beauty'. For Bennett, Elgar bridged the gap between the music of the past and the 'music of the future' in a manner which had defied his contemporaries. The critic, as a sign of friendship and support, at the composer's invitation joined the Worcestershire Philharmonic Society (despite its Wagnerian motto '*Wach Auf!*'). Elgar, an accomplished manager of his own press, courted Bennett assiduously in the 1890s. As a result he had no more firm ally amongst the watchmen.

Elgar, on his part, acknowledged his debt to Bennett in a public lecture which he gave as Peyton Professor of Music at the University of

---

[69] *DTel* 5 Oct. 1898. See Chapter 7 below for a more detailed discussion on Bennett's reception of Elgar.

[70] *DTel* 15 Oct. 1903.

[71] *DTel* 17 Mar. 1904.

Birmingham in 1905. In this address on 'Critics' Elgar singled Bennett out for special mention:

> English criticism should be – honest, fearless and reasonable. There are many younger writers of whom I could write [...] but I instance Mr Bennett as the patriarch and head of the profession.[72]

The term 'patriarch', with its connotations of father-figure and spiritual guardian, vividly acknowledged Bennett's status in British music journalism. Paternalistic, Christian, moral and judgmental, Bennett most certainly was – and proud of the fact. The composer's compliment obviously delighted the old critic since, three days after the lecture, Lady Elgar noted that her husband had received 'a nice telegram from J. Bennett'.[73]

Bennett was also keen to project other young English composers. The critic, as evidenced in Elgar's case, had a natural predisposition to favour the underdog and Edward German certainly came into this category. When the composer premiered his *Symphony No. 2 'Norwich'*, Bennett, having praised him for 'a notable and valuable addition to English orchestral music', went on to note that:

> the young Englishman's position has been won by sheer hard work. Advantages other than those which lie within himself he has never courted, and assuredly they have never been thrust upon him.[74]

Frederick Cliffe too benefited from Bennett's support in the *Telegraph* as when his *Symphony No. 2* was hailed as 'a very interesting and poetical work' and 'one of the most elaborate productions of contemporary art'.[75]

In spite of Bennett's pragmatic accommodation with Wagnerism, he opposed much that was new in English music as the new century approached. The work of Coleridge-Taylor in particular found no favour in the *Telegraph*. Of the composer's first festival commission, the *Ballade for Orchestra*, which had been recommended to the Gloucester Festival committee by Elgar, Bennett observed that it reflected the misuse of a 'very great talent'.[76] In language suggestive of the white European male's anxiety about the black man's sexual potency, he continued in the same review:

> I am not going to discuss the work, but simply to observe that already, through the Russians, we possess enough of music tinc-

---

[72] Young, *A Future for English Music*, p. 181.

[73] Ibid. p. 191. A selection of Elgar's letters to Bennett were published in 'Elgar and Joseph Bennett', *DTel* 4 Sept. 1937.

[74] *DTel* 5 Oct. 1893.

[75] *DTel* 8 Oct. 1892. See also positive reviews of Cliffe's *Symphony No. 1* in *DTel* 22 Apr. 1889 and *Violin Concerto* in *DTel* 9 Oct. 1896.

[76] *DTel* 16 Sept. 1898.

tured with the barbaric. Our art is not, I hope, to be controlled by
primitive instincts, but the hope is faint, seeing how the public
applaud that which is bizarre, extravagant and startling. The best
wish for the clever Anglo-African is that he may exercise restraint
and attain to the chaste dignity of highly-cultivated art.[77]

Bennett may have eventually accepted that western music had to progress,
but he was not prepared to tolerate non-European violation of the
immaculate beauty of music. Even so, by the time Coleridge-Taylor's
*Scenes from Hiawatha* was given its first complete performance by the
Royal Choral Society (1900), Bennett's attitude had mellowed since he
pointed out that it was a 'creation of the highest importance, bound to
exercise large influence upon English music'.[78] In Bennett's later reception of English music a certain evasiveness may be detected; already
approaching seventy, he was clearly struggling to stay in touch with the
increasing diversity of the Renaissance.[79]

Bennett delivered a withering judgement on the English Musical
Renaissance in a series of articles on 'Victorian Music' which appeared in the *Musical Times* in 1897.[80] At the outset, the critic having
declared himself a 'musical conservative' went on to bemoan a contemporary musical climate dominated by unsound musicianship and
'superficiality'.[81] For Bennett, English church music alone was an area
of success because it provided an 'illustration of our national character' in its resistance to change and in its adherence to continuity.[82] As
for the rest, he was despondent about the state of English opera as the
new century beckoned, despite his own best efforts gloomily conclud-
ing:

> never, perhaps, was the fortune of English opera so low as now
> [...] we find evidence of decadence steadily progressing [and] there
> is little hope for opera in England in point of really national
> support.[83]

Of English orchestral music, and with Elgar in mind, Bennett conceded
that 'substantial progress had been made' and hoped that 'the still
spreading and deepening enthusiasm of the public may be rightly

---

[77] Ibid.

[78] *DTel* 23 Mar. 1900.

[79] The *Daily Telegraph* chose to ignore Granville Bantock's first two big premieres – of
*Jaga-Naut* (1900) and *The Witch of Atlas* (1902).

[80] Bennett, 'Victorian Music'. The series consisted of eleven articles (*MT* issues Jan.-
Jul. and Sept.–Dec. 1897).

[81] Ibid. (*MT* Jan. 1897).

[82] Ibid. (*MT* Apr. 1897.

[83] Ibid. (*MT* Jul. 1897).

guided'.[84] The critic however held out the greatest hopes for chamber music, since it alone had:

> freedom from reckless changes and, as a corollary, its general adhesion to the rules of the great masters [...] So the tide of change sweeps past chamber music, leaving it comparatively unaffected. It is a "city of refuge" for the art which, in other cities, encounters forces that tend to demoralisation. There the musician is free to be musical. No temptations whisper to him with siren voices.[85]

Bennett had, throughout his long career, served loyally as a watchman on the walls of England's music. His abiding principle throughout had been 'freedom from change', and he had spent his professional life trying to persuade English musicians to adhere to the same doctrine.

By the time he retired from the *Daily Telegraph* in 1906, Bennett's disillusion with the direction of English music was well-nigh absolute. In his last reviews for the newspaper, from the Birmingham Festival that same year, Bennett's disenchantment was palpable in his notices of three English works premiered at the event. Even Elgar's new oratorio, *The Kingdom*, could not lift his spirits, so that while he generally welcomed the work, he put its success down to 'Elgar charm' and 'a hypnotised public responding meekly to the suggestions of a gifted and daring composer'.[86] The second English piece premiered was by Granville Bantock, the cantata *Omar Khayyam*, which Bennett savaged as typical of contemporary composers' infatuation with Bayreuth:

> They should walk in the way their fathers trod and see what can be done there. The world has not been asleep since they were born [although] the present work has many 'beauty spots', delicate charms of orchestration and pleasant touches of melody [...] the difficulty is that the composer cannot get out of the Wagner rut.[87]

In the same vein, the *Telegraph*'s review of the third new English work on display, Josef Holbrooke's symphonic poem, *The Bells*, captured the spirit of utter dejection with which Bennett left his craft:

> I refuse to consider it as necessary to go into a detailed examination of the composer's work. I have been told that an understanding of his art is beyond me. If that be the truth, I am glad to admit it.[88]

Thus did Bennett leave his vocation, not so much with a bang as with a weary and embittered whimper. In his final years as a journalist, he

---

[84] Ibid. (*MT* Nov. 1897).

[85] Ibid. (*MT* Dec. 1897).

[86] *DTel* 4 Oct. 1906.

[87] *DTel* 5 Oct. 1906.

[88] Ibid. Even after 'retirement', Bennett clung on at the paper until 1908 with the honorific title of 'music editor'.

regarded the total achievement of the Musical Renaissance, despite all his efforts, as deeply flawed and bitterly disappointing.

Despite his disillusion, Bennett's influence on the course and development of English music during its most formative 'renaissance' period can hardly be underestimated. Apart from his thirty six years on the *Telegraph*, he was, as we have seen, a regular and prolific essayist on the *Musical Times* and a stalwart contributor to the *Musical World*. Alongside his music journalism, he also found time to write the programme-notes for the Philharmonic Society's concerts (1885–1903), as well as an autobiography, *Forty Years of Music* (1908).

Bennett also made a minor mark on English music as a librettist. The most notable of his 'books of words' was that of *The Golden Legend* written for Sullivan.[89] He also provided texts for the younger composers of the Renaissance: for Cowen, he wrote *Thorgrim* and *Ruth*; and for Mackenzie, he wrote the *Jubilee Ode* (1887), *The Rose of Sharon* (1884) and *Bethlehem* (1894). Several contemporaries took a dim view of such collaborations. Not least the Irish dramatist (and sometime music critic) George Bernard Shaw who, on the premiere of *Thorgrim*, attacked the unhealthy relationship between composers and critic-librettists.[90] Shaw pilloried Bennett in particular as a purveyor of 'doggerel' verse, who was commissioned to write libretti only because of his 'enormous power' in the *Telegraph* which would 'secure such a backing of press bluff and press butter as would push and slide anything into good repute for a season at least'.[91]

Bennett's discourse was largely drawn from the Bible. In his reviews, composers are seen as virtuous or tainted, and almost always in need of moral guidance. Bennett took great pride in his role as patriarch of his profession. In this respect, as the *Musical Times* pointed out in its tribute to Bennett's life and career, his was a 'peculiarly early-Victorian' outlook which increasingly jarred with a changing musical world.[92] It is indeed difficult to disagree with *Grove 3*'s assessment of Bennett as having clung to 'a repressive style of dogmatic criticism' for far too long.[93] Yet for all that, there was much that was invigorating about

---

[89] Jacobs, *Sullivan* p. 243.

[90] G. B. Shaw in *The Hawk* 6 May 1890, q. in Laurence, *Shaw's Music* vol. ii pp. 41–4. In the light of Shaw's comments, it is interesting to note that, despite Bennett's appalling reviews of both *Columba* and *The Troubadour*, Mackenzie was prepared to collaborate with him on a major oratorio commission, *Bethlehem* (1894). The price of good notices?

[91] Ibid. p. 44.

[92] *MT* 1 Dec. 1910.

[93] Colles, entry on 'Robin Legge' in *Grove 3*, vol. iii p. 129.

'Old Joe"s journalism and, as Gerald Cumberland pointed out 'he was the public [...] and the people read him'.[94]


## 2. Robin Legge

Robin Legge, a Cambridge law graduate, was already an experienced music journalist by the time he was appointed critic at the *Telegraph*, having already served for fifteen years on *The Times* under Fuller Maitland. At the 'Thunderer', Legge had shown himself to be in accord with most developments in contemporary music and in him the *Telegraph* had secured the services of a critic who was prepared to be both modern and populist in approach. Legge's arrival at the paper meant that the Bennett era was finally over.

Legge felt that music should reach out to the largest possible audience and his support for new English music was consistent and powerful. At *The Times*, Legge had proved himself a keen admirer of Elgar, and under him the music columns of the *Telegraph* powerfully projected the composer's music. For his part, Elgar, a highly skilled manipulator of the press, recognised Legge as a loyal ally among the watchmen and gave him both privileged access to his circle and insights into work in progress. There is no better example of Legge's close relationship with Elgar than the way the critic was invited to a lunch party during Gloucester Festival week of 1910 at which Elgar and the violinist Fritz Kreisler ran through the draft score of the *Violin Concerto*. The result was a preview article in the *Telegraph* in which Legge hailed the new work as a milestone in musical history.[95] By this time Legge was clearly in affectionate awe of the composer, describing him to Lady Elgar as 'a remarkable person'.[96] When the *Violin Concerto* was premiered a few weeks later, Legge described it as 'a work of rare beauty and stupendous skill".[97] It was much the same story with regard to the Elgar's other pre-Great War works. The *Symphony No. 1*, which was given two *Telegraph* reviews, was triumphantly acclaimed as 'very decidedly English' and a 'masterpiece', while the *Symphony No. 2*, Legge promoted as 'a work of rare and real beauty and significance'. Even *Falstaff* secured glowing reviews, being curiously hailed as both 'intentionally and appropriately ugly' and a 'masterpiece of music'.[98]

---

[94] Cumberland, *Set Down in Malice*, pp. 143–4.
[95] *DTel* 26 Sept. 1910.
[96] Legge to Lady Elgar 8 Sep. 1910, q. in Moore, *Edward Elgar* p. 590.
[97] *DTel* 11 Nov. 1910.
[98] *DTel* 4 and 5 Dec. 1908, 25 May 1911 and 1 Oct. 1913. See also Chapter 7 below.

Legge was also a passionate advocate of Delius's music. The critic, having left Cambridge, received his musical education on the continent where he became dedicated to post-Wagnerian progressivism. Accordingly Legge became one of the first (and also one of the most influential) of Delius's supporters in England. Of the *Piano Concerto*, Legge wrote that it was 'profound' and 'essentially virile', the work of 'no dilettante scribbler [but that] of a composer of rarest sincerity and conviction'.[99] In the same review, he decried England's 'boasted progress in musical matters', and he questioned the validity of a 'musical renaissance' which had allowed a composer of Delius's stature to be marginalised. Two years later, the *Telegraph* came out strongly in favour of the *Mass of Life* – extracts from which were given their English premiere under Beecham – commenting on the work's 'immense virility' and 'dignity' and on the fact that it made 'no concession to any but the highest taste'. The same review went on with prescience and not a little anger:

> As, however, Mr Delius's country is slow, even among many of the professional element, to adopt any kind of art in its advanced form, it is unlikely that his music will become an integral part of the life of the present generation [...] The art progresses nevertheless, and it has always been the fate of the genuine progressive that his voice was as that of one crying in the wilderness.[100]

Legge's enthusiastic reception of Delius continued after the Great War and played an important part in preparing the ground for the Delius Festival of 1929.

Although Legge was at first hesitant about projecting Vaughan Williams' work, he soon became a convert to the composer and to the Pastoral School. When the *Tallis Fantasia* was first performed in 1910, the *Telegraph* was only quietly enthusiastic, judging it to be 'pregnant with musical matter of real moment', whilst allocating a mere twenty-five lines to it.[101] Within a few weeks, however, Legge had clearly warmed to Vaughan Williams's music, describing *A Sea Symphony* at its premiere as being of 'first importance from the point-of-view of British music' with its incessant vigour, its immensely broad lights, its nobility of conception and imagination, [it] easily overtops its composer's previous compositions, and at once places him among those who count in our native music world.[102]

---

[99] *DTel* 23 Oct. 1907.
[100] *DTel* 8 Jun. 1909.
[101] *DTel* 8 Sept. 1910.
[102] *DTel* 14 Oct. 1910.

By the time *A London Symphony* was premiered in 1914, the *Telegraph* had no doubts as to the importance of Vaughan Williams' to national music:

> [*A London Symphony* is ...] not only the most masterly but also the most beautiful work, musically or psychologically considered, from the pen of any musician of his generation that we have heard in recent years.[103]

However, the music of Vaughan Williams's fellow-pastoralist, Gustav Holst, did not fare well in the *Telegraph*. Legge seems to have felt that there was much that was 'un-English' in Holst's enthusiasm for the exotic and foreign. When the *Beni Mora Suite* was first given in 1912, it was dismissed as a pastiche:

> infinitely preferable would have been a rehearing of the same composer's *Somerset Rhapsody* – that is genuine all through. We do not ask for Biakra dancing-girls in Langham-Place, however clever their representation.[104]

Given Legge's commitment to 'progressive' English music, it is not surprising that his reception of the late works of Parry and Stanford was merely dutiful. For example, of Parry's cantata, *Beyond These Voices There is Peace* (1908), Legge commented that although 'worthy of consideration' that it had 'too much of the distressing voices and too little of heavenly peace'.[105] And of the same composer's *Symphony No. 5*, he concluded that 'its modernity is of a decade or more ago', while its 'brooding and pessimism [were] not productive of any prolonged loveliness'.[106] It was the same story with regard to important Stanford premieres: of the first performance of the *Songs of the Fleet* (1910), for example, Legge could only lamely remark that they were of 'merit, but not of commanding interest'.[107]

In contrast, Legge was keen to promote the music of Granville Bantock and Ethel Smyth (1858–1944). The former's *Fifine at the Fair*, premiered at the Birmingham Festival of 1912, was given a superlative review:

> Superbly put together, invented and scored by a truly masterly hand, Bantock has not given us for many days a work so likely to bring worshippers to the shrine of his great and genial talent.[108]

---

[103] *DTel* 30 Mar. 1914.
[104] *DTel* 2 May 1912.
[105] *DTel* 10 Sept. 1908.
[106] *DTel* 6 Dec. 1912.
[107] *DTel* 15 Oct. 1910.
[108] *DTel* 4 Oct. 1912.

In the same spirit, Smyth's opera, *The Wreckers*, was praised for its 'complex and vivid' music and for a 'strength of imagination, a steadfastness of purpose, and a dramatic instinct which combined in a way that must needs command attention'.[109] The reception of new English music in the *Telegraph* had rarely been so joyous and uninhibited.

Nearly sixty years after its inception the *Telegraph* had expanded in overall size without compromising its journalistic philosophy and coverage of events. An issue of 1911, still priced at one penny, would typically have twenty-four pages and contain the traditional mix of news, advertising, human interest stories (with an emphasis on violent crime and the courts), sport and entertainment. Within the latter category, although music coverage held its place during the Bennett era, relative to the growing size of the paper, it had suffered a decline. That falling off was quickly reversed when Legge took complete charge as music editor in 1908, with more expansive and lively treatment of music becoming the order of the day. The two main format changes introduced by Legge were the 'Music Page' and the 'Music of the Day' feature; the latter, which occupied one half-page in the Saturday issue, often jostling for space with the 'Page for Women' and the 'Motors and Motor-Boats' feature. Legge's efforts at popularising and extending music coverage in the *Telegraph* did not go unnoticed, not least by *Grove 3* which remarked that he had 'stimulated the general reader's interest in music and musicians to an uncommon extent'.[110]

Any understanding of the English Musical Renaissance has to take into account the importance of the *Daily Telegraph*. If *The Times* spoke to the political class, the *Athenaeum* to the green rooms of clubland, and the *Musical Times* to the musical nation, it was the *Daily Telegraph* that tried to make the nation musical in numbers that no other newspaper or journal could match.

---

[109] *DTel* 23 Jun. 1909.
[110] Colles, 'Robin Legge' in *Grove 3* vol. iii p. 129.

# CHAPTER THREE

# The *Athenaeum*

Principles: Those of sound intellectual culture, as the best and most
direct means of moral improvement. [...] Its musical and theatrical
critiques are ably written.[1]

The novelist Wilkie Collins observed in 1858 that the Victorian
epoch was an 'age of periodicals', a time in which a vast number of
quarterlies, monthlies and weeklies competed for a seemingly ever-
expanding readership.[2] In this marketplace for ideas, the literary
journals reigned supreme as the gatekeepers of culture and arbiters
of intellectual fashion. While several titles, such as the *Spectator*,
dated from Georgian times, many more were founded in the nineteenth century to cater for the tastes and aspirations of an expanding
and affluent middle-class. Among the leading newcomers were: the
*Saturday Review* (founded in 1855); *Macmillan's Magazine* (1859);
the *Fortnightly Review* (1865); and the *Athenaeum*, which was established as a weekly in 1828.[3]

From its inception, the *Athenaeum* dominated the weekly periodical
market with its breadth and depth of coverage. Although it hit its peak
circulation (at 18,000 copies per week) in the late-1830s, the journal
continued to sell well and make profits up to the end of the century.[4]
The *Athenaeum* under a succession of editors experienced few changes
of format and content. Throughout the period surveyed, it remained the
'acknowledged mentor in the literary and art world', its music coverage
unique among journals of its type.[5]

For this chapter I have consulted the complete series (1828–1921) of
the *Athenaeum* housed at the City University Library in London. This
copy ascribes in manuscript, a specific, named writer to most of the
articles printed in each issue of the journal after 1850. Given the enormous amount of information provided, it is probable that this is the
*Athenaeum* editors' own office set. Whatever its provenance, this copy
gives a unique insight into the identities of the journalists and occasional contributors who wrote for the journal.

---

[1] Mitchell, *Newspaper Press Directory*, p. 19.
[2] Wilkie Collins q. in Houghton, *British Periodicals*, p. 554.
[3] See Shattock and Wolff, *Victorian Periodical Press*.
[4] Sullivan, *British Literary Magazines: The Victorian and Edwardian Age* p. 21.
[5] Hatton, *Journalistic London* p. 204.

The history of the *Athenaeum* was characterised by continuity of ownership, editorial style, content and format. Early on the proprietorship rested with the Dilke family, thereafter passing (in 1869) into the hands of John Collins Francis, where it remained until the new century.[6] Under a succession of editors, most notably Hepworth Dixon, Norman MacColl and Vernon Randall, the *Athenaeum* did not undergo many changes in style or approach, continuing as the 'staid organ of critical opinion' in the eyes of many contemporaries.[7] In its format too, the journal changed little: in 1850, it was priced at 4d and it generally consisted either of twenty-four or thirty-two pages, one-third of which were dedicated to advertising.[8] As far as content was concerned: the 'Reviews' section held pride of place with about eight pages; features of general interest were allocated two pages; 'Our Weekly Gossip' covered two pages; 'Fine Arts' was given one page; 'Music and the Drama' was allocated around two pages; and 'Miscellanea' accounted for a page.[9] Over the years, the *Athenaeum* tended to expand, so that by 1912, a single issue would normally contain thirty-six pages, with the proportion of content to advertising remaining broadly constant.

It is possible to identify the *Athenaeum*'s chief music critics with considerable accuracy from the City University series. They were: Henry F. Chorley (critic 1833–68), Campbell Clarke (1868–70), Charles L. Gruneisen (1870–79), Ebenezer Prout (1879–88), Henry F. Frost (1888–98) and John S. Shedlock (1898–1916). Throughout this period it appears that the journal employed its music critics primarily for their experience and eminence. Chorley was appointed for his distinction as a literary critic and author; Campbell Clarke for his experience as music critic on the *Daily Telegraph*; and Gruneisen for long service as music critic on the *Morning Post*, that 'organ of the aristocracy and the fashionable world'.[10] Prout in turn was hired for his reputation as a scholar, music editor, critic and hard-hitting academic. As far as Frost and Shedlock were concerned, their more humble credentials had more to do with the decline in the journal's overall standards. There was, it seems, no editorial line that the *Athenaeum*'s critics were expected to follow; rather music reception was a matter for individual critics.

Although the *Athenaeum* was a 'literary' journal, from its inception it provided full coverage of music performances as well as articles on musical topics. For example, in November 1833, the journal supported

---

[6] Symon, *Press and its Story*, pp. 261–3.

[7] Ibid.

[8] See *Ath* 5 Oct. 1850.

[9] Ibid.

[10] Mitchell, *Newspaper Press Directory* p. 17.

the idea of a new non-profit making national opera company founded by public subscription 'for the general advancement of the science of music in this country'.[11] And in January 1834, after Chorley had taken over as critic from John Ella (1802–88), the journal allocated music a dedicated niche in a 'Music and the Drama' column that became a permanent feature. The importance of this development cannot be over-stated in an age when music was viewed by many as being dangerously emotional and politically suspect. Indeed, as John Ruskin warned:

> music is in her health the teacher of perfect order, and is the voice of the obedience of angels [...] In her depravity, she is also the teacher of perfect disorder and disobedience, and the *Gloria in Excelsis* becomes the *Marseillaise*.[12]

This mid-Victorian prejudice against music ran very deep. Thomas Carlyle, writing in 1851, painted opera in even more lurid terms:

> Your celestial opera house grows dark and infernal to me! Behind its glitter stalks the shadow of eternal death; through it, too, I look up not at the divine eye [...] but down into the bottomless eye socket – not upwards towards God, heaven and the throne of truth but too truly towards falsity, vacuity, and the dwelling place of despair.[13]

Both Ruskin and Carlyle held that, among the arts, music was closest to God ('the voice of the obedience of angels') while at the same time having the potential for the greatest moral and social harm. Further-more, in the opinion of many Victorians, music was un-English and even unmanly and therefore best left to foreigners. Despite such deep-rooted prejudice (even, or perhaps especially) among the educated classes, the *Athenaeum* accorded music equality with its sister arts. Concert and festival reviews were informed and comprehensive, with native music given prominence. This pattern of thorough reviewing was established by Chorley who, having introduced the discrete music section, devel-oped and expanded it so that, by the 1850s, it would regularly cover two pages.

Under Chorley, the *Athenaeum* became a major provider of informa-tion and opinion about music, coverage that continued for the rest of the century. Hardly any premiere of an English work escaped attention; even minor festival 'novelties' were mentioned in the tightly packed columns of the journal. From the evidence of the City University series, Chorley and his successors almost never farmed out concert notices to

---

[11] Anon., 'The Projected 'Grand National Opera", *Ath* 9 Nov. 1833.
[12] Ruskin, *Queen of the Air* p. 59.
[13] Carlyle q. in Davison, pp. 123–4.

occasional reviewers or 'special correspondents'. The chief critics themselves penned the vast majority of the *Athenaeum*'s music reviews.

## 1.   Henry F. Chorley: Critic as Patron

The Critic has largely replaced the Patron.[14]

Henry Chorley, high-priest of the critic cult, was ever willing to proclaim the power of his ministry. Chorley was a professional writer who was determined to place music and music criticism in the mainstream of intellectual and artistic life. An inveterate snob, he was dedicated to lifting music journalism from Grub Street and making it acceptable in clubland – his own preferred *milieu*. Above all, Chorley regarded himself as a critic-patron, bestowing patronage on the deserving while heaping odium on the undeserving. For him, the printed word was all-powerful in its ability to project and promote music, and he demanded all the respect and honour due to a journalist-benefactor of the new publishing age. In terms of music ideology, Chorley was a Mendelssohnian, a passionate supporter of the 'Elijah of the new art', who regarded the prophet's death as a catastrophe and of which he wrote 'the fountain is dry, – the familiar book is closed [...] no more great works shall be produced'.[15] For him 'Music' itself had 'died' with Mendelssohn. Chorley was by far the most influential music critic to write for the *Athenaeum*, a task that he fulfilled for thirty-five years.

Chorley was a music conservative who first understood the power of the critic-patron by observing musical life on the continent. He documented his experiences abroad in his seminal *Modern German Music* (1854). In this work, he revealed himself as a writer whose critical judgements were primarily based on moral, social and political considerations. Chorley not only believed that music was a 'good' in itself, but also that it performed a moral function in helping the individual reject materialism and superficiality. He also held that music benefited society in its potential to become a centripetal force for stability in an age beset by revolution. In his *Modern German Music*, he wrote bitterly of the political upheavals of the 1840s as heralding 'the destruction of established things'.[16] German music before the 'revolutions of 1848', he declared, had been 'gentle and simple' drawing upon a past enriched by the continuity from Bach to Mendelssohn.[17] This ordered vision stood

---

[14] Chorley, *Modern German Music* vol. ii p. 66.
[15] Ibid. p. 404.
[16] Ibid. pp. 401–4.
[17] Ibid. vol. i p. 54.

in stark contrast to the tide of 'anarchy' which Wagner had unleashed and which threatened to overwhelm European music. Chorley saw Wagnerism in political terms, as a revolutionary force with which there could be no compromise. He drew comfort only from the fact that 'the open proclamation of anarchy is less to be mistrusted than the discontents and plottings of secret conspiracy'.[18] His panic is palpable in these images of subversion, popular insurrection and blood in the streets. Away from defending the barricades of music, the critic revered Italian opera, and especially the Rossini school, for its 'musical beauty, constructive science and vocal accomplishment'.[19]

Chorley's support for any English composer was conditional on an allegiance to the Mendelssohnian tradition. Like Davison in *The Times*, he was dedicated to the development of a strong native oratorio tradition that would draw on Mendelssohn's inheritance. He enthusiastically endorsed any new work which promised progress in this regard. In the 1850s when the quest for an English oratorio became intense, Chorley fixed upon Horsley, Bexfield, and Leslie as the young composers most likely to pen an oratorio worthy of the nation. Accordingly, when Horsley's oratorio *David* was premiered in 1850, Chorley travelled to Merseyside and wrote a detailed notice complimenting Horsley for a work which displayed 'not a few indications of force and grandeur',[20] Likewise, the critic promoted Bexfield, on the premiere of *Israel Restored*, he predicted that the young composer would 'produce really sound, national and characteristic additions to the stores of English music'.[21] The essence of Chorley's reception of new English music was that, above all, the work had to be morally and stylistically 'sound'; only then did it matter to him whether it was 'national'. Leslie too received Chorley's approval, most especially for his oratorio *Judith* (1858), with a review that praised the Birmingham Festival committee for giving 'an English composer such an opportunity as an English composer was never before indulged with'.[22]

Yet it was the young Arthur Sullivan, newly returned from study at the Leipzig Conservatorium, who was to win Chorley's most enduring support. Although the reception of Sullivan's music is the subject of chapter five, it is worth noting here the enthusiasm with which Chorley greeted Sullivan's first important premiere, that of *The Tempest Music* in 1862:

---

[18] Ibid. vol. ii pp. 370–1.
[19] *Ath* 11 Jan. 1851 and 31 May 1856.
[20] *Ath* 16 Nov. 1850.
[21] *Ath* 25 Sept. 1852.
[22] *Ath* 4 Sept. 1858.

> It was one of those events which mark an epoch in a man's life;
> and, what is of more universal consequence, it may mark an epoch
> in English music, or we shall be greatly disappointed [...] The day
> was a pleasant day altogether for those who wish well to English
> music.[23]

In this notice the critic went on to declare Sullivan to be the new hero of
the nation's music with the potential to become even an English
'Mendelssohn'.

Chorley could be brutal with native composers who did not conform
to his conservative agenda for English music. Since he despised
Schumannites, Sterndale Bennett was out of favour and his work found
little comfort in the *Athenaeum*. Of Bennett's *Fantasia-Overture: Paradise and the Peri*, composed specially for the Philharmonic Society in
1862, Chorley witheringly commented that 'as the music slid past, some
individual portions gave pleasure [but] as a whole, the impression left
upon us is want of brilliancy and boldness'. Six years later, when
Bennett had finally produced a large-scale festival work, *The Woman of
Samaria*, Chorley mocked it as 'lifeless', especially disappointing since it
came from 'a composer long waited for'.[24] Chorley also castigated
another Schumannite, Hugo Henry Pierson, as one who deserved to be
'little heard and less admired'; of Pierson's *Jerusalem* Chorley, the Christian moralist, raged: 'what is crude, puerile and uncouth is intermixed
with the best thoughts and obtruded in the most holy places'.[25] For this
watchman, the contagion of post-1848 trends in music had to be kept
at bay, a priority far more important than the promotion of new English
music.

Chorley's stature as an intellectual led, in 1862, to an invitation to
give a series of lectures, on the evolution of 'national music', at the
Royal Institution.[26] The importance of these lectures cannot be overestimated since they began the process of re-evaluating the role of folk
tune in the formation of a national Art-Music style. It is important to
note that Chorley's papers for the Royal Institution pre-date Carl
Engel's hugely influential work in this field, *An Introduction to the
Study of National Music* (1866). They deserve to be examined in some
detail.[27]

Chorley's four lectures had an overarching emphasis on the character
of 'national music' around the world and, how in Europe, this came to

---

[23] *Ath* 12 Apr. 1862.

[24] *Ath* 12 Jul. 1862 and 7 Sept. 1868.

[25] *Ath* 25 Sept. 1852.

[26] Chorley, *National Music*.

[27] For a discussion of Engel's work on 'national music' see Hughes and Stradling, pp.
77–9.

influence Art-Music. Of particular interest to this book is Chorley's fourth lecture, 'Music from the West', in which he set out his thoughts on the evolution of the 'national music' of Britain, 'a region of anything rather than brotherly love or concord, as regards music'.[28] In the 'home world of national music', Chorley held that Wales had pride of place since no-one had 'laid hands' on its tunes; next came Ireland, a 'wild world' whose music was 'full of tune, full of genius'; and then Scotland, whose 'national music' had long-since been admired.[29] Last and least came England, whose tunes he argued suffered from a 'want of style which establishes a certain parentage' and whose musical heritage was fatally flawed; as he expressed it:

> I find that among English tunes nothing in the least equivalent to Welsh or Irish or Scotch melodies, as regards freshness or strangeness, [...] nationality in music does not lie in borrowing or adaptation, but in some inborn qualities.[30]

Chorley made clear his conviction that England's music had always lacked a distinct identity and it was not surprising to him that it had been left to foreigners, from Handel to Mendelssohn. As for the present day, he was pessimistic. While conceding that there were some signs that interest in music was increasing, nevertheless 'with all our honesty, our wealth, our welcome [...] we may fail for a while [...] in having a music of our own'.[31]

Despite Chorley's conclusions on English 'national music', his lectures had a powerful consciousness-raising effect which resulted in a torch being lit which eventually ended up in the hands of Vaughan Williams and the Pastoral School. Perhaps one of the earliest fruits of Chorley's ground-breaking work came from Sullivan, who became the first composer to incorporate elements of the 'national music' of Ireland into a major orchestral composition: his *'Irish' Symphony* (1863–4). Rarely can there have been so swift a response to the urging of a critic. Chorley's Royal Institution lectures were so successful that they were repeated at venues in Birmingham and Manchester and were eventually published as *The National Music of the World* in 1880.

Chorley was the first watchman to think his life worthy of a memoir, and duly brought out an autobiography, *Thirty Years' Musical Recollections*, in 1862.[32] The *Recollections* are important for the light they

---

[28] Chorley, *National Music* pp. 174–5.
[29] Ibid. pp. 176–7 and p. 186.
[30] Ibid. pp. 213–5.
[31] Ibid. p. 223.
[32] Chorley, *Thirty Years' Musical Recollections*. This memoir was supplemented after

shed on Chorley's musical affiliations and for the wealth of detail on the London opera scene which they provide. Of English music he had little to say. Chorley's mid-Victorian piety meant he held music, above all, should perform an ethical and Christian function. Accordingly, he believed that England's foreigner-dominated oratorio tradition was the most valued element in the nation's musical life. Chorley's prime interest was 'Music'; English music was of secondary importance to him. It is surely a measure of his impact and importance that Ernest Newman prepared a new edition of his autobiography in the 1920s.[33] Alongside his work as a journalist, Chorley was also a novelist, playwright and librettist, providing texts for, among others, Benedict (*St Cecilia*), Sterndale Bennett (*The May Queen*) and Sullivan (*Kenilworth*).

In his writing Chorley adopted a learned and aloof tone which easily slipped into arrogance and condescension. The discourse of his criticism drew on the tropes of revolution as well as on images of moral and spiritual Armageddon. No one understood better than Chorley the social and political function of the critic. Well-connected in artistic circles both at home and abroad, he adopted the role of a critic-patron and intellectual elitist, arbitrating musical destinies from on high. In terms of the reception and projection of new English music in the *Athenaeum*, Chorley's writings were suffused with despair at the state of music after 1848. For him, the inheritance of the past had to be shored up at all costs, with contemporary developments viewed mostly with a chill foreboding. Chorley's greatest success lay in the elevation of his craft and in his (albeit highly selective) patronage of new English music in the *Athenaeum*. Yet for all his distinction, Chorley, unlike his bitter rival Davison, did not act as a focus for either a clique or a school of criticism. That was not his style. Despite his achievements, his unyielding conservatism made his a mixed inheritance and one which ultimately had to be overturned by a later generation.

## 2.   Campbell Clarke

After Chorley's departure from the *Athenaeum*, Campbell Clarke took up the role of chief critic. From the evidence of his reviews, it can be seen that Clarke was another conservative who shared his predecessor's loathing of modern trends in music. One of Clarke's first articles illustrates the point, writing of a performance of *Lohengrin* in Baden:

---

the critic's death by *Henry Fothergill Chorley: Autobiography, Memoirs & Letters* 2 vols. (Bentley 1873), compiled by H. G. Hewlett.
[33] Newman, *H. F. Chorley*.

To us, *Lohengrin* seemed to be the very sublimity of impudence. Of music, in the only sense that we can understand the term, there is next to none in the entire opera [...] Unless ugliness in some wild day come to be mistaken for beauty, Herr Wagner's will never be the music of the future.[34]

As far as English music was concerned, one of Clarke's relatively few major notices was for Pierson's oratorio *Hezekiah*, extracts of which were premiered in 1869. In this review he wrote of Pierson: 'He has contempt for form which would warm the heart of Herr Wagner himself; and the courage to write music unmelodious enough to satisfy even that arch-priest of cacophony'.[35] In contrast, Clarke eulogised Sullivan's *Prodigal Son*, premiered at Worcester that same year, as a work which gave the composer a place in 'Fame's temple'.[36] Clarke only had one opportunity to review Cowen's music, which was the premiere of his *Piano Concerto in A minor* and his *Symphony No. 1 in C minor*, when he wrote of the composer as of 'distinctly-suggested promise'.[37] Clarke summed up his conservative approach to music in a New Year feature-article in the *Athenaeum*, entitled 'Music, Past & Future', a piece which discussed music in the discourse of *laissez-faire* economics:

It is advisable to take stock at the end of the year of our possessions in Art, not so much in order to count our past gains as to estimate our future profits. [...] we need not now enter upon the question of whether the government should come to the rescue of native talent [... since] Free Trade should no more cripple our enterprise and dull our industry in art than in trade. We should not be content with the consumption of foreign produce: we should resolve to be producers ourselves.[38]

Free Trade or Protectionism in music? In Campbell Clarke's call for more 'producers' of English music, it can be seen that even a free-marketeer like him was prepared to back the calls for a home grown product. In any event, his days at the *Athenaeum* were numbered, since his name disappears from the City University series in July 1870 to be replaced by that of Charles Gruneisen.

---

[34] *Ath* 12 Sept. 1868.
[35] *Ath* 4 Sept. 1869.
[36] *Ath* 18 Sept. 1869. See also Chapter 5 below.
[37] *Ath* 18 Dec. 1869.
[38] *Ath* 1 Jan. 1870.

## 3.  Charles Gruneisen

In Charles L. Gruneisen the *Athenaeum* appointed a music journalist of experience and distinction who came out of retirement to take over its music column.[39] Once again the journal had plumped for a conservative watchman; literally this time, since Gruneisen was a founding-member of the Conservative Land Association. In his musical orientation, the journal's new critic was prepared to accept some of the trends in contemporary music, whereas he emphatically rejected others. While he favoured the music of Liszt, he regarded most of Wagner's output as illegitimate; as he wrote in one of his first articles:

> The Music of the Future is still an open question in this country. If Wagner will produce another *Flying Dutchman* there would be unanimity in musical Europe, and his return to the legitimate school of lyric drama would be heartily welcomed.[40]

Gruneisen was also uncompromising on the maintenance of standards in music performance and could be scathing in his condemnation of any deficiencies. In 1871, for example, he took the Three Choirs (Gloucester) Festival committee to task for blunders in organisation and for the fact that 'no new work with the smallest chance of vitality has emanated from the mass of music included in the festival'.[41] As far as new English music was concerned, Gruneisen's reviews in the *Morning Post* had already testified to his strict insistence on quality and earned praise. For example, in a notice from the Norwich Festival of 1852, he suggested to Hugo Pierson that, despite the 'ugliness' of much of his *Jerusalem*, his 'natural powers' might 'eventually prove honourable to himself and to his country'.[42]

The fact remains that Gruneisen was dismissive of native talent and treated much new English music with disdain. When Macfarren's *Violin Concerto* was premiered at the Philharmonic Society it was accorded a review of only fourteen lines, being disingenuously described as 'worthy of the prolific composer'; and when his oratorio *The Resurrection* was first given, it was dismissed as having 'signs of labour and hard workmanship rather than those of inspiration'.[43] Even Sterndale Bennett, who had been knighted by Queen Victoria in 1871 in order that he

---

[39] Gruneisen was a founder-member of the Royal Italian Opera Company in London. He was a biographer of Meyerbeer and worked as chief critic on the *Morning Post* (1844–67).

[40] *Ath* 18 Dec. 1869 and 30 Jul. 1870.

[41] *Ath* 16 Sept. 1871.

[42] *MP* 23 Sept. 1852 and 25 Sept. 1852.

[43] *Ath* 17 May 1873 and 2 Sept. 1876.

might 'improve and advance the musical profession in England', came in for Gruneisen's trenchant criticism. On the premiere of his orchestral prelude *Ajax* he summed up the piece as 'a succession of very tame passages, in which neither pathos nor passion could be recognised. No wonder the new work fell lifeless on the ears of the auditory'.[44] Although other critics were often sceptical, Gruneisen was an agnostic as far as national music was concerned.

England's younger composers fared only a little better in the *Athenaeum*'s music columns. In particular the critic treated Sullivan, who by the 1870s had become the acknowledged standard-bearer of English music, with barely concealed contempt. When Sullivan's *Te Deum*, commissioned by the directors of the Crystal Palace for the 1872 May Day celebrations was premiered, Gruneisen was in uncompromising mood:

> The composer seems to us to have been depressed by his task [... and] he has been too severe in his treatment, too rigid in his observance of rule of rote, too restrained and formal in his development of themes. [...] the *Te Deum* cannot be declared to be a work of inspiration or genius.[45]

Sullivan rarely suffered such dimissive treatment at the hands of the watchmen. Among the group of composers who were soon to provide the core talent of the Musical Renaissance, Cowen fared best in the *Athenaeum*. Although his cantata *The Corsair* was given a cool reception, it was still complimented on its 'considerable charm'.[46] The composer's first major operatic premiere, *Pauline*, was treated sympathetically with Cowen being hailed as 'the coming composer, the most able representative of our native talent'.[47] In contrast, the young Stanford's *Symphony No. 1* was given short shrift in the *Athenaeum*. In his review Gruneisen, having dismissed the British Symphony Competition of 1876 in which this work took second prize as 'absurd', went on:

> The most ardent admirer of Mr Stanford must have been pained, certainly not surprised, at the solemn silence which succeeded the close of each of the four movements, [...] it is much to be regretted that our young composers should waste their strength in essaying the symphony; [...][48]

Gruneisen's disdain for English music and his pessimism as to its future potential is brutally plain in this review. As the critic himself had

---

[44] Sterndale Bennett, *Life of W. Sterndale Bennett* p. 409, and *Ath* 13 Jul. 1872.

[45] *Ath* 4 May 1872. It was the same story when Sullivan's *The Light of the World* was first performed the following year, see Chapter 5 below.

[46] *Ath* 2 Sept. 1876.

[47] *Ath* 25 Nov. 1876.

[48] *Ath* 15 Mar. 1879.

observed, 'music with the Germans is a faith, but with the English the cultivation of it is based mainly on the commercial principle'.[49] Perhaps Gruneisen, in true Hegelian fashion, felt that history (or at least music history) was not on England's side.

Despite his reservations about the viability of English music, as critic of the *Athenaeum*, Gruneisen was required to review new native works. He clearly found it an uncongenial task. As far as the young Hubert Parry was concerned, although the critic evinced some support for the early chamber works, when the composer premiered his *Guillem de Cabestanh*, Gruneisen poured scorn on the work's 'programme'.[50] Ebenezer Prout was another English composer upon whose shoulders at least some hopes were pinned in the 1870s, and he too found Gruneisen a hard critic to please. When Prout's cantata *Hereward*, based on that legendary icon of English nationalism, was premiered, it was slammed for being 'rather wearisome, and the music [...] is not remarkable for inspiration'.[51] By a twist of fate within weeks of this review Gruneisen was dead and Prout had succeeded him as chief critic of the *Athenaeum*.

### 3.   Ebenezer Prout and Henry Frost

Music criticism in the *Athenaeum* in the last two decades of the century was dominated by Ebenezer Prout and Henry F. Frost.[52] These two watchmen shared the same fundamental approach to music and its reception. Both were 'progressives' who championed the music of Schumann, Berlioz and Wagner, and both wanted to see a transformation in national music. In this respect Prout and Frost contrasted with their predecessors on the journal. Although both critics shared a rather scholarly approach to criticism, they differed in at least one important regard. Prout found little to favour in Grove's RCM team, preferring to regard the RAM as the leading institution of the Musical Renaissance; while Frost was more generous towards South Kensington in his reviews, a tendency which became more marked after his promotion to chief critic.[53]

---

[49] *Ath* 14 Sept. 1872.

[50] *Ath* 22 Mar. 1879.

[51] *Ath* 14 Jun. 1879.

[52] Prout held the post of chief critic (1879–89) with Frost as his deputy throughout. Frost took over in 1889. From the City University series we see that the two men shared the music column in this period – even to the extent of pooling notices in a single issue. Frost remained as chief critic until 1898.

[53] Prout had fallen out with Grove in the late 1870s, see Young, *Grove* p. 150. The breach was probably exacerbated by Grove's reluctance to bring him into the RCM team, despite his service at the National Training School.

Prout regarded two *alumni* of the RAM, Alexander Mackenzie and Arthur Goring Thomas, as the leading figures of the national musical revival. The *Athenaeum* critic expected the greatest things of Mackenzie, both in terms of the quest for a 'great' English oratorio and in terms of laying the foundations for a native operatic tradition. When Mackenzie's opera *Columba* appeared Prout greeted it with a massive three page review in which the composer was praised for adopting the 'best points of the Wagnerian system' in an 'opera which is an honour to English art'.[54] And when, a year later, his oratorio *The Rose of Sharon* was premiered at the Norwich Festival, Prout welcomed it as a landmark in English choral music:

> The composer has put forth his full strength, and has not only surpassed everything he has previously done, but in our deliberate opinion has produced by far the finest oratorio ever written by an Englishman [...] *The Rose of Sharon* is the most important new work produced in this country during the present generation. By this achievement Mr Mackenzie has placed himself at the head of living English composers.[55]

So far as Prout was concerned, the search for a native oratorio composer had ended with Mackenzie. He was equally anxious to give the Scottish composer's instrumental music a glowing press, as with his *Violin Concerto* (1885), the first essay in the form to be written by an 'English' composer in living memory. Prout covered the premiere of the concerto in two consecutive notices in which he declared that 'on no previous occasion have the claims of native art been so freely and fully recognised'.[56] The music of Goring Thomas, who had been Prout's student at the RAM, was also given glowing and exhaustive reviews. Writing of his first opera *Esmeralda*, premiered by the Carl Rosa Company, Prout was convinced that operatic music in England was set on a new path:

> The fortunes of English opera tremble for a while in the balance, and Mr Goring Thomas and Mr Alexander Mackenzie may be said to hold the scales [... *Esmeralda*] may be said to mark the commencement of a fresh epoch in our native art.[57]

In the same notice Prout went on to commend this 'opera of the future' as worthy of comparison with Wagner's *Rienzi*. It was the same story when Goring Thomas premiered his second opera, *Nadeshda* which Prout, in a whole-page review, declared to be 'an honour to its com-

---

[54] *Ath* 14 Apr. 1883.
[55] *Ath* 25 Oct. 1884.
[56] *Ath* 29 Aug. 1885 and 5 Sept. 1885.
[57] *Ath* 31 Mar. 1883.

poser and to English art; and its success will be welcome to all who have at heart the cause of music in this country'.[58]

Other young English composers of the 1880s fared less well in the *Athenaeum*. Prout had little enthusiasm for the music of Cowen and still less for that of Parry and Stanford. Cowen's reputation in the 1880s rested mainly on his symphonic output with the *Symphony No. 3 'Scandinavian'* being the most performed English work of this genre. Yet Prout did nothing to promote or project him in the *Athenaeum*. When the *'Scandinavian'* was first performed it received a schoolmasterly reception, Cowen being advised 'to reconsider, if not rewrite, the finale'. While of his *Symphony No. 4 'Cambrian'* (1884), Prout commented that it displayed characteristics more 'Scotch' than Welsh.[59] A definite note of professional envy can be heard in these reviews. It was the same story when Parry's music started to make an impact. When the *Piano Concerto in F sharp major* was given its second performance under Richter in 1880, Prout railed:

> Why is this the only work introduced in the whole series of concerts? [...] why should this solitary exception be made, surely there are other English composers with at least an equal claim to recognition? [...] It would be invidious to mention names [...].[60]

This outburst ostensibly aimed at Parry may also have been directed at the composer's friend and patron, George Grove, for reasons of envy surmised above. Years later, Prout was still treating Parry with condescension as when, on the premiere of the ode *At a Solemn Music*, he noted that the composer had merely made 'marked progress'.[61] Neither was Prout enthusiastic for the music of Stanford. When the composer's opera *Savonarola* was premiered at Covent Garden (albeit in German), it was savaged as a regrettable 'fiasco' damaging to 'English art'.[62] In reviews such as these, it can be seen how Prout went out of his way to portray the RCM professors as liabilities to the Musical Renaissance.[63]

Prout's critical discourse was predominantly academic in content and tone. His notices of new English music frequently gave the impression that he was marking the efforts of his students. Composers were praised for their overall 'state of progress', 'lucidity' of thought; or they were

---

[58] *Ath* 25 Apr. 1885.

[59] *Ath* 25 Dec. 1880 and 31 May 1884.

[60] *Ath* 15 May 1880.

[61] *Ath* 21 May 1887.

[62] *Ath* 12 Jul. 1884.

[63] Prout gave Stanford's instrumental and choral music a slightly more positive reception.

damned for writing 'unequal' or 'dull' music injurious to their 'future prospects'. Prout's reviews typically encouraged musicians for making 'rapid strides', or rebuked them for efforts which had 'vulgar associations'. In so many of his notices, the only missing element seems to be an academic grade at the end.

Henry Frost, during his time as second critic, was given equal responsibility for music reviewing. Frost held inclusive and tolerant positions on many musical matters and his equable approach can clearly be detected in his reception of Sullivan's music, as when *The Golden Legend* was praised for its 'abstract beauty' and 'finish of workmanship'.[64] Frost also reviewed much of Stanford's music, giving it a positive reception. When *The Canterbury Pilgrims* was premiered, despite a dismal run it was commended as: 'a work of which English musicians may feel proud [... which will] strengthen the claims of this country to consideration among musical nations'.[65] Frost also occasionally reviewed the premieres of Parry's music and did so favourably. The oratorio *Judith*, for example, was greeted with a long review which announced that although 'until now Dr Parry was regarded as a composer of promise rather than of actual achievement [...] no finer oratorio music than this has been written for many years'.[66]

Once he became chief critic in 1889, Frost gave his support for the Musical Renaissance a freer rein. New music from the RCM was much more positively promoted; with Parry, in particular, attracting support – as with the *Symphony No. 3 'English'*:

> Though not so designated by the composer, its proper title would be the 'English' Symphony. There can be as little doubt that Dr Parry has given the themes a national colouring with intent.[67]

By the time the same composer's oratorio *King Saul* was premiered five years later, Frost was in no doubt of Parry's importance, praising it as 'unquestionably one of the greatest choral works – if not the greatest – ever produced by an English composer'.[68] Stanford too was strongly endorsed as the 1890s wore on. His opera *The Veiled Prophet of Khorassan*, staged for one night only at Covent Garden, was given an amazing notice (under the circumstances), Frost suggesting that it 'should

---

[64] *Ath* 23 Oct. 1886.

[65] *Ath* 3 May 1884. However, in the same review Frost pointedly remarked that a 'school of English opera must be a matter of evolution, not of creation, as some people seem to imagine'.

[66] *Ath* 1 Sept. 1888.

[67] *Ath* 1 Jun. 1889.

[68] *Ath* 6 Oct. 1894. By this time, Frost, along with several of the other leading critics, had embraced Parry as 'English master'. See Chapter 6 below.

take its place by the side of any lyric drama of full dimensions produced within the last fifteen years, the masterpieces of Verdi excepted'.[69] Yet for Frost, it was Cowen who stood at the forefront of the Musical Renaissance despite his decision to concentrate on conducting at the expense of composition. When Cowen premieres came up, the critic was always on hand with the highest praise. The oratorio *The Trans-figuration*, for example, was described as 'brilliant and devotional' at once transcending 'all his efforts in strength and virility of style'.[70]

With Frost as chief critic, the *Athenaeum* put its full weight behind the rising talents of the 1890s. Frederick Cliffe and Edward German both benefited from favourable reception. When Cliffe, a Professor of Piano at the RCM, had his *Symphony No. 1* premiered, Frost declared that it had a 'depth of expression and a command of orchestral colour rarely to be met with save in the works of the greatest masters'.[71] Although German's *Symphony No. 2* did not attract this order of praise, the composer was complimented as an 'earnest and accomplished musician'.[72]

It was, however, the emerging Elgar who enjoyed the most consistent support. When, in 1896, his *Light of Life* was given its first performance, Frost commended him as a 'talent of no ordinary nature' and greeted the oratorio with the comment that 'no more pleasing or artistic work has been produced at a festival of the Three Choirs for several years'.[73] Later that same year when *King Olaf* was premiered, Frost described the score as of 'extraordinary merit, full of rich device of every sort and with the use of representative themes which [...] are almost, if not quite, worthy of Richard Wagner'.[74] Elgar, who was a devoted (if sometimes discreet) follower of *der Meister*, must have been gratified by this plaudit.

Frost's generosity was at its most apparent in his reception of Sullivan's music. He was one of the few watchmen who was prepared to embrace Sir Arthur's output, accepting the fact that he would never prove a standard-bearer of England's music. Frost admired the Savoy Operas for what they were. *The Gondoliers*, he rated as possessing 'a higher art value than many a pretentious oratorio or symphony'.[75] When Sullivan's 'grand opera' *Ivanhoe* was premiered in the purpose-

[69] *Ath* 5 Aug. 1893.
[70] *Ath* 21 Sept. 1895.
[71] *Ath* 27 Apr. 1889.
[72] *Ath* 7 Oct. 1893.
[73] *Ath* 12 Sept. 1896.
[74] *Ath* 7 Nov. 1896.
[75] *Ath* 14 Dec. 1889.

built Royal English Opera theatre (a veritable *Festspielhaus* in the West End) Frost was supportive, diplomatically declaring that Sullivan had succeeded 'as well as it was likely he would succeed, having regard to the directions in which his genius has been previously engaged'.[76]

Henry Frost resigned from the *Athenaeum* in 1898. Throughout his twenty years on the journal, many of them under the difficult and irascible Prout, he had proved himself a thoughtful and informed critic. He had also showed himself to be a true friend of the English Musical Renaissance. Although his critical discourse lacked the strident nationalism of a Davison or Bennett, his reviews reflected a deep and increasing confidence (as well as pride) in the future of English music. The *Athenaeum*, already entering its period of marked decline, was not to employ a critic of his calibre again.

## 4.   John S. Shedlock

John Shedlock succeeded Frost at the *Athenaeum* in the summer of 1898 and remained with the journal until 1916. He was a 'conservative' critic who was uncomfortable with the influence of Wagner and held strongly that music should be 'abstract' rather than 'programmatic' in content. That said, Shedlock belonged to no musical party or faction and, although he occasionally expressed general support for young native talent in his column, he seems to have had limited enthusiasm for developments in English music.

Shedlock's lack of commitment to English music can most clearly be seen in his reception of Elgar. Although his approach to the Worcester composer's music was generally supportive, his reviews were tempered with petty reservations and stylistic quibbles, with many reflecting a superficial approach to his craft. For example, Shedlock's notice of the *Enigma Variations* lamely drew attention to the fact that 'not one [of the variations] could be termed feeble';[77] and when *The Apostles* was premiered, the *Athenaeum* preferred to 'suspend judgement' on the new work given its 'chromatic harmonies'.[78] Even with regard to Elgar's greatest triumph, the *Symphony No. 1*, Shedlock's review displayed that same outdated carping streak when he wrote that it was a 'healthy reaction against the prevailing fashion of writing programme music'.[79]

---

[76] *Ath* 14 Feb. 1891.
[77] *Ath* 24 Jun. 1899.
[78] *Ath* 17 Oct. 1903.
[79] *Ath* 12 Dec. 1908. See also Chapter 7 below.

By 1910, a music review in the *Athenaeum* might occupy a paltry quarter-page, surely a symptom as much of Shedlock's complacency as of the remorseless decline of the journal at this time.

Shedlock gave the music of other, lesser known English composers, similarly lukewarm attention. The work of Elgar's closest disciple, Granville Bantock, fared particularly badly: with *Fifine at the Fair* criticised for being 'light in substance; and *Omar Khayyam* (Part One) slated for its 'Wagnerian reminiscences' in 'dull surroundings'.[80] The only native composer whose work Shedlock seems to have admired was Delius, with his *Mass of Life*, in particular, being singled out as 'interesting and original' with 'no pose, no concession to public taste'.[81]

Shedlock's reception of the new works emanating from the RCM reflected his limited support for contemporary English music. As far as Stanford was concerned, the *Athenaeum*'s review of the opera *Much Ado about Nothing*, premiered at Covent Garden in 1901, was judged to 'lack soul [and any] marked originality'.[82] As for Parry's music, Shedlock thought it lacked sophistication, although he did concede that *The Soul's Ransom* (1906) had a certain 'latent power'.[83] With the music of the younger talents of the RCM too, he was generally cool in his reviews; Coleridge-Taylor especially suffered from indifferent notices: his hugely popular *Hiawatha*, for example, was deemed 'not a flawless work'; and when *Toussaint l'Overture* was premiered, Shedlock concluded that 'the interest of the music was in inverse proportion to its length'.[84]

The most important new development in English music during the 1900s was the appearance of what became known as the Pastoral School, yet its composers too found little favour in the *Athenaeum*. Foremost among the new pastoralists was Vaughan Williams whose music Shedlock seems to have found bemusing: of *Toward the Unknown Region*, he wrote that it was a 'meritorious work' in which there was 'nothing actually inappropriate'; whilst of the *Tallis Fantasia*, he could only manage the anodyne compliment that it had 'marked ability'.[85] With the standard-bearer of the pastoralists attracting lukewarm support, there could be little hope for the music of Vaughan Williams's

---

[80] *Ath* 20 Sep. 1902 and 13 Oct. 1906.

[81] *Ath* 12 Jun. 1909. Even so, Shedlock had judged Delius's *Sea-Drift* to be 'difficult and awkward', *Ath* 10 Oct. 1908.

[82] *Ath* 8 Jun. 1901.

[83] *Ath* 15 Sept. 1906.

[84] *Ath* 31 Mar. 1900 and 2 Nov 1901.

[85] *Ath* 19 Oct. 1907 and 10 Sept. 1910.

lesser-known colleague, Gustav Holst, whose premieres were accorded the most perfunctory reviews. Holst's *Phantastes Suite*, first given at a RCM concert with King George V and Queen Mary present, was summed up in one word: 'clever'.[86]

During Shedlock's years as critic, we become aware of a more general decline in journalistic standards at the *Athenaeum*. Although by the end of the period surveyed here, the price and format of the journal's content had changed little in half a century, the overall impression was one of deteriorating standards: broader typefaces, more patchy coverage and a general lack of quality in its journalism. Corner-cutting is everywhere in evidence. For instance in 1908, the *Athenaeum* ceased to publish its annual alphabetical index, an invaluable guide in times past to its dense coverage of the nation's artistic and scientific life. With this general deterioration went a decline in the range and thoroughness of its coverage of music. More and more Shedlock kept his notices of new performances to a minimum, relying instead on straightforward music 'news'. From the manuscript marginalia in the City University series, it is clear that the journal was suffering financially in the 1900s, and it is likely that the torpid Shedlock was the best that it could afford under the circumstances.

The only literary journal to compare with the *Athenaeum* in the coverage and reception of new music was the *Saturday Review* (founded 1855) which some contemporaries held to have an ' academic attitude towards life, politics, literature and the arts'.[87] The *Saturday Review* ran a regular 'music' or 'recent concerts' column, with its critics picking up on most of the major concerts and festivals both in London and the provinces. With the arrival of J. F. Runciman as chief critic (1896) this policy changed as regular articles on musical topics replaced in-depth performance reviews. For his part, Runciman was a colourful and controversial critic who held the achievements of the English Musical Renaissance in utter contempt, as he wrote in 1900: 'the English musicians of the today remind me chiefly of a pack of querulous, gossiping, afternoon tea old ladies. [...] the history of English music in the nineteenth-century is a blank page'.[88] Despite its articulate and informed coverage of music, the *Saturday Review* did not match the *Athenaeum* for depth and thoroughness over the whole span of this survey.

For the other leading journals of the literary press music was clearly not a priority. The *Fortnightly Review*, a publication which regarded politics and international affairs as its chief remit, did not cover con-

---

[86] *Ath* 27 Jul. 1912.
[87] Symon, *Press and its Story* pp. 264–5.
[88] Runciman, 'English Music in the Nineteenth-Century' pp. 45–6.

certs and festivals at all and its value to reception history is therefore minimal. The journal, however, did occasionally print scholarly articles on music and, under Frank Harris's progressive editorship (1886–94), it took a more positive stance on musical developments. For example, in 1894, it published Stanford's 'Some Aspects of Musical Criticism in England', an article in which the composer expressed the hope that critics (the 'literary wing of the musical army') would support the 'great renaissance of music in England which is every day more marked'.[89]

All the evidence underscores the special position of the *Athenaeum* in the reception history of English music. In its writing and presentation, for most of its life it was the product of critical, reflective minds, addressing an intellectual readership on issues of artistic importance. Unlike some of its lesser competitors the *Athenaeum* did not to succumb to the temptation of simply reporting newsworthy events or providing diverting comment on cultural matters. Music was an integral part of its serious coverage of the arts for the best part of a century. Yet for all that, the journal's great contribution to English music was to place music at the heart of its arts coverage, rather than provide consistent and direct collaboration with the English Musical Renaissance. To that extent, the *Athenaeum* therefore was not always a reliable regiment on the 'literary wing of the musical army'.

---

[89] Stanford, 'Some Aspects of Musical Criticism in England' pp. 826–831.

CHAPTER FOUR

# The *Musical Times*

We gather from the steady increase in our monthly sale, that we
continue to give satisfaction to our enlarging circle of friends. The
number sold of the last few Numbers has exceeded 7,000 copies –
thus forming an unparalleled intercommunication between musical
people.[1]

With these words did J. Alfred Novello, editor and proprietor of the
*Musical Times*, proudly proclaim the success of his journal. The *Musical Times* was one of the first music periodicals to appear in this
country and established its long-term commercial viability in Novello's
hands. It gradually carved out a leading role in the music press during
the period surveyed. Although competitors and imitators appeared over
the years, none was able to challenge it in terms of circulation or
prestige. In the pages of music journals the watchmen were best able to
advertise new English talent and address the musical public. At the
heart of the music press was the *Musical Times*.

## 1.  J. Alfred Novello: A Lookout for Profit

From the 1830s onwards the musical press played an increasingly decisive role in constructing a national music. Editors and critics emulated
their German counterparts who, earlier in the century, had mobilised
opinion to create a musical identity for a 'Young Germany'.[2] The first
journal to establish itself was the *Musical World*, founded in 1836 by J.
Alfred Novello which, issued as a weekly, combined coverage of musical
matters with topics of general interest. The appearance of this first successful music journal coincided with the triumph of Mendelssohn's
oratorio, *St Paul*, the English version of which was published by the
Novello firm. Although the *Musical World* proved an immediate success,
Novello's decided to sell it in 1837 to Frederick Davison.[3] This move
tends to confirm the view that the *Musical World* was primarily a publicity
vehicle for *St Paul*. Once the new oratorio had been successfully launched,
the journal was deemed to have outlived its usefulness to the firm.

---

[1] 'Preface to the Fourth Volume', *MT* 1 May 1852.
[2] Hughes, 'Lucifer of Music'.
[3] Hurd, *Vincent Novello* pp. 129–30.

However, over the following years the market for music journals continued to expand. Such was the success of the *Musical World* under Davison's that Novello's began to have second thoughts about the need for a house periodical. Accordingly, in 1844 they bought out the *Musical Times and Singing Class Circular* which had been established two years earlier, and re-named it the *Musical Times*.[4] The journal was subsequently published as a monthly under the personal editorship of its new owner, J. Alfred Novello.

Novello's was the most flourishing music publishing company in Britain. The essence of the firm's success was the belief that music could be sold cheaply, in quantity and at a profit. Along with so many other Victorians of his generation, J. Alfred Novello believed that music also had a moral and a social purpose. He would probably have agreed with Dr James Kay, who observed in 1840 that singing was 'an important means of forming an industrious, brave, loyal and religious people'.[5] In the politically troubled 1840s by promoting and selling music Novello's saw itself playing a part in upholding the social order – as well as increasing its profits.[6] Novello's had an unerring sense of the music market-place, and music for the middle-class public poured from its printing presses. The *Musical Times* should be seen as a vital component of the commercial strategy of the Novello empire.

From the outset, the *Musical Times* was primarily a Novello house publication with two fundamental aims. To advertise and popularise the firm's publications, and to encourage a general awareness, and interest in, music. These aims naturally coincided: the more musical the nation became, the greater the prosperity of the Novello business. Looking at the sales figures for 1852, it is difficult to see how the company could have made a profit purely on its monthly print-run. The publication of the journal at a price of one penny ha'pence could only have been justified by Novello's broader marketing and advertising strategies.[7]

During the 1850s the content and format of the *Musical Times* changed little. A typical issue, consisting of sixteen pages, would feature: one main article (up to three pages); notices of musical events both here and

---

[4] Ibid. pp. 133–4. *Musical Times and Singing Circular* was founded by the German-born teacher and journalist, Joseph Mainzer (1801–51), to promote his 'system of popular musical instruction'.

[5] Kay, q. in Rainbow, *Land Without Music* p. 120.

[6] See Hurd, pp. 53–4 on J. Alfred Novello's lobbying for the repeal of Stamp Duty, Excise Duty and Advertisement Duty, imposts which he regarded as 'taxation on knowledge'.

[7] At one penny ha'pence per copy, a print run of 7,000 would have grossed a mere £45. The journal's closest rival, the weekly *Musical World*, which did not have a music publisher's interest or subsidy, was priced at a hefty 4d per copy.

in the USA (two pages); a piece of printed vocal music (typically four pages); and usually six pages of advertisements (40% of the issue).[8] The centrepiece of each number was the printed music section, comprising of a sacred or secular work, designed to appeal to the maximum number singers, both amateur and professional. In addition, for their one penny ha'penny subscribers were exposed to intense advertising of the Novello catalogue.

The *Musical Times* under J. Alfred Novello regarded articles, news and reviews as of secondary importance. The proprietor-editor viewed his journal in simple commercial terms, gleefully commenting in his Preface of 1852 that it amounted to 'a very pretty balance-sheet at this our stock-taking'.[9] The journal played safe in its meagre reviews, as well as in its features and articles, rarely inviting controversy and employing a small number of tried and tested regulars on its journalistic staff. The result was that the *Musical Times* provided its readers with a diet of fairly predictable (and often) mundane features on anodyne topics.

In terms of reception history, the *Musical Times* under its owner-editor was low-key and highly selective in its support of new English music. The rule seems to have been: if Novello published a work, then the journal would give it a plug; if not, then it might not be mentioned at all. The journal's lack of objective involvement in the projection of native music can be seen in its treatment of Horsley's oratorio, David (1850), a work not to be found in the Novello catalogue. Despite the fact that several critics considered the Liverpool premiere a great success, the *Musical Times* made no mention of it. When the new work was later given in London (at the Philharmonic Society) the journal contented itself with printing an abridged notice from *The Times*.[10] In contrast, the few new English works published by Novello's were given enthusiastic coverage. For instance, the review covering Pierson's oratorio, *Jerusalem*, praised the composer 'as an original thinker, [...] entitled to the support of his countrymen'.[11]

It was only after J. Alfred Novello had relinquished his editorship of the *Musical Times* in 1863 that a more satisfactory balance was struck between Novello house interests and the promotion and projection of

---

[8] The original eight pages gradually expanded to twelve (1848), and then to twenty or more pages (1853). The inclusion of American news was a measure of Novello's ambitions to expand its business across the Atlantic. See Hurd, pp. 61–2.

[9] 'Preface to the Fourth Volume', *MT* 1 May 1852.

[10] 'Brief Chronicle of the Last Month', *MT* 1 Mar. 1851 p. 153. This review was written by J. W. Davison, editor of the rival *Musical World*!

[11] *MT* 1 Sept. 1852.

new English music. In fact, during the 1840s and 1850s, the *Musical Times* was overshadowed by the *Musical World* in almost every respect. Although the two publications were broadly similar in terms of format, the latter, under its editor J. W. Davison, excelled in its verve and controversial edge. Unlike the Novello paper, the *Musical World* was passionate and outspoken in its support for native talent and contemptuous of the forces that it perceived were holding back the development of music in England.[12]

By 1860, the Novello firm further enhanced its fortunes when, following J. Alfred's retirement, the management (and eventually the ownership of the company) passed to Henry Littleton (1823–88).[13] Under Littleton and his dynastic successors, Novello's took a far greater pride and interest in the achievements of national music. Over time the firm even began to subsidise the publication of new English works out of the huge profits it made from its choral and vocal backlist. As a result, over the following decades, Novello's played a vital part in fostering the nation's music and, as a corollary, the *Musical Times* became a powerful organ for the projection of new English music.[14]

## 2.   Henry Lunn Takes Command

In 1863, the Novello management appointed Henry C. Lunn (1817–94) as editor of the *Musical Times*. Lunn, a Mendelssohnian conservative, swiftly moved to transform the journal from simply being a Novello mouthpiece into the leading music periodical of the day. The new editor, an ex-army officer and veteran of the Crimean War, was an experienced writer on music who had first set out his thoughts on the future development of music in England in his *Musings of a Musician* (1847). This book is of great interest not least because many of his 'musings' became the editorial line of the *Musical Times*. Lunn's volume had three preoccupations: the deficiencies of the state of national music; the importance of music in the life of civilised nations; and the formulation of a programme which would ensure that England could be proud of its music. Lunn was scathing about the state of music at the mid-point of the century. His targets included the materialism of the 'gentlemanly ignorant' as well as the superficiality of those seduced by the virtuoso cult.[15] He also railed against music publishers, especially those who profited from selling sub-

---

[12] See Chapter 1 above on Davison's editorship of the *Musical World*.
[13] Hurd, pp. 64–5.
[14] See Hurd on English music in the Novello's catalogue, ibid. pp. 68–70 and pp. 102–4.
[15] Lunn, *Musings of a Musician* p. 19.

standard music to the unenlightened public and whose commercial priorities made music reform more difficult. The need for change was pressing, Lunn argued, and centred on music's social dimension as a 'humanizing influence' and on its role in boosting national pride:

> why England, great in literature – great in arms – great in almost everything – has never, until lately, really taken a prominent position in music [...] we have never systematically set about forming a definite school of music'.[16]

Lunn thus presented a radical agenda for the systematic reform of music in England. He believed that music should, above all, be for the 'multitude'. For him, a national music was never just going to happen, it had to be *made* to happen and he held that opera was the key to England's musical future:

> the only way of creating a universal taste, all our thoughts and all our energies must be devoted to this one object [...] to the entire British public, must the appeal be made. It must take the form of a national movement [...] let all unite. The establishment of a Grand National English Opera is the one thing now required.[17]

This plea for a 'Grand National English Opera' was a call to arms that anticipated Wagner's appeal for a German National Theatre by two years (1849). In all, Lunn was a pioneer critic and an early advocate of planned and organised musical reform.

In 1863 the *Musical Times* therefore came under the command of a warrior and a patriot who set a new dynamic course for his journal. At the beginning of Lunn's tenure, a typical issue was twenty pages; a generation later, by 1879, the size of the journal had nearly tripled to fifty-six pages with its price doubled to 3d. In terms of content, an issue edited by Lunn typically contained: twelve pages of concert and festival reviews; twelve pages of features; four pages of book reviews; published music from the Novello catalogue covering four pages; four pages of correspondence and 'country news'; and eighteen pages of advertisements. Lunn wrote most of the major festival reviews himself, while commissioning features from a wide range of journalists including the prolific Joseph Bennett of the *Daily Telegraph*. So successful was Lunn's stewardship that the readership of the journal doubled to 14,000 between 1850 and 1870.[18]

In terms of editorial policy and content Lunn invariably led from the front. The new editor set out his hopes for England's musical future in his first leader article:

---

[16] Ibid. p. 3.
[17] Ibid. p. 5. (Lunn's italics).
[18] Hurd, p. 135.

music has ceased to be almost a luxury and has grown to be a
necessity. [...] When once want of knowledge in art ceases to be
'gentlemanly', Knowledge will be assumed as a passport to society;
[...] That England's musical future lies brightly before us, must be
acknowledged by all who look lovingly and trustfully forward.[19]

Evidence indeed of the loathing which Lunn felt for those ingrained
prejudices that had prevented music from being accepted by the middle
and upper classes. Here too it is possible to detect the classlessness that
characterised his approach to the understanding and appreciation of
culture. In another signed editorial later that year, he keenly trumpeted
the 'real progress' made by music since Mendelssohn's death, describing
the proliferation of 'cheap operas and cheap concerts' as a 'democratic
movement' which had lowered the barriers that had 'hitherto held the
multitude back'.[20] In such editorials Lunn fully grasped the role that
music journalism had to play in creating a new climate of ideas in
which music could flourish. In place of the reticence of the J. Alfred era
there was a new crusading spirit in which the editor took the lead.
Furthermore, Lunn did not confine himself to strictly editorial matters
since his obituary mentions he covered major musical events in person.[21]

Despite Lunn's commitment to English music, native composers found
him a very difficult critic to please. Arthur Sullivan, for one, came in for
some of his strongest criticism. Lunn thought that Sullivan's approach
to Art-Music lacked seriousness and that his work lacked substance: for
example, of the premiere of the cantata *Kenilworth*, the editor declared:

> the general effect of the composition [...] is that he has performed
> his work as a task, and much of the music falls flatly on the ear as
> a consequence, and leaves no trace behind.[22]

Five years later, Sullivan's first major large-scale festival commission,
the oratorio *The Prodigal Son*, fared little better. While other critics
ranked the work alongside *Messiah* and *Elijah*, Lunn was not convinced, declaring it merely as 'a thoughtful, conscientious work [...]
unequal in merit'.[23]

Frederic Cowen, too, was subjected to Lunn's exacting standards. A
good example of this is found in his review of *The Corsair*. This work,
which was an important first festival commission for the composer, was
given a muted reception, with Lunn judging it to have mere 'merit' and

---

[19] Lunn, 'The London Musical Season'.
[20] Lunn, 'An Autumn Gossip on Music'.
[21] Obituary 'Henry C. Lunn', *MT* 1 Feb. 1894.
[22] *MT* 1 Oct. 1864.
[23] *MT* 1 Oct. 1869.

of having made too many concessions to 'popular taste'. The editor went on to caution Cowen of the dangers of public acclaim: 'Mr Cowen may have a brilliant future before him if only he can take to heart what Mendelssohn said: 'the people indeed shout and applaud: but that quickly passes away, without leaving a vestige behind".[24] Nevertheless, overall Cowen's music did rather well in the pages of Lunn's journal; for instance his *Symphony No. 3 'Scandinavian'*, was given a rousing reception in a half-page review: 'it is a marked advance on anything Mr Cowen has yet done, and cannot fail to draw to the composer the attention of amateurs as to one who may accomplish great things for English music'.[25]

Lunn gave established English composers a generally more favourable reception. The works of the semi-retired Sterndale Bennett were especially welcomed; as on the premiere of the oratorio, *The Woman of Samaria*, when the composer was commended for responding to the 'artistic summons of his countrymen'. Three years later Lunn's review of Bennett's *Symphony in G minor* praised the composer as one 'worthy to be reckoned among the great creative artists of the world'.[26] George Macfarren's music too, was generously promoted: for example, his *Violin Concerto* was thought to be 'scored throughout with a masterly hand'; while the 'unity of effect' of the new oratorio, *St John the Baptist*, premiered at the Bristol Festival of 1873, placed it above that which was found 'even in Bach'.[27]

In the 1880s the *Musical Times* generally welcomed the music of the younger composers of the English Musical Renaissance. By this time, Lunn seems to have left much of the review work to Joseph Bennett, a critic who tempered his musical patriotism with condemnation of any composer tempted by Wagner's *Zukunftsmusik*. For example, Parry's *Prometheus Unbound* evinced the comment 'that had the composer been less fettered by the school to which he has wedded himself his real poetical feeling would have been more constantly evidenced'.[28] In contrast, Mackenzie's *The Rose of Sharon*, was glowingly described as 'the greatest oratorio written since *Elijah* ... [being] the most remarkable English work of modern times'.[29] Thus thundered Bennett, the *Musical Times*' evergreen 'special correspondent', in a notice covering nearly one page and a half. It might

---

[24] *MT* 1 Oct. 1876.
[25] *MT* 1 Jan. 1881.
[26] *MT* 1 Oct. 1867 and 1 May 1870.
[27] *MT* 1 Jun. 1873 and 1 Nov. 1873.
[28] *MT* 1 Oct. 1880. See also Chapter 6 below.
[29] *MT* 1 Nov. 1884.

have been no coincidence that Mackenzie, 'a great favourite' with
the Novello management, had been paid £500 for the copyright of
*The Rose of Sharon*.[30]

All in all, Lunn was one of the most influential music journalists of
his time. His reviews reveal the military man; tough, clear-minded and,
at times, blunt. Although as a critic he led no faction and headed no
clique, throughout his long tenure as editor he held on to one strategic
objective: the reform of English musical life. Nowhere is his commitment to the process of renewal more clearly seen than in the countless
signed articles he wrote for his journal. In one, entitled 'A Musical
Congress', he uses a metaphor drawn from international diplomacy as
he dreams wittily of a 'musical congress' which would 'reform many of
the musical abuses which plague English music'.[31] In another piece,
Lunn attacked the ' "Home Music" of the middle-classes' which threatened the real and rapid progress already being made by music in England,
warning:

> it is here that the sort of artistic paganism is apt to linger long after
> the nation has converted to the true faith [...] Why should not the
> audience be elevated to the art instead of the art being degraded to
> the audience ?.[32]

Here indeed is the new religion of art as promulgated by Matthew
Arnold. Lunn was on controversial ground yet, fearless as ever, he was
prepared to confront his middle-class readers with some uncomfortable
truths. The reaction of the bourgeois 'pagans' went unrecorded. Among
the many other issues that Lunn discussed in his columns were: a non-
revolutionary (that being a non-Wagnerian) future for music in England;
the barriers of class to musical progress; and the perennial crisis in
English opera.[33] Among the watchmen there was no more incisive and
fearless prophet of Musical Renaissance than Lunn, war-veteran turned
journalist.[34]

As the *Musical Times* went from strength to strength under Lunn's
leadership, Novello's decided to re-enter the weekly market with a
new journal, *Concordia* – a periodical launched with Joseph Bennett as
editor in 1875. Bennett recalled in his memoirs that it was originally
intended that *Concordia* should sell alongside the *Musical Times* as 'a

---

[30] Hurd, p. 88.

[31] Lunn, 'A Musical Congress'.

[32] Lunn, 'Drawing-Room Music'.

[33] Lunn, 'The Music of the Future'; 'Musical Ignorance'; 'English Opera'; and 'Free
and Cheap Concerts for the People'.

[34] Hurd is mistaken when he states that Lunn retired from the *Musical Times* in 1877;
his obituary notice states that he left in 1887.

more ambitious journal'.[35] The first issue appeared on 1 May 1875 priced at 4d, containing twenty-four folio pages of which approximately half were advertising. As for content, although it declared itself to be a 'journal of music and the sister arts', music predominated, with only one page given over to 'The Drama'. *Concordia* set out to succeed by dint of established contributors, with Bennett placing the emphasis on a team approach with regular feature writers such as Prout, Edward Dannreuther and S. K. Salaman. In terms of its core values *Concordia* set out to be elitist, patriotic and reflective of the new 'Pateresque' interest in the arts. Yet, with Bennett at the helm, the new journal could hardly be at the leading edge of contemporary music. *Concordia* was in fact an experiment that was brought to an end after a year when it became apparent that it would not add to Novello's profits. Bennett thought this decision premature.[36] Undeterred by this failure, in 1883 Novello's once again tried to move up-market with a new journal, the *Musical Review*, which was, according to *Grove 2*, aimed at 'serious musicians' and 'students of musical history'. However, after a few months, this too ceased publication, Novello's having decided that there was no market for a 'loftier kind' of music periodical.[37]

Alongside the Novello titles, a small but increasing number of new music journals were coming onto the market. In 1871, a direct competitor to the *Musical Times* appeared in the shape of the *Monthly Musical Record*, published by the Augener firm. Ebenezer Prout was its first editor. In terms of its style, layout and typeface the *Monthly Musical Record* was similar to the *Musical Times*, and at a launch price of only 2d, it significantly undercut its rival. With a circulation of 6,000 per month (by 1876), the *Monthly Musical Record* was a not insignificant competitor for the *Musical Times*. Proudly carrying a medallion-image of Beethoven on its masthead, the journal had a strong Germanocentric orientation. It specialised in keeping its readers informed of developments in German musical life with Wagner as its main focus. In its reception of English music, the *Monthly Musical Record* provided an uneven coverage of contemporary developments and was hesitant in its promotion of native talent. Other, less ambitious journals, also appeared in this period: the *Musical Standard* (1862); the *Orchestra* (1863) from Cramer, Wood & Co., and the *Choir and Musical Record* (1863) from Wright. In 1877, the *London & Provincial Music Trades Review* appeared as a trade journal which,

---

[35] Bennett, *Forty Years* pp. 225–6.
[36] Ibid. p. 229.
[37] Streatfeild, entry on 'Musical Periodicals – England' in *Grove 2* vol. iii pp. 680–4.

rather bizarrely, mixed music reviews with news of bankruptcies and musical patents.[38]

### 3. Changing the Watch: W. A. Barrett and E. F. Jacques

After Lunn's retirement in 1887, the *Musical Times* moved under the part-time editorial direction of the Oxford-educated William A. Barrett (1834–91) who continued with his duties as chief critic at the *Morning Post*. The arrival of the clubbable, and musically conservative Barrett heralded a period of broad continuity with the Lunn era. Yet Barrett's appointment, at the age of fifty-three, represented something of a generational shift which placed the journal in the hands of a Schumannite who was, according to Joseph Bennett, an 'essentially modern man'.[39]

'Modern man' or no, in the event Barrett brought little that was new or dynamic to the *Musical Times*. The journal's price (at 4d) and format (of sixty-four pages) remained the same, and the distribution of articles, reviews, printed music, advertising retained the same formula. It should be remembered that Barrett was subject to the tight overall direction of the senior management at Novello's, and it is difficult to see how he had much discretion in the areas of pricing, advertising and overall format. Yet changes in journalistic content were also minimal, with only an increase bias towards London's musical life being evident. As for reviewing, Barrett covered most of the major metropolitan and provincial events, occasions that in any case he would have attended as critic of the *Morning Post*. Probably because of Barrett's *Morning Post* commitment Joseph Bennett became more heavily involved at the *Musical Times* so that George Bernard Shaw could later refer to his 'enormous power', both on the *Daily Telegraph* and as 'editor of the *Musical Times*'.[40] Without reading too much into Shaw's jibe, there is the impression that Bennett saved Barrett many a train journey to musical venues away from the capital. Given the new editor's workload it is hardly surprising that he had so little time to devote to the *Musical Times* in a life 'never free from strain'.[41]

Under Barrett, the *Musical Times* continued to promote the cause of English Musical Renaissance. Parry was a beneficiary of his support, for despite the fact that he was not an enthusiast for the composer's earlier 'Wagnerite' works, he eventually warmed to the composer's later style.

---

[38] Ibid.
[39] Obituary 'William Alexander Barrett', *MT* 1 Nov. 1891.
[40] *The Hawk* 6 May 1890, q. in Laurence, *Shaw's Music* vol. ii p. 42.
[41] Barrett's obituary, see n39.

Barrett's conversion to Parry's music began with the oratorio *Judith*, when he commented (in a review which followed his line in the *Morning Post*) that its 'excellencies largely outnumber and outweigh the blemishes' and that the composer was set fair to produce even finer works.[42] However, the real turning-point for Barrett came with the premiere of Parry's *'English' Symphony*:

> It was suggested in the analytical remarks that the production should be styled the 'English' Symphony. Public opinion has accepted the term which, indeed, accurately suggests the prevailing character of the themes employed. [...] absolute beauty reigns throughout each movement.[43]

It seems that once Parry had been designated the composer of an 'English' symphony in Joseph Bennett's programme-note, even sceptics like Barrett readily joined in the paeans of praise. In a similar vein, Parry's *Ode on St Cecilia's Day*, premiered later that year, was powerfully projected in the *Musical Times* in a notice which once again closely mirrored a *Morning Post* review:

> Dr Parry has given to English music nothing less than a masterpiece. I say 'English music' with special emphasis on the adjective. [... It] has a perceptible English flavour, and, so to speak, introduces to us the national muse gloriously attired in the robes of classic art. [...] We do not want composers who give us imitations of Wagner, or Brahms, or Mendelssohn, or anybody else; but we do need men who can work out for us ideas suggested by the national musical spirit and taste. Dr Parry is one of these.[44]

This review confirms Barrett's keen music patriotism and his rejection of any compromise with foreign models. Having once accepted Parry's quintessential 'Englishness' then Barrett was prepared to promote the composer as the standard-bearer of a national music. Moreover, it is possible to detect Barrett's other concerns, the primacy of 'beauty' expressed in the most 'classical' of musical forms – the symphony.

The *Musical Times* strongly promoted the music of the other leading lights of the Renaissance in the 1880s. Parry's close colleague at the RCM, Stanford, enjoyed a good press from Barrett, evidenced in a review of the composer's new *Symphony No. 4* which was judged 'full of fresh and genial thoughts' in which 'qualities of heart and head [were] in complete equipoise'.[45] Barrett was also generally supportive of Frederic Cowen, writing a favourable review of the premiere of *Thorgrim*

---

[42] *MT* 1 Sept. 1888. See also *MP* 30 Aug. 1888.
[43] *MT* 1 Jun. 1889.
[44] *MT* 1 Nov. 1889. See also *MP* 12 Oct. 1889.
[45] *MT* 1 Mar. 1889.

(1890) in which he declared: 'if we are to have an English school of opera the foundation must be laid by those who devote their lives to their art'.[46] The young Elgar too was promoted by Barrett who welcomed his *Froissart*, despite 'the mark of youth and inexperience'.[47] As for Sullivan's music, Barrett's reviews were complimentary and diplomatic rather than ecstatic. Even *Ivanhoe*, premiered amid extraordinary public and press interest in 1891, stirred him only to write a safe notice, observing the opera as both 'Sullivanesque' and 'destined to exercise great influence on the future course of English opera'.[48]

Barrett wrote his last *Musical Times* reviews from the Birmingham Festival of 1891. It was the editor's final assignment before he suddenly died of influenza.[49] In this final notice new works by Stanford and Mackenzie were reviewed and warmly promoted. Of the more substantial work, Stanford's *Eden*, Barrett declared that it possessed 'ingenuity' and a 'wonderful cleverness'; while Mackenzie's *Veni Creator* was commended for being: 'solid, noble and convincing music'.[50] Yet apart from its support for the Renaissance, the *Musical Times* only managed to mark time under Barrett's stewardship. Like Lunn before him, Barrett ensured that his journal was close to the RAM, to the extent that in 1888, it openly (and successfully) canvassed for the appointment of Mackenzie as principal.[51]

After Barrett's death Novello's turned to the experienced Edgar Jacques, ex-editor of the defunct *Musical World*, to fill the vacancy. Jacques cut a singular figure among the watchmen with his expertise in Indian music and bias toward French music. Yet the colourful Jacques initiated few changes to the successful formula of the *Musical Times*: the sixty-four pages format was retained, as was the broad distribution of classified advertisements, scholarly articles, concert reviews, music news, sheet-music and readers' correspondence. As editor Jacques hardly ever contributed signed articles it is difficult to discover what copy he did provide. Despite the absence of a distinctive editorial presence, he did (albeit fitfully) reflect his own musical interests in the journal, especially in allocating more coverage to French and Russian music. The indomitable Joseph Bennett remained a key contributor under Jacques.

Jacques was sympathetic rather than passionate in the cause of the Musical Renaissance. He was, for example, supportive of Parry's music,

---

[46] *MT* 1 May 1890.
[47] *MT* 1 Oct. 1890.
[48] *MT* 1 Mar. 1891.
[49] Barrett's obituary, see n39.
[50] *MT* 1 Nov. 1891.
[51] Editorial 'The Royal Academy of Music', *MT* 1 Mar. 1888.

as with *Overture to an Unwritten Tragedy*, premiered in 1893, an occasion when he noted that it gave 'the impression of a masterly composition which will become more esteemed the better it becomes known'.[52] Of the oratorio *King Saul* (1894), the journal (probably 'special correspondent' Bennett) reported that: '[*King Saul*] has many of the elements of greatness so that it stands very near the throne, and that absolutely it is an honour to English art'.[53] Paradoxically, as with all Parry's big biblical festival works, the watchmen were far more enthusiastic about them than the composer himself.[54] The *Musical Times* extended the same admiration to Stanford, whose operas of the mid-1890s were well received in its columns. *The Veiled Prophet of Khorrassan* was judged to be a 'greatly strengthened version of an already remarkable work'; while *Shamus O'Brien* was greeted as a 'little masterpiece [...] and may even prove to have inaugurated in these isles a native school of opera'.[55] The journal, under Jacques's editorship, continued its promotion of Elgar, declaring on the premiere of the oratorio *The Light of Life* (1896) that:

> Mr Elgar has endowments sufficient for important results. He is no wayside musician whom we can afford to pass and forget, but one to be watched [...] *The Light of Life* is a work of no ordinary power and promise'.[56]

During Jacques's tenure at the *Musical Times*, a rather unusual competitor appeared in the journal's monthly market in the shape of the *Strand Musical Magazine*. The new publication, edited by E. Hatzfeld and published by Newnes, was directed at a younger female readership. It offered a combination of chatty articles (or interviews) on musical topics, short illustrated stories centred on romantic attachments, and a musical supplement. In its first issue of January 1895, the *Strand Musical Magazine* contained: an article by Mackenzie on the RAM, which the canny principal clearly used to improve his student recruitment; a short story about a young singer; and a musical supplement being in this issue a Sullivan setting.[57] Throughout its life the *Strand Musical*

---

[52] *MT* 1 Oct. 1893.
[53] *MT* 1 Nov. 1894.
[54] See Chapter 6 below.
[55] *MT* 1 Aug. 1893 and 1 Apr. 1896.
[56] *MT* 1 Oct. 1896.
[57] Mackenzie, 'The Royal Academy of Music'. In the second issue, it was Grove's turn to set out his stall for the RCM. This he did in no uncertain terms, telling his young readers that the RCM was founded on the patriotic belief that 'sufficient creative and executive talent existed within the country to revive the English school – to restore to England the lost laurel of its musical supremacy. [...] the college may be said to aim at being a musical commonwealth, whose members are part of a great movement to replace England in a dignified musical position'. (Grove, 'The Royal College of Music').

*Magazine* was keen to support and promote the achievements of the English Musical Renaissance. Despite its informality, the journal was keen to treat music seriously. Its message was that music could be respectable, fun, socially advantageous, and empowering for its female readers. For example, in the short story, 'The Stradivarius', the 'dowdy' little heroine Martha is given a violin by a seductive gypsy with the prophecy, 'thou shalt rule the world with thy bow for a sceptre, and a Stradivarius for a throne'.[58] The magazine, priced at 6d, aimed to exploit a new younger market for a music journal. This market however seems not to have materialised since the *Strand Musical Magazine* published its final issue in December 1897.

Jacques left the *Musical Times* in March 1897. During his tenure he had become music critic on the *Observer* (in 1895) and it may be that outside responsibilities had something to do with his departure. In any event, Jacques bequeathed little that was new to his successors, and he can only be seen as a 'transitional figure in the history of the journal. When Jacques died in 1906, the publication saw fit to accord him only the briefest of obituaries in its 'Occasional Notes' column.[59]

## 4.   Frederick G. Edwards

Frederick G. Edwards (1853–1909) took over editorial responsibility at the *Musical Times* in April 1897. Born in London into a Presbyterian family, Edwards studied at the RAM before pursuing a career as a chapel organist. As a young man he became friendly with George Grove who encouraged him to write on music. As a result he published his first *Musical Times* article in 1891, with his *History of Mendelssohn's 'Elijah'* following in 1896. Once appointed to the *Musical Times*, Edwards (like Lunn) chose not to write for another publication. At the journal Edwards was at the centre of everything. Apart from writing editorials, he penned articles under his own initials and wrote major reviews of London concerts and the choral festival circuit. He even found time to write an occasional obituary for the great and good. The Edwards Papers in the British Library give an idea of how seriously the new editor took his duties.[60]

Edwards energised his journal and placed a personal stamp on its contents. His support for the English Musical Renaissance soon found expression in a new series of 'biographical sketches' on leading musical

---

[58] Finlay, 'The Stradivarius'.
[59] *MT* 1 Feb. 1907.
[60] 'Edwards Papers', B. L. Egerton 3090–3097.

figures. This series started in January 1898 and continued for several years, with the luminaries of the Renaissance taking precedence. In its first year the series featured Mackenzie (June), Parry (July), Cowen (November) and Stanford (December) with Elgar eventually appearing in October 1900. These biographies were of great importance in making the Renaissance more appealing and accessible to the musical public, the portraits being detailed with supporting photographs and other illustrations. The series invited the readers to identify with composers as celebrities setting out to de-mystify music and bring readers more intimately into contact with the 'heroes' of national music. Edwards invited his subjects to co-operate in the compilation of their 'sketches'; an opportunity which some, like Elgar, grasped with relish.[61] In Edwards's *Musical Times* reviews were thorough, new trends and developments were explored (as with folk-music) and composers and executants were given every opportunity to shine. Edwards preferred to employ younger journalists, such as Rutland Boughton, Arthur J. Johnstone and August Jaeger, although Joseph Bennett, despite his age, still provided frequent features and festival reviews.

Edwards effectively placed the *Musical Times* at the disposal of the Musical Renaissance. The new editor certainly ensured that the music of its senior figures was strongly promoted. For example, of Stanford's *Te Deum* premiered at the Leeds Festival (1898), the journal (probably Edwards himself) reported: 'there is mingled with Teutonic sobriety and intellectuality a distinct feeling of Latin sensuousness [...] the work must be pronounced among the best balanced and best sustained of all Dr Stanford's compositions'.[62] While of Parry's *A Song of Darkness and Light*, given at the Three Choirs that same year, the journal's 'special correspondent' declared:

> Sir Hubert Parry here tells us little about himself that we do not already know, his masterfulness invests even the familiar with fresh interest [...] he is one of the few true minstrels who can make us feel with them in their songs.[63]

Yet it is indicative of the decline in importance of the older composers that, a mere decade later, the journal felt able to voice only the most qualified support for a new Parry work when it reported of the cantata, *Beyond These Voices There is Peace*, that 'whatever may be said for or against Parry's creative gifts, no-one can deny that there is a personality in all that comes from his pen'.[64] The emergence of Elgar was decisive in

---

[61] See Chapter 7 below for a discussion of professional relationship between Edwards and Elgar.
[62] *MT* 1 Nov. 1898.
[63] *MT* 1 Oct. 1898.
[64] *MT* 1 Oct. 1908.

the waning influence of the Parry-Stanford-Mackenzie generation and Edwards's editorship was important in the apotheosis of the Worcester composer. Elgar's music always secured a powerful endorsement in Edwards's journal. This support is conveyed in the review of the premiere of *Gerontius* at the Birmingham Festival of 1900 – a notice (probably written by the editor) which complemented admirably Edwards's 'biographical sketch' of Elgar which appeared in the October issue:

> *The Dream of Gerontius* is a work of great originality, beauty and power and, above all, of the completest sincerity. [...] The boldness with which Mr Elgar has shaken himself free from all conventionality is most admirable, since it is the outcome of conviction – not of a desperate desire to be different from other people at all costs.[65]

For Edwards the terms 'originality' and 'sincerity' were key in estimating the value of any music. As far as he was concerned these qualities defined Elgar's work and explain the editor's championship of his music.

The *Musical Times* under Edwards's stewardship was positive in its reception of the music of the younger generation, with composers such as Granville Bantock, Walford Davies and Josef Holbrooke all enjoying support. For example, of the premiere of Holbrooke's symphonic poem *The Raven* in 1900, the reviewer noted:

> *The Raven* is deficient in regard to the balance of tone in orchestration [... with] crudities and harsh sounds that seem to blaze forth their inability to combine with anything approaching a harmonious whole. [...] Still, the work in its entirety is one of decided promise, for it attests to the possession of lively imagination, invention, considerable knowledge and resource.[66]

Samuel Coleridge-Taylor's music was also strongly endorsed. Of his the *Ballade for Orchestra*, premiered at the Gloucester Three Choirs, the journal wrote that it was 'stimulating, highly-coloured and sonorous even for the present generation of hearers'; while two years later *Hiawatha* was described as a milestone in English music history:

> here we have at last what England has been waiting for ever since she began to repudiate the taunt that she was unmusical, that the creative gift was denied to her musicians [...] a work so absolutely beautiful and so absolutely unique'.[67]

Again, we find Edwards placing the highest premium on 'originality'. Under Edwards, the *Musical Times* was keen to advocate Delius for the

---

[65] *MT* 1 Nov. 1900.
[66] *MT* 1 Apr. 1900.
[67] *MT* 1 Oct. 1898 and 1 Apr. 1900.

same reason; so that at the premiere of the *Mass of Life* (1909), having noted its 'manifold effects of great beauty and originality', it went on to affirm:

> The status attained by Frederick Delius as a composer ensures for every new work from his pen the respectful attention of all classes of musicians, in whatever direction their sympathies may lie. [...] Delius is in the forefront of the movement that has of late years altered the character of choral music.[68]

As an editor, Edwards was a creative professional whose letters reveal him as a conscientious journalist who often had to deal with those who looked down on his trade while craving his support. In terms of the journal's broader content, Edwards tried to tread a fine line between the old and the new. The result was that folk song and Wagner were given enhanced profiles, while the church organs of England were also allotted generous coverage. Away from the editor's chair, he maintained close ties with the RAM, his *alma mater*, as well as with Grove and his South Kensington team.

Frederick Edwards died suddenly in November 1909. His obituary in the *Musical Times* bore eloquent testimony to his signal contribution to British music journalism and the English Musical Renaissance. It also recorded the esteem and affection in which his staff held him and the sense of professional loss felt at Novello's on his passing.[69]

## 5.  W. G. McNaught

William Gray McNaught (1849–1918) took over the *Musical Times* in New Year 1910. He had edited Novello's *School Music Review* since 1892 and his appointment can be seen as a safe choice after Edwards's sudden departure. And play safe is what McNaught did, bringing little that was new or visionary to the *Musical Times*. The most discernible shift came in the increased coverage of local, even parochial, aspects of musical life. For example, articles on 'Music in Village Churches' and 'Welsh Music from an English Point-of-View' both found their way into one issue (February 1911). In terms of layout, the journal under McNaught stuck to its tried and tested formula, containing seventy-two pages (slightly increased from sixty-eight) with the usual mix of articles, features, reviews, sections on 'foreign notes', 'country and colonial' and

---

[68] *MT* 1 Jul. 1909. Delius's *Piano Concerto* was also given a fine review, being commended for its 'virility and strenuousness', *MT* 1 Nov. 1907.
[69] Obituary 'Frederick George Edwards', *MT* 1 Jan. 1910.

the sheet music insert. The *Musical Times* of the new Georgian era comprised thirty three percent of advertising and had a cover price of 3d – back to the level set in the 1870s – a sure sign perhaps that it was feeling the pressures of competition.

Under McNaught the *Musical Times*'s coverage of new English music declined in both quantity and quality. The responsibility for this deterioration rested with the editor himself since he palpably lacked the background and journalistic resource to cover major musical events. Furthermore, he did little to build a team of contributors who could maintain the standards set by his predecessor.

The most striking difference between McNaught and Edwards may be seen in the coverage of choral festivals, occasions which the editor himself normally reviewed. McNaught's treatment of English music is reflected in the reception of the early works of Vaughan Williams, already hailed by many watchmen as the new leader of the Musical Renaissance. The *Tallis Fantasia* was only accorded five lines in which it was described as 'a grave work, exhibiting power and much charm of a contemplative kind, but it appeared over-long for the subject-matter'.[70] Vaughan Williams's other big premiere of 1910, *A Sea Symphony*, fared only slightly better:

> It is a serious work of art and may be regarded as the latest expression of musical feeling of one of the ablest and most profound of our existing English composers [...] but we cannot help thinking that it is over-scored and that the climaxes are too often tremendous.[71]

In reviews of this sort, one feels that McNaught (both as critic and editor) was seriously ill-equipped for his responsibilities at the *Musical Times*. Under his direction the journal often gave the impression that it was unaware of the contemporary scene. A good example of this seeming ignorance was the notice of Vaughan Williams' *Five Mystical Songs* of which it wrote: 'the composer is known to have a close acquaintance with Folk-Song, and the peculiarities of this mode of musical expression [...] seems to have permeated his style'.[72] Neither could the ageing leaders of the Musical Renaissance rely on the journal for favourable coverage of their new works. For instance, Stanford's *Songs of the Fleet* (1910) destined to become one of the composer's most popular works, received the bald comment that they had 'many good qualities'.[73] The

---

[70] *MT* 1 Oct. 1910.
[71] *MT* 1 Nov. 1910.
[72] *MT* 1 Oct. 1911.
[73] *MT* 1 Nov. 1911.

same composer's *Symphony No. 7*, which was given a Philharmonic Society launch, was greeted with the obtuse observation that 'the character of the symphony was a surprise because so simple and straightforward a composition was hardly expected in these times'.[74] Elgar's new works too suffered at McNaught's hands, as in the case of *The Music Makers* which, despite being published by Novello's, was summed up with the observation that its 'climaxes are in places tremendous'.[75] With such banality the *Musical Times* declined as a supporter of new English music in the years preceding the Great War.

The relationship between the *Musical Times* and the English Musical Renaissance was a fascinating one. Novello's core business was music publishing and what was good for music was good for the firm. Yet the publishers promoted new English music without any realistic hope of a profitable return – for at least many years; as Michael Hurd has pointed out, even Elgar's music did not a show a clear profit until the 1960s.[76] In this respect, the Novello company can be seen as one of the great patrons of the English Musical Renaissance, as an organisation which placed its financial strength and corporate resources behind national music without hope of gain.

The role of Novello's in promoting and projecting English national music cannot be overestimated. In the company's publishing policy as well as in the pages of the *Musical Times*, the Renaissance can be seen as a joint venture, a fusion of capital and culture, profit and ideal, an enterprise both material and spiritual. To that extent, the English Musical Renaissance was a product, manufactured of its own time, created by a shared need to express nation, empire and corporate pride. In this venture, composers, publishers, public and journalists, all combined to yield a commendable, if not always a literally profitable, return.

---

[74] *MT* 1 Apr. 1912.
[75] *MT* 1 Nov. 1912.
[76] Hurd, pp. 108–9.

1  James William Davison, music critic of *The Times* (1846–78) and self-
anointed holder of the 'sceptre of music criticism'.

2   Henry Fothergill Chorley, critic on the *Athenaeum* (1833–68) shown here
    in a photograph pasted into a signed copy of his autobiography presented
    to George Grove.

3   Joseph Bennett, critic on the *Daily Telegraph* (1870–1906) and according to Elgar, 'the patriarch and head of the profession'.

4   John Alexander Fuller Maitland, 'doorkeeper of music' on *The Times* (1889–1911).

5   Frederick George Edwards, editor of the *Musical Times* (1897–1909).

6   Sir Arthur Sullivan, the lost leader of English music?

7   Sir C. Hubert H. Parry, celebrated as the most suitably English of composers by many watchmen.

8   Sir Edward Elgar, 'self-made' bard of the Edwardian Age.

9    Elgar 'facing English music' on the reverse of the Bank of England £20 note
     (Reproduced by permission of the Bank of England).

# PART TWO

# The Watched

# CHAPTER FIVE

# Sullivan: 'Jumbo of the Moment'

The death of Sir Arthur Sullivan [...] may be said without hyperbole to have plunged the whole Empire in gloom; for many years he has ranked with distinguished personages, rather than with ordinary musicians. Never in the history of the art has a position such as his been held by a composer [...][1]

## 1.   Lost Leader?

On the 27 November 1900, Sir Arthur Sullivan was laid to rest in the crypt of St Paul's Cathedral with great and solemn pomp. Although the composer had been in indifferent health for some time, his death on the 22 November was sudden and unexpected. Sullivan had left instructions to be buried in his parents' grave in the Brompton Cemetery. Yet what actually took place was a funeral more fitting in its grandeur for a military hero or a statesman. As *The Times* suggested this funeral was unique for the passing of a musician; only the nation's farewell to the great Handel could be compared to the rites accorded to the composer of *The Golden Legend* and *The Mikado*. Queen Victoria in fact, commanded Sullivan's funeral with such elaborate planning and obsequies as could only have been organised through the direct involvement of the Court.

Sir Arthur's burial was an extraordinary expression of public mourning, more akin to a state or royal occasion. The cortège was made up of three cars of flowers and eight carriages, dense crowds lined the route and flags in the City of London were flown at half-mast. The rites consisted of two separate services. The first took place in the Chapel Royal, St James's with entrance by ticket only: the pall-bearers included several grandees of the Renaissance, Sir John Stainer, Sir Frederick Bridge, Sir Alexander Mackenzie and Sir Hubert Parry. The Queen was represented by Sir Walter Parratt (Master of the Musick) and Kaiser Wilhelm II by Count Hochberg (Director of the Imperial Opera in Berlin). The United States' ambassador was also present. *The Times* reported that the Chapel Royal was heavy with the scent of the floral tributes which included a cross of Parma violets from the staff and

---

[1] Leader 'Death of Sir Arthur Sullivan', T 23 Nov. 1900.

students of the Royal College of Music; and a laurel wreath inscribed: 'a mark of sincere admiration for his great musical talents, from Queen Victoria'.[2] The interment itself took place in Wren's cathedral with the Band of the Scots Guards providing the music. The queen's own floral tribute was interred with the coffin.[3]

The national press reflected on the sense of loss at the composer's passing and on his special place in the nation's cultural life. The *Morning Post*, a paper owned and run by the composer's friend Lord Borthwick, led the way with a fulsome assessment of Sullivan's contribution to music:

> The loss of Sir Arthur Sullivan deprives England of her most famous composer, one who has had a career unparalleled in the history of this country [... he was] struck down when still in the plenitude of his powers and in the full force of his creative abilities.[4]

The same notice explained how Sullivan had taken on the foreigners and beat them at their own game – through his ability above all, to be 'original'. Furthermore, as far as the *Morning Post* was concerned, Sullivan, in his literary friendships and cosmopolitan culture, had been the focus of English musical life.

However, there were elements in the press that were not quite so convinced of Sullivan's place in the pantheon of the nation's musical heroes. The *Athenaeum* pointed out that, although the composer may have been 'a general favourite', it was 'useless to speculate as to his place in the history of music'.[5] The *Musical Times*, though dedicating its leader pages (bordered in black) to Sullivan's obituary, published a rather childishly anecdotal necrologue.[6] Even *The Times* shared this ambivalence in its coverage of Sullivan's death. On 23 November, it ran two articles: an untitled announcement on page seven; and a leading article on page nine. In the announcement, the writer careful in his choice of phrase described Sullivan as England's 'most conspicuous composer [... who had] the power to charm all classes' and that his death 'was in the nature of a public calamity', yet:

> Many who are able to appreciate classical music regret that Sir Arthur Sullivan did not aim at consistently higher things, that he set himself to rival Offenbach and Lecocq instead of competing on a level of high seriousness with musicians as Sir Hubert Parry and

---

[2] *T* 28 Nov. 1900.
[3] Ibid.
[4] *MP* 23 Nov. 1900.
[5] *Ath* 24 Nov. 1900.
[6] Obituary 'Sir Arthur Sullivan', *MT* 1 Dec. 1900.

Professor Stanford [...] If he had followed this path, he might have
enrolled his name among the great composers of all time. He might
have won a European reputation in addition to his fame at home.[7]

Sullivan's failure is depicted as really a moral and spiritual one, his
flawed talent as incapable of holding dear those 'higher things' that
could 'compete' for the ultimate prizes in his art. Here, too, is that most
pernicious of charges – the lack of cultural patriotism in his failure
successfully to forge a European reputation. In this respect, Sullivan not
only failed himself and music, but he had also failed England. The
comparison with Parry and Stanford is deliberately made, for only they
could be truly regarded as having the 'high seriousness' that was the
stuff of true heroes of the nation's music. This announcement has all the
hallmarks of the work of John Fuller Maitland, who was implacably
hostile to Sullivan and his music.

In contrast, the 'Thunderer's' leading article on Sir Arthur's death was
to offer a radically different reading of his career. This piece chose to
stress that Sullivan's passing was not only a national, but also an
imperial tragedy. So far so good. But then the leader entered more
controversial territory by attacking those among the elite of English
music who had accused Sullivan of eschewing 'great' music in favour of
popular and commercial success in the musical theatre:

For all English-speaking races, with the exception of a very small
and unimportant class, Sullivan's name stood as a synonym for
England. perhaps it is not strange that [...] the small class referred
to was principally – if not entirely – composed of musicians of
earnest aims and highly-cultivated tastes. These regarded Sullivan
as a 'lost leader'; one who [...] had preferred the applause of the
patrons of the comic opera to the less noisy appreciation of genuine musicians.[8]

*The Times* was engaged in not only mounting a defence of Sullivan, but
also in taking on his detractors in the musical establishment. The newspaper spoke with two different voices, summing up perfectly the two
schools of thought concerning the duality of the composer's career. On
the one hand, the untitled announcement chose to stress the misgivings
which swirled around Sullivan's music, while, on the other, the leader
emphasised his role as a composer of national importance. So where did
*The Times*, and indeed the press as a whole, stand on Sir Arthur's life
and work? Was he a musical lightweight who possibly did English
music more harm than good? Or was he a music hero of whom queen
and country could be proud? The answer lies in an examination of the

---

[7] Untitled *T* 23 Nov. 1900.

[8] See n1.

reception of Sullivan's music in the press and his complex relationship with the watchmen.

## 2.   'Risking Comparison with Great Men'

From a young age Arthur Sullivan was groomed for greatness. The son of a clarinet teacher at the Royal Military College (Sandhurst), Sullivan became one of the Children of the Chapel Royal in 1854. In 1856, he became the first Mendelssohn Scholar at the RAM and, in 1858, with the patronage of John Goss (1800–80) and Sterndale Bennett, he secured funding to spend two years at the Leipzig Conservatorium. By going to Leipzig, Sullivan not only embraced the Mendelssohn tradition, but also established with the dead composer's family and colleagues. Sullivan seized his opportunity and made a great success of his German sojourn, not least in expanding his contacts to include some of the foremost names in German musical life – including the Moscheles family, Moritz Hauptmann and Joseph Joachim. Furthermore, on his return to England, Sullivan quickly built up a system of powerful patrons from among those who still revered and promoted the Mendelssohnian inheritance in England. Foremost among these new supporters was George Grove, who became a lifelong friend and ally.

When Sullivan returned from Leipzig in 1862, he soon had musical life at his feet and found himself increasingly regarded as legatee (or even executor) of Mendelssohn's English inheritance. It is clear from the outset of his career that Sullivan was groomed to be an insider; his was to be a fast track smoothed by interested professors, generous financiers, friendly aristocrats and royal patrons. The press played a vital role in this process and one which the composer fully grasped. Sullivan throughout his career spared no effort in cultivating the watchmen, getting to know most of them personally and lobbying them assiduously on behalf of his music. There were three critics in particular who assisted his rise to fame in the 1860s: Davison, Chorley and Gruneisen. Davison was to prove the most influential of the three and the two men became so close that 'old Jimmy' remained a Sullivan stalwart until his death.[9] Chorley too, as we have seen, was a Mendelssohnian keen to support a pupil with a Leipzig pedigree. However, Grunseisen had such a low opinion of English music that he

---

[9] Undated letter, Sullivan to his mother, q. in Jacobs, *Sullivan* p. 123. See ibid. p. 22 for Sullivan's letter to Davison from Leipzig lobbying him for a favourable mention in the *Musical World*. By 1874 Sullivan was close enough to Joseph Bennett to greet him as 'my dear Jo' in correspondence. Sullivan q. in ibid. p. 76.

had to be won over, and this Sullivan did mostly through personal contact by the end of the decade.[10]

*The Tempest Music* was the first important Sullivan premiere and took place at the Crystal Palace on 5 April 1862. The venue, which had been organised through Grove's position as Secretary of the Crystal Palace Company, was suitably impressive, especially since the work was given under the baton of the German conductor, August Manns. It is indicative of Sullivan's shrewd appraisal of the power and position of the critics that he approached Chorley to provide the libretto for *The Tempest Music*. Thus the young composer guaranteed that he had (at least) the *Athenaeum* on his side. In the circumstances, it is not surprising that Chorley welcomed the new hero in a sensational first review. In his notice the critic placed Sullivan (in terms of his potential) in the same category as Cherubini and Mendelssohn, when he declared:

> It was one of those events which mark an epoch in a man's life; and, what is of more universal consequence, it may mark an epoch in English music, or we shall be greatly disappointed [... it was] a very remarkable and legitimate success.[11]

Davison, despite his bitter feud with Chorley, also came out strongly in praise of Sullivan's first major concert in England, and he too announced the dawn of a new era in national music:

> *The Tempest*, while betraying a strong partiality for Mendelssohn's fascinating style, exhibits remarkable merits, and amongst the rest a decided vein of melody, a strong feeling for dramatic expression, and a happy fancy in the treatment of the orchestra'.[12]

As far as the other quality dailies were concerned, the *Daily Telegraph* announced that Sullivan had 'great natural capacity';[13] while an unconvinced Gruneisen in the *Morning Post* cast doubt on Sullivan's deeper qualities, implying critical disapproval of the Leipzig *Meister*: 'Mr Sullivan is [...] a close follower of Mendelssohn; and among those who prefer technical proficiency before imagination and originality he will doubtless find many ardent admirers'.[14] Even so, with *The Tempest* Sullivan had been given a remarkable launch by the watchmen, a confraternity which he was to cultivate throughout his career.

---

[10] Ibid. p. 417.

[11] *Ath* 12 Apr. 1862.

[12] T 7 Apr. 1862. Subscribers to the *Musical World* read virtually the same review in the 12 April issue.

[13] *DTel* 7 Apr. 1862.

[14] *MP* 7 Apr. 1862.

The 1860s was a golden decade for Sullivan as he built on the triumph of *The Tempest Music*. At this time his circle of patrons and supporters expanded impressively to include Charles Hallé, Michael Costa, Rossini and (through Grove) the Prince of Wales.[15] One of the keys to Sullivan's success was that he was the only young composer of real pedigree and promise around. As we have seen Sterndale Bennett had long since found composition uncongenial and George Macfarren was regarded as an eccentric whose bizarre theories of harmony precluded him from being considered as a leader of the national music. It was not until the mid-1870s and the advent of Frederic Cowen, that Sullivan had a serious competitor for the title of musical champion of England. Despite Sullivan's renown he still relied for his livelihood on his income as church organist, part-time teacher and composer of parlour songs and hymn-tunes. Art-Music did not provide him with a living.

In contrast to the success of *The Tempest*, Sullivan's next large-scale work, the masque *Kenilworth*, suffered something of a setback with the critics. The Birmingham Festival committee had approached the composer with this first important public comission as a direct result of Sullivan's cultivation of Michael Costa, resident conductor of the event.[16] Chorley, who had (once again) provided the libretto from Sir Walter Scott, was alone in his effusive praise for Sullivan's talents, asserting that it would 'do more than bear out every favourable impression existing and retained by the writer's *Tempest Music*'.[17] *The Times*, however, was unsure whether *Kenilworth* was worthy of a commission from the Birmingham Festival, thus making it clear that there were limits to its championship of Sullivan's music. In his review, Davison reminded Sullivan that he was lucky to have 'so golden a chance' from 'so exceptional an occasion', and that although *Kenilworth* was 'lively, tuneful and fresh', it was also 'unambitious in plan' and 'unpretending in style'.[18] The suggestion that his efforts were unworthy was a charge that was to haunt Sullivan for the rest of his life. Henry Lunn was unimpressed with *Kenilworth* too writing in the *Musical Times* that he thought the commission premature and that Sullivan was advised 'to imperil his reputation by risking comparison with great men'.[19] Despite its uncertain reception *Kenilworth* marked the beginning of Sullivan's long association with the Birmingham Festival and its resident conductor Sir Michael Costa.[20]

---

[15] Jacobs, pp. 35–6.
[16] Sullivan, an inveterate networker, had written to Costa asking him for the 'favour ' of a Birmingham commission. Ibid. pp. 37–8.
[17] *Ath* 17 Sept. 1864.
[18] T 12 Sept. 1864.
[19] *MT* 1 Oct. 1864.
[20] Jacobs, p. 38.

Perhaps stung by the *Kenilworth* setback with the critics, Sullivan turned to the more purely classical forms for his next premieres. The three major works of 1866, the *'Irish' Symphony*, the overture *In Memoriam* and the *Cello Concerto*, may be seen as a collective reply to the unfavourable criticism of 1864. The first of these works to be premiered was the *'Irish' Symphony* and it met with a warm reception from the watchmen. It was Davison who promoted the new work most assertively, commenting that Sullivan's efforts would 'raise the English school of music from the dead level of vainly aspiring mediocrity at which, for the most part, it has remained for some years'.[21] This review was controversial since there were several highly-respected composers who were by implication slighted by Davison's call – among them, Macfarren and Sterndale Bennett.[22] Gruneisen in the *Morning Post* was equally impressed with the new work, calling it a 'fine symphony' and confirming the composer as 'one of the most promising of the present day'.[23] Even Lunn managed to raise a cheer, commenting that the *'Irish'* 'seems to have achieved a success which we trust may have a healthy effect upon the young composer'.[24] Chorley, in the *Athenaeum* wrote that although the symphony lacked 'brilliant strokes of originality', he was nevertheless charmed by its 'individuality'.[25] At last, Sullivan had written a work that affirmed his reputation as the nation's leading composer. Yet ironically, over time this status was to prove as much of an imposition as a blessing and a burden from which the composer was never to be free.

Underlining his growing domination of English music, Sullivan scored a second triumph in 1866 with his overture *In Memoriam*, commissioned by the Norwich Festival. This festival was enhanced in prestige by the carefully orchestrated presence of the Duke of Edinburgh, a royal friend of the composer. As far as the watchmen were concerned, Davison both in *The Times* and the *Musical World*, loyally led the way, remarking that *In Memoriam*:

> not only exhibits high ability, serious thought and careful workmanship but in the clearness of its plan, its ample development, its absence of mannerism, and frequent boldness of touch, shows the young composer determined to advance.[26]

Chorley too had no doubts as to the greatness of *In Memoriam*, declaring that the new work, characterised by its 'mood of lofty hope tempering

---

[21] *T* 12 Mar. 1866.
[22] Davison repeated his views in *MW* 17 Mar. 1866.
[23] *MP* 12 Mar. 1866.
[24] *MT* 1 Apr. 1866.
[25] *Ath* 17 Mar. 1866.
[26] *MW* 3 Nov. 1866. See also *T* 1 Nov. 1866.

resigned grief [...] might as justly be performed at a royal funeral as the *Coronation Anthem* of Handel'.[27] No greater accolade could have been extended, a sentiment that must have seemed to have been reinforced by the royal presence at the premiere. Gruneisen in the *Morning Post* remarked that the core idea of the new work was 'full of beauty' and that the whole piece was 'cleverer than anything' Sullivan had written before.[28] It was left, as so often, to Henry Lunn in the *Musical Times* to apply the cold shower treatment, and he duly commented that 'pathetic and powerful as [*In Memoriam*] is in subject and treatment, it is one more instance that continuity of design cannot be compensated for by facility of invention'.[29]

The third work of 1866 with which Sullivan continued to impress the critics and musical public was the *Cello Concerto*. This piece, written for the Italian cellist Alfredo Piatti (1822–1901), a friend of Mendelssohn and of George Grove, was given its first performance at the Crystal Palace. Although some of the critics did not notice the work, others responded on cue. Chorley, in the *Athenaeum*, stated that it marked: 'another step forward in a true and earnest career. The music is elegant, full of contrast and effect'.[30] The *Daily Telegraph* was equally enthusiastic, declaring that the concerto would add to Sullivan's reputation as the 'most promising composer of our time'.[31] There can be little doubt that Sullivan set out to make a deep impression with the premieres of 1866: a symphony, a solemn overture and a concerto all marked the seriousness of his intent.

After 1866 Sullivan rarely returned to orchestral music. Notwithstanding the critical and public acclaim which greeted his music of the mid-1860s Sullivan realised that the publishing and performance climate meant that orchestral works could not live beyond their premieres – not even with the enthusiastic endorsement of the watchmen. As an early biographer pointed out, Sullivan in his mid-30s despaired that 'symphonies and the like would ever become strictly 'popular' in England', consequently he despaired of finding enduring fame and fortune writing large-scale orchestral works.[32]

---

[27] *Ath* 3 Nov. 1866.
[28] *MP* 3 Nov. 1866.
[29] *MT* 1 Dec. 1866.
[30] *Ath* 1 Dec. 1866.
[31] *DTel* 26 Nov. 1866.
[32] Simcoe, *Sullivan v. Critic* p. 12. Of the orchestral works of 1866: *In Memoriam* was published in 1885; the *'Irish' Symphony* in 1915; and the *Cello Concerto* had only two further professional performances before disappearing until the 1950s.

Sullivan had to look elsewhere for pecuniary reward. Fame he would soon seek as a composer of large-scale choral works for the provincial festival circuit, but for serious profit he looked with increasing interest towards the musical theatre. This strategy was however fraught with danger, since many of the watchmen felt that operetta was contaminated with superficiality and 'vice'. Nevertheless, Sullivan went ahead with his first theatrical production, *Cox and Box*, which was written for an amateur charity performance in 1867. In the event, this musical comedy had little impact on his relationship with the watchmen since they all decided to ignore it. It was to be four years before he returned to the theatre.

As far as the critics were concerned the only true test of a composer's greatness was the oratorio, that popular vehicle of Victorian Christianity. Sullivan realised as a serious composer, he would sooner or later have to prove himself in the genre. However, his lack of any deep religious conviction meant that he brought little spiritual commitment to the composition of devotional works. As Sullivan commented of his editorship of *Church Hymns with Tunes* (1874), 'I hope that the hymn-book will be a blessing to the Church.. It's a curse to me'.[33]

Despite his lack of Christian zeal, Sullivan took up the challenge of oratorio with *The Prodigal Son* for the Three Choirs (Worcester) Festival of 1869. The new work, with its libretto by George Grove, received a warm welcome in the press and marked the composer's breakthrough into writing large-scale music for the festival circuit. The coverage of *The Prodigal Son* was far more extensive than that for previous premieres. The *Athenaeum*'s Campbell Clarke perfectly understood the significance of the occasion:

> much hung upon its fate. The question to be decided was [...] whether the hopeful English composer of our day had the stuff enough in him to do a great thing – nay, the greatest. A verdict has been arrived at [...] and Mr Sullivan [...] enters the ranks of those who have achieved.[34]

From this review it is clear that, for Clarke at least, the quest for an English oratorio was over. Sullivan had succeeded where so many others had failed. Davison's two-column review in *The Times* also gave the new work a rousing reception. It was:

> not merely the best and most carefully finished work of its composer, but a work that would do credit to any composer now living. *The Prodigal Son* has the stuff in it which endures.[35]

---

[33] Sullivan q. in Jacobs, p. 72.
[34] *Ath* 17 Mar. 1866.
[35] *T* 11 Sept. 1869. There was also a shorter notice in *T* 9 Sept. 1869.

Furthermore, Davison suggested that comparison could be made between *The Prodigal Son* with the choral works of Handel and Mendelssohn. The *Morning Post* joined the chorus of praise describing it as an 'excellent work' being 'exceedingly clever and beautiful', despite the fact that there was 'something awful and unapproachable in the name of oratorio'.[36] The *Daily Telegraph*, covering the premiere with two substantial reviews on consecutive days, hailed the work's 'grand vocal and instrumental effects' and greeted Sullivan as 'one of our first living composers'.[37] Even the *Musical Times* was mildly impressed, as Lunn declared (in a long review) that: 'Mr Sullivan has shown a progress in his art which cannot be mistaken'.[38]

Yet rarely again was Sullivan to bask in such critical acclaim. One reason for his waning reputation with the critics was certainly the 'embarrassment' of his enormous output of parlour songs. Although popular successes such as *Marquis de Mincepie* (1875), proved beneficial to Sullivan's bank-balance, it did not improve the composer's artistic standing. But the real explanation for his increasingly fraught relationship with the watchmen was his growing involvement in the musical theatre, an association which was resumed with the opening of *Thespis* at the Gaiety Theatre in 1871. The majority of the critics, including those close to him, could not accept that the most acclaimed English composer since Purcell should prostitute his talent by writing a Christmas burlesque in which the 'ad lib gag was as prominent as the female leg'.[39] While Sullivan was not mauled in the press for *Thespis* (since its premiere would not have been covered by music critics), it is likely he began to pay the price for his disloyalty to his art when *The Light of the World* was first performed at Birmingham in 1873. The transition from the false gods of *Thespis* to the 'one True God' of *The Light of the World* was one the watchmen would not make as effortlessly as the composer.

The reception of *The Light of the World* at the hands of the critics was a disaster for Sullivan. The broad critical approval which had characterised the reception of his music for more than a decade was gone. The *Morning Post* dismissed it in a single page as a work 'tending to tediousness', and questioned whether the 'life of the Redeemer' was a fitting subject for an oratorio.[40] Gruneisen in the *Athenaeum* was particularly scathing, commenting that: '[the libretto ...] has been badly

---

[36] *MP* 9 Sept. 1869.
[37] *DTel* 10 Sept. 1869 and 9 Sept. 1869.
[38] *MT* 1 Oct. 1869.
[39] Jacobs, p. 69.
[40] *MP* 28 Aug. 1873.

selected, ill arranged, is faint in outline, weak in details [...] the patchi-
ness is probably the result of haste'.[41] Sullivan had never had such a
poor review. In the *Musical Times*, Lunn echoed these sentiments contemptuously advising the composer to go away and 'calmly analyse the
merits and demerits of his oratorio, when removed from the flattery of
friends'.[42] Only Sullivan's truest friends stood by *The Light of the
World*. Joseph Bennett summoned up some enthusiasm, in a huge one-
third page review, pointing out that despite an appalling libretto, 'the
man who writes an oratorio for Birmingham sets his candle on the
highest of hills [... and Sullivan] has satisfied the exigencies of the
case'.[43] The ever-loyal Davison also did his best in *The Times*; having
excused the libretto, he settled for the assertion that 'Mr Sullivan has
not only composed a good oratorio, but in many respects a great one'.[44]
Yet no amount of special pleading could save *The Light of the World*,
which survived in performance mainly in extract form. Even more
worrying for Sullivan was the fact that, following its premiere a new
note of serious disquiet is apparent about his artistic judgement and
integrity. Perhaps it was naive of Sullivan to hope that he could retain
the group loyalty of the press with an *oeuvre* that stretched from the
*risqué* burlesque of *Thespis* to the life of the 'Redeemer'. Sullivan's
credibility as an Art-Music composer never fully recovered. Over thirty
years later the failure of the work still rankled with Sullivan loyalists
who endlessly raked over the 'betrayal' of *The Light of the World* by
the critics.[45]

By 1873, Sullivan was losing some of his most important friends
among the watchmen. With Chorley dead and Davison's position at
*The Times* becoming increasingly problematical, Bennett's presence at
the *Daily Telegraph* must have seemed a godsend. After the failure of
*The Light of the World*, the composer's gaze turned once more towards
the musical theatre. The result was *Trial by Jury*, his second collaboration with W. S. Gilbert, which went into performance at the Royalty
Theatre in 1875. With its success the die was cast as Sullivan's involvement with operetta threw his reputation with the critics into ever deeper
shadow. Sullivan wanted to be feted on the choral festival circuit as a
'true' artist; while he also craved the financial rewards and concomitant
life-style of a successful man of the theatre. Meanwhile, the watchmen
were not prepared to accept this tense duality in both his life and work.

---

[41] *Ath* 30 Aug. 1873.

[42] *MT* 1 Oct. 1873.

[43] *DTel* 28 Aug. 1873.

[44] *T* 28 Aug. 1873.

[45] See Chapter 3 in *Simcoe, Sullivan v. Critic*.

### 3. 'A Love of the Stage'

In an interview towards the end of his life, Sullivan explained that it was Rossini who first inspired him with 'a love of the stage and of things operatic'.[46] The composer also made it clear to the interviewer from the *Strand Musical Magazine* that he closely identified with the Italian maestro because of their shared devotion to the 'achievement of maximum true excellence' in music. What Sir Arthur however did *not* make so clear was, that like the 'Swan of Pesaro', he was obsessed with a way of life that only vast amounts of money made possible. Smart addresses, fashionable clothes, luxury travel (including a private train), high-society and Court connections were all on his wish-list. Sullivan realised that only serious box-office success could finance such a celebrity life-style. Sullivan decided that instead of being a servant of music; he would make music serve him. Both Sullivan and Rossini were hard men of the theatre, but they paid a high price for *la dolce vita* at the hands of the critics.

Nineteenth-century composers were not expected to embrace a champagne and racehorses lifestyle. Instead, theirs was to be an existence of material denial in the name of artistic integrity and spiritual greatness. A unifying theme of the music history writing of the time was that in the life of a truly 'great' composer poverty and harshness of experience meant creativity. For example, the contemporary biographies of the impoverished Schubert, the consumptive Weber, and the neurotic Schumann, all powerfully underscored the notion that Art entailed suffering and self-denial. According to these expectations money and Great Music did not mix, but Sullivan (like his hero Rossini) loved lucre: and needed lots of it.

In the 1870s as Sullivan's career as a theatre composer blossomed, his relationship with the watchmen withered. The premiere of *Trial by Jury* (1875), and its reception in the press, marked a watershed in his career. Even 'old Jimmy' Davison for once showed his anger in his review in *The Times* when he wrote: '[it is] no more than a humorous bagatelle. Its first and not least valuable recommendation is its brevity'.[47] Gruneisen of the *Athenaeum*, did not bother to review the work, leaving it to a fellow-critic to write it up in the journal's 'drama' column.[48] The critical punishment meted out to *Trial by Jury* was to become the norm for Sullivan's theatrical works over the ensuing decade. What made matters worse was that the older critics were fast disappearing, to be replaced

---

[46] Zedlitz, 'Sir Arthur Sullivan'.
[47] *T* 29 Mar. 1875.
[48] *Ath* 3 Apr. 1875.

by a new 'aesthetic' generation of journalists, many of whom were imbued with the teachings of the art-historian and critic Walter Pater. For these younger watchmen, Sullivan's operettas were an even greater anathema than they were to the older generation of Mendelssohn-oriented critics.

By 1880 Sullivan's course was set. He had written a string of successful stage works in collaboration with W. S. Gilbert and the impresario Richard D'Oyly Carte, the most successful of these being *HMS Pinafore* and *The Pirates of Penzance*. The premiere of the former in 1878 was ignored by the *Daily Telegraph*, the *Morning Post* and the *Musical World*, while Hueffer in *The Times*, commenting for the first time on a Gilbert and Sullivan production, spoke for most of the watchmen:

> we cannot suppress a word of regret that the composer upon whom before all the others the chances of a national school of music depend should confine himself, or be confined by circumstances, to a class of production which however attractive, is hardly worthy of the efforts of an accomplished and serious artist.[49]

In this review Hueffer made it clear that despite not having scored a great Art-Music success for nearly a decade, Sullivan remained the only English composer of stature who was capable of leading a school of national music. Lunn's *Musical Times* had no such hopes confining its review of *HMS Pinafore* to the grim comment that 'this firmly cemented union between author and composer is detrimental to the art-progress of either'.[50]

*The Pirates of Penzance*, premiered in London in 1880, attracted further odium from the watchmen. Despite its sensational premiere in New York the previous year, English journalists were hostile when it arrived in the West End. Far from mollifying the critics, *The Pirates'* American success added to Sullivan's problems, since the work could hardly be held up as a worthy product of the English Musical Renaissance in the New World – or indeed anywhere. While Hueffer was probably too disappointed to review *The Pirates* in *The Times*, Barrett in the *Morning Post* wearily observed:

> it is certain that there is very little, if anything, in the music that Mr Sullivan has not said before [...] There is better evidence of tune-making than the desire to exhibit musical science or original invention.[51]

---

[49] *T* 27 May 1878.
[50] *MT* 1 Jun. 1878.
[51] *MP* 5 Apr. 1880.

It was left to Ebenezer Prout, Gruneisen's recently appointed successor at the *Athenaeum*, to summon up a degree of mercy for *The Pirates*:

> if there be some that would prefer that our native composer's ability should be expended on more serious and enduring work, it must be at any rate admitted that light opera is a legitimate form of art.[52]

The watchmen's dilemma with regard to Sullivan's operettas was, how could such 'illegitimate' music be so much loved? The *Musical Times* in its review at least acknowledged this quandary when it observed:

> Whatever then may be said of the future place of these works in the temple of Fame, there can be no question that there is a public ready and waiting to receive them in the present day [...]even the most severely critical must acknowledge [... Gilbert and Sullivan's] power.[53]

Disingenuous, perhaps?, but this line was useful; it reiterated the notion that if only Sullivan could stop wasting his talent and return to his 'high calling', then all would be well. In the midst of this negative reception, the composer could still count on one ally among the critics: Joseph Bennett, who wrote breezily of *The Pirates*, 'there is scarcely a dull bar in it [...] and as usual Mr Sullivan excels in his treatment of the orchestra'.[54]

In 1876, Sullivan's relationship with the critics was further complicated following his appointment as principal of the new National Training School of Music (henceforth NTS) at South Kensington, an institution founded as a 'state conservatoire' along continental lines.[55] The elusive figure behind the new school was Sir Henry Cole, friend of Prince Albert and one of the prime movers behind the Great Exhibition of 1851. It is significant that Sullivan was not Cole's choice for the principalship of the NTS because of the high salary (£1000 pa) which he was demanding and because of doubts about his involvement with the musical theatre.[56] Although the Duke of Edinburgh, the composer's royal friend and patron, succeeded in brokering a compromise, Sullivan found

---

[52] *Ath* 10 Apr. 1880.

[53] *MT* 1 May 1880.

[54] *DTel* 5 Apr. 1880.

[55] National Training School Appendix III: 'Objects of the School' (Nos.13 and 15). Feb. 1877. RCM Archive.

[56] National Training School Minute Books, 12th meeting of Management Committee, Jan. 1876. RCM Archive. See also the letter from Sir Henry Cole to the Duke of Edinburgh (11 Jan. 1876) in which he expressed the 'strongest conviction that Mr Sullivan's appointment on several grounds is undesirable'. RCM Archive.

his academic responsibilities irksome. At the end of his five-year tenure at the NTS, Sullivan resigned, and not even the appeals of George Grove could ever bring him back to academe as a professor at the new RCM.

The 'Sullivan dilemma' for the critics intensified as the needs of English national music collided head on with the demands of D'Oyly Carte and the Savoy. Although the watchmen were actively promoting a rising younger generation of English composers, there were few who cared to question Sullivan's enduring popularity on the festival circuit. Meanwhile, Sullivan achieved new distinction with his appointment as chief conductor to the Leeds Festival (1880) and with his knighthood (1883). Those critics who still believed that Sullivan had a contribution to make to the future of English music continued to be exasperated by his refusal to turn his back on the theatre. Sullivan duly responded to the lobbying of the watchmen with two new Choral works: *The Martyr of Antioch* (1880) and *The Golden Legend* (1886).[57]

The first major festival work with which Sullivan tried to rehabilitate himself with the watchmen was *The Martyr of Antioch* (1880). This new devotional work, with a libretto by that arch-scribbler of operetta W. S.Gilbert, was not well received: *The Times* accused Sullivan of sacrificing 'dramatic propriety to mere prettiness', although Hueffer added that the composer was still a 'highly gifted musician';[58] the *Morning Post*, was appalled that such a work so 'profane' in its theatricality, should be called a 'sacred musical cantata':

> truths which affect the foundation of Christian belief had not been considered as a matter worthy of more exalted treatment than a mere dramatic one. [... Sullivan] has looked at music too much as a means for delicate display of humour or eccentricity, or as the power by means of which present popularity can be wooed and won.[59]

Even Bennett in the *Daily Telegraph* found it difficult to raise a cheer for the new work, slyly commenting that at least the 'judgement of the audience never seemed in doubt'.[60] The *Musical Times* too was very unhappy, commenting that in the new work Sullivan had 'bestowed all his energies on songs and hymns' rather than make the most of the dramatic opportunities of the text.[61] Finally, the *Athenaeum* chose to

---

[57] In the intervening six years between the works Sullivan wrote *Patience* (1881), *Iolanthe* (1882), *Princess Ida* (1884) and *The Mikado* (1885).

[58] *T* 16 Oct. 1880.

[59] *MP* 16 Oct. 1880.

[60] *DTel* 16 Oct. 1880.

[61] *MT* 1 Nov. 1880.

emphasise the dramatic weaknesses of a work it believed 'not conceived in a very lofty spirit', although Frost did go on to say that it was 'an advantage to have the composer of *HMS Pinafore* once more occupying himself with a worthier form of art'.[62] It was left to the *Musical World*, in an unsigned report reprinted from the *Leeds Mercury*, to point out a new factor in the reception of Sullivan's music: that, for all its deficiencies, at least the new cantata it did not exhibit Wagnerian tendencies:

> No doubt Mr Sullivan's theme would have accepted a great deal more 'learned' labour than he brought to it [... yet] Another point to be observed is the freedom of the music from the tyranny of some modern fashions to which young composers frequently submit [...] because they wish to appear abreast of what they call 'progress'.[63]

Despite the failure of *The Martyr of Antioch* to impress the watchmen, the work did mark a slight shift of opinion in Sullivan's favour among those critics who feared the 'menace' of Wagner. Sullivan's knighthood was also important since it ensured a note of deference from some of the critics after 1883. Regardless of Sullivan's new knightly status, a younger 'aesthetic' generation of critics and composers regarded Sir Arthur as *passé* and no model for the future development of national music. Furthermore his notorious fondness for gaming and the Turf, his royal friends, Riviera trips, Parisian visits (plus attendant bordello expenditures) and the private train, went down badly with many younger critics.[64]

Meanwhile the Savoy Operas continued to flow from Sir Arthur's pen, although they were placing an increasing physical and nervous strain on him. By 1884, Sullivan was ready to quit and made his feelings known to D'Oyly Carte and Gilbert.[65] His threat to abandon the Savoy connection came to nought and *The Mikado* was the immediate result. This colossal hit did nothing to enhance Sullivan's standing with the critics. Although the ever-loyal Bennett in the *Daily Telegraph*, commenting that the country was being 'more or less Japanned', did Sullivan proud by asserting that 'on his part [he] keeps the sacred lamp alight and need not feel ashamed thereof'.[66] *The Times*, however, was in no mood to tolerate such 'sentimental and comic ditties' in a work

---

[62] *Ath* 23 Oct. 1880.

[63] *MW* 16 Oct. 1880.

[64] Arthur Jacobs surmises from Sullivan's diary entries for February 1885 that the composer's gambling losses amounted to £110 that month – rather more than the £100 monthly allowance he gave his mistress, Mrs Ronalds. Jacobs, pp. 200–1.

[65] Ibid. pp. 188–9.

[66] *DTel* 16 Mar. 1885.

which failed 'to establish any rapport between music and words'.[67] The *Musical Times* did not deign to review *The Mikado*, while the best that the *Musical World* could do was to reprint a slight notice from the *Daily News*. It was left to the *Athenaeum* to voice that disapproval that Sullivan had heard so often before: 'the pity is that so much ability should be employed on productions which from their very nature must be ephemeral'.[68] Once again, Sullivan had let himself down badly with the watchmen As *The Mikado* soared in popularity, so did the composer's reputation languish in the critics' estimation.

Even so, a certain critical tide was beginning to flow in Sir Arthur's direction. This trend was marked by a willingness by some of the watchmen to disregard the Savoy Operas in order to encourage Sullivan to engage in more 'serious' composition. The composer's eventual response was *The Golden Legend* (1886), with its libretto by Joseph Bennett, a work which marked the arrival of a reformed 'Sullivan' with some critics.

*The Golden Legend* was a distinct turning-point in Sir Arthur's rehabilitation. The *Daily Telegraph*, with its own music critic as the librettist, gave the new work an exhaustive review reminding the readers that Sir Arthur was 'old-fashioned enough to put trust in the power of tune':

> It is in music only, that, according to modern teaching, there must be complication of means, that passion must be twisted into incomprehensible shapes, and that all expression must be strained and forced, every picture made garish, if not lurid, and every element of 'sensationalism' be present.[69]

There is evidence here of Sullivan's 'vice' of simple tunefulness being turned on its head, with the transparency of his music now seen as innocent and morally harmonious. In this review, Wagner is presented as a danger to music and, in a passage revealing how Sullivan's value was being re-assessed by some of the watchmen, Bennett stressed that *The Golden Legend* was: 'an honour to English music [and no ...] finer demonstration of the fact, that our native art is well-qualified to speak with its enemies in the gate, could be desired by the most patriotic'.[70] The 'enemies at the gate' were, of course, the Wagnerites, the new horde of Huns who had been advancing across musical Europe for decades. *The Times* was also generous (though with more than a hint of irony), further evidence of the changing climate in the reception of Sullivan's

---

[67] *T* 16 Mar. 1885.
[68] *Ath* 21 Mar. 1885.
[69] *DTel* 18 Oct. 1886.
[70] Ibid. See also Chapter 2 above on Bennett and Wagnerism.

music; once again, erstwhile irredeemable flaws were made into virtues as Sullivan's standing was palpably talked up:

> [Sullivan] does not simulate any sympathy with Wagner, Liszt or Berlioz which he does not feel, and his relations with the *leitmotif* are of the most platonic kind [...] The Leeds Festival may boast of giving life to a work which, if not one of genius in the strict sense of the word is at least likely to survive until our long-expected English Beethoven appears on the scene.[71]

In this playful notice, with its subtle allusion to the composer's reputation as something of a *roué*, Hueffer affirmed his acceptance of Sullivan on his own terms – at least until English music was capable of producing a 'great composer' of its own. For its part too, the *Morning Post*'s review positively glowed:

> The hearer is carried to the highest realms of poetical music, so admirably piloted by one of the greatest modern masters [*The Golden Legend* demonstrates ...] that the hand of the master has united with his head and his heart, and the result is a composition which will live and deserve its vitality, for it is human in scope and capable alike of refining as of elevating the hearer [...].[72]

The *Musical Times* gave *The Golden Legend* the best review of any Sullivan work since the 1860s, pointing to the new cantata's great 'beauty' and 'strength'.[73]

Perhaps beguiled by the critical and popular success of *The Golden Legend*, Sullivan accepted an invitation to perform the new work at the Imperial Court Theatre in Berlin, as part of the Kaiser's birthday celebrations in March 1887. This was a highly unusual honour for a foreign composer and Sullivan was delighted to accept. It was to prove a fateful decision since, of the performance, Sullivan wrote that 'a crowded and brilliant audience' turned up to 'the most agonising evening I have ever spent'.[74] Even worse, *The Golden Legend* was savaged by the German critics: *Fremdenblatt* sneered that the composer was 'not up to the task' while suggesting that Sullivan would 'soon cover this defect with another pretty operetta'; while the *Börsen Kurier* commented that '[Sullivan] lacks two qualities – emotion and passion absolutely, original conception entirely [...] greatness he has not'.[75] This occasion was not only a disaster for Sullivan but was also a catastrophe

---

[71] *T* 18 Oct. 1886

[72] *MP* 18 Oct. 1886.

[73] *MT* 1 Nov. 1886.

[74] Sullivan q. in Jacobs, p. 253.

[75] Q. in translation in '*The Golden Legend* in Berlin'. Although this article is unsigned, it was almost certainly written by Joseph Bennett.

for English music, which had been held up to condescension and ridicule in the land of Beethoven and Wagner. Sullivan had been judged as mediocre, spiritually bereft and boring. It was surely the lowest point in his career.

When news of Sullivan's fiasco sank in at home, the *Musical Times* responded to his German critics with an article setting out a selection of their notices (in translation) accusing them of nationalistic prejudice. This extraordinary article, probably written by Joseph Bennett, made scant attempt at answering the German journalists point by point; instead it let its readers 'judge for themselves', the 'hostile spirit' and 'manifest untruth' of the foreigners' onslaught.[76] In language reminiscent of that used to mark humiliating defeat in war, the article concluded: 'Alas, poor *Golden Legend*! Alas, poor Sullivan! Alas, poor England! Will it, or he, or she ever hold up head again?'. The article was a bold move and may be seen as a an attempt at a damage-limitation exercise. Yet not even the loyal Bennett could not disguise the harm done by the debacle in Berlin to Sullivan's reputation, as well as the German perception of the English Musical Renaissance.

Whatever the German watchmen had made of him, Sullivan remained very popular both in the West End and on the provincial festival circuit. And some critics at least were prepared to accept him, rehabilitate him and recruit him anew into the cause of the Renaissance. It is also clear that Sullivan, despite the criticism which his career in the musical theatre had attracted, continued to identify himself with the national music project. Evidence for this desired affiliation may be found in a revealing lecture which the composer gave at the Birmingham and Midland Institute in 1888, an occasion in which Sir Arthur set out his frank thoughts on English music. What the audience made of Sullivan's vivid opening gambit can only be surmised: 'music is to me a mistress in every sense of the word; a mistress whose commands I obey, whose smiles I love, whose wrongs move me as no others do'.[77] In any event, in his lecture Sullivan went on to blame England's musical backwardness on the fact that 'in the mind of the true Briton, Business, Society, Politics, and Sport, all come before Art', music being seen as a 'pastime fit only for women and children'.[78] (Sir Arthur conveniently chose to ignore the fact that three of his own preoccupations were business, high society and sport). Even so, Sullivan went on to argue that this state of affairs had to change, since music was not only useful, but also a force for good in the world – providing it was 'controlled by proper educa-

---

[76] Ibid.
[77] Sullivan, *About Music* p. 3.
[78] Ibid. pp. 10–11.

tion'.[79] Herein lies the nub of the lecture: English music was deserving of greater financial support from both individual benefactors and government alike. Sullivan's Birmingham utterance was the clearest public statement he ever made of his support for the revival of England's national music.

It was with his grand opera *Ivanhoe* that Sullivan made his most signal act of affiliation to the Musical Renaissance. With this work he wanted to prove himself as a 'serious' composer, free of the constraints of Gilbert's texts, and an artist capable of establishing the continental reputation which had so long eluded him.[80] Although there were three Savoy operettas in the late-1880s: *Ruddigore*, *The Yeomen of the Guard* and *The Gondoliers*, Sullivan devoted to them none of the time and creative effort that he lavished on *Ivanhoe*. With this work, Sir Arthur intended to provide D'Oyly Carte not only with the core work for an entire season (1891) of English 'Grand Opera' at a new custom-built theatre in Cambridge Circus, but also a production which would inspire a whole new generation of native opera composers. A '*Lohengrin*' for England.

*Ivanhoe* was premiered on 31 January 1891 in the presence of Sullivan's loyal royals, namely, the Prince and Princess of Wales and the Duke and Duchess of Edinburgh. The opera and its new theatre had been widely advertised and the press interest was predictably intense. Sullivan had finally taken up the challenge of seeking the grail of founding an English grand opera tradition. It was a momentous occasion and the watchmen to a man wanted the Royal English Opera House to succeed.

In the event, however, the critics could only give *Ivanhoe* qualified approval. Bennett in the *Daily Telegraph* spelled out the scale of the gamble undertaken with *Ivanhoe*:

> the battle of English opera, like that of freedom, has been handed down from one generation to another, and always as a lost cause which cannot quite be killed [... and if] necessity [should force Mr Carte ...] to strike the flag of English opera now floating over his grand new house [... then the cause of] an indigenous lyric stage will be lost to this generation.[81]

From Bennett's review it is possible to detect disappointment in his use of the language of heroic resistance rather than that of victory. Although Bennett analysed the text and music in detail, he ominously made no attempt to take a view of the whole work, except to remark

[79] Ibid. p. 17.
[80] Jacobs, p. 307.
[81] *DTel* 2 Feb. 1891.

that 'a distinguished audience' attended a 'brilliant success'.[82] The *Morning Post* also did its best to talk up the occasion, reminding its readers that Sullivan had 'long been ambitious of showing the world his powers as a composer' and that:

> Musicians will one and all agree that in *Ivanhoe* [Sullivan] has opened a path which he may pursue further with honour to himself and advantage to the art he adorns. [...] If *Ivanhoe* does not fully realise all that was expected of it [... it] shows that it is an earnest sign of greater things to come. [... Sullivan] says the right thing at the right time, and that most appositely, and, above all, his work is thoroughly English.[83]

Here too, the note of disappointment is palpable. It seems that Barrett's strongest recommendation of *Ivanhoe* was that it was English. In a strange way, Sir Arthur had become '*Ivanhoe*', and upon his lance rested England's honour in opera. Yet the nation's champion had finally come out of his tent to do battle only to be found sadly inadequate. In *The Times*, Fuller Maitland, for all his contempt for Sullivan diplomatically asked: 'will *Ivanhoe* enhance the composer's reputation and that of English art; and will the work take a place among the classics of dramatic music, and attain a real immortality?'.[84] Although Maitland acknowledged *Ivanhoe* as Sullivan's best work, he stressed that if 'modern theories' (of opera) gained 'universal acceptance', then *Ivanhoe* would be forgotten as merely 'a series of numbers'.[85] The *Athenaeum* rather underplayed the premiere, merely noting the opera's 'striking success';[86] while the *Musical Times* resented the way in which public interest was 'artfully developed' in advance of the first night, asserting that the opera was 'a work that was destined to exercise a great influence on the future course of English Opera'.[87]

Although Sullivan's 'grand opera' ran for a remarkable 155 consecutive performances, in the end, it brought the Royal English Opera venture to its knees and D'Oyly Carte had to abandon the project with his personal debts standing at a colossal £36,000.[88] Once again, Sullivan had disappointed as a 'serious' composer and was never again to be considered a serious contender for a place among the leaders of the Musical Renaissance. *Ivanhoe*'s defeat was total and final.

---

[82] Ibid.
[83] *MP* 2 Feb. 1891.
[84] *T* 2 Feb. 1891.
[85] Ibid.
[86] *Ath* 7 Feb. 1891 and 14 Feb. 1891.
[87] *MT* 1 Mar. 1891.
[88] Jacobs, p. 330.

The last decade of the century was, for Sullivan, a time of deteriorating health, declining income and an output of increasingly stale operettas. To make matters worse, relations with Parry's RCM team reached new depths when Stanford's supporters on the Leeds Festival Committee ousted Sullivan as festival conductor after the 1898 event. Still, the status of 'grand old man' of English music wasn't that uncongenial to Sullivan, since clubland was ever welcoming and royal favour was assured. As we have seen, the end, when it came, was marked with all the funerary pomp that the British state could muster. Yet, in the grand manner of his passing, Sullivan in death seemed (to some) to mock the 'real' achievements of the Musical Renaissance, and this state of affairs could not go unremarked upon by at least one supporter of the South Kensington team.

The posthumous and, as it turned out, the definitive verdict on the life and career of Sir Arthur Sullivan is to be found in the *Cornhill Magazine* (March 1901).[89] Here, in this monthly journal, noted for its lack of interest in matters musical, Fuller Maitland, in a signed obituary, gave full vent to his feelings about Sullivan's true place in the history of English music.

> 'Jumboism' is more and more the characteristic defect of the English race and any voice that is raised against the Jumbo of the moment must be forced into the unenviable position of the *advocatus diaboli*, and is certain to incur the wrath of those who are working up the 'boom', whatever it may be.[90]

In this obituary, Maitland was prepared to play his role of 'devil's advocate' to the full, in an attempt to distance Sullivan, a failed and unworthy leader of English music, from the 'real' heroes of the English Musical Renaissance – namely, Parry and Stanford. To this end, Maitland cast Sullivan as 'Jumbo', the most celebrated zoo animal of Victorian times, that lumbering, over-hyped and popular elephant so loved by the masses. The critic asserted that to admire Sullivan was a lapse of taste, a 'defect' of the English 'race'. The case for Sullivan was rejected out-of-hand, as far as Maitland was concerned: 'the great renaissance of English music, which took place in the last quarter of the nineteenth century, accomplished itself without any help or encouragement from Sullivan'. Sir Arthur had contributed virtually nothing of value, with his oratorios 'lamentable' and 'pompous', and the Savoy operas not fit to be compared with those of Offenbach. The 'refinement' so often mentioned in relation to Sullivan's music was castigated as akin to 'the

---

[89] Fuller Maitland, 'Sir Arthur Sullivan'.
[90] Ibid. p. 300.

extra-fine manners exhibited by a certain class of ladies who are dreadfully afraid that their position might be misunderstood if they are not very careful'.[91] This obituarist saw the composer as a morally corrupt artist who had sold his talent to the highest bidder.

> it was the spirit of compromise that did more than anything else to lower Sullivan's standard: for the demands of the public became of increasing importance to him, and in [*Ivanhoe* ...] a work that ought to have raised him to the highest plane of his life's achievement was spoilt out of deference to the taste of the multitude.[92]

He also hints that Sullivan wasn't man enough to be a great artist alluding to the broken, inadequate '*Ivanhoe*': Sir Arthur as unworthy champion, unworthy man.

Sullivan's obituary in the *Cornhill* was, to say the least, unusual. It brought a storm of protest, as Sullivan's supporters leaped to their champion's defence. Even Elgar, in one of his public lectures as the new Peyton Professor of Music at Birmingham, referred to Fuller Maitland's obituary as a 'foul, unforgettable episode' and as the 'shady side of musical criticism'.[93] But it was all to no avail, the Renaissance had had the last word, and the damage inflicted on Sullivan's reputation was permanent.

In Sullivan's relationship with the critics there is much evidence of the enormous importance of the watchmen at work. First they celebrated him, then they tried (and failed) to keep him on the straight and narrow, and finally some of them cautiously forgave him. Several even held high hopes of him as a 'serious' composer until the last years. Yet despite his turbulent relationship with the press, Sullivan was always his own man, a composer who believed that he could be a serious artist and a rich one too. For all the brickbats of the watchmen, Sir Arthur continued to ride high in the esteem of the musical public until his death. Sullivan had an instinctive feel for what his public wanted. Whether writing for the Savoy or the choral festival circuit the success of this 'jumbo of the moment' rested primarily on his ability to entertain.

---

[91] Ibid. pp. 303–4.

[92] Ibid. p. 307. Fuller Maitland, whom Sullivan once referred to as a 'priggish amateur', was one watchman that the composer was never able to win over. Letter, Sullivan to Joseph Bennett q. in Jacobs, p. 296.

[93] Elgar q in Young, *A Future for English Music* p. 187.

# CHAPTER SIX

# Parry: 'English Master'

> *Scenes from Prometheus Unbound* [...] was not a success, but it
> was none the less interesting on that account; it undoubtedly marks
> an epoch in the history of English music, and the type of composi-
> tion of which it was the first specimen has had great consequences
> in the development of our national art.[1]

As the 1880s dawned English music lacked a leader, a master-musician
who could take command of the Musical Renaissance. Although George
Grove, a former lighthouse-builder, was soon to become Director of
the new RCM, as a non-musician he could only help light the way for
the national music revival, never assume its captaincy. By 1883, with
the new RCM finally setting sail, few among the watchmen doubted
the seriousness of the situation: England needed a composer at the
helm.

Charles Hubert Hastings Parry (1848–1918) loved the sea and spent
much of his time messing about in boats. Parry also loved music and his
background and education ideally fitted him for command. Born into a
Gloucestershire gentry family with naval and colonial connections, he
was a product of Eton and Oxford who wanted for nothing financially.
His social connections too were of the best, having married (in 1872)
Maude Herbert, sister of the Earl of Pembroke. Yet Parry's emergence
as the composer-commander of England's Musical Renaissance was
neither easy nor sudden. Although, by the beginning of the 1880s, his
reputation as an academic had been established through his work as
Grove's lieutenant on the *Dictionary*, he had virtually no reputation as a
performer, conductor or composer. Within a decade, however, all this
had changed as Parry was hailed as the greatest native composer since
Purcell – a new 'English master'. This chapter will explore how the
watchmen assisted this transformation and by playing a determining
role in the construction of Parry's reputation.

## 1. 'Wild Oats'

Parry made an uncertain start as a composer. Despite being interested
in music at both Eton and Oxford, on leaving university he launched

---

[1] Fuller Maitland, entry on 'Sir C. H. H. Parry' in *Grove 2* vol. iii pp. 624–7.

himself into a career in the Lloyd's insurance market – a decision that
he was later bitterly to regret. He returned to music in fitful stages
and, being uncertain of his musical orientation, he hovered in his
affiliations between Wagner and Brahms. Parry lacked confidence in
his abilities and consequently tended to rely heavily on the advice and
encouragement of others, notably that of his close friend, the German
pianist Eduard Dannreuther (1844–1905). The latter was a leading
advocate of *Zukunftsmusik* having founded the Wagner Society (1872)
and translated *Music of the Future* into English (1877). Dannreuther's
commitment to Wagner made a deep impression on Parry, who helped
to entertain *der Meister* during his visit of 1877.[2] Yet, even with so
distinguished a mentor, Parry early compositions reveal an insecure
musical sensibility which tended towards eclecticism and experimen-
tation. The result was that, despite his conversion to Wagnerism,
Parry's output up to 1879 consisted mostly of a series of Brahmsian
chamber works.

Given his background, it is hardly surprising that Parry's rise to the
mastership of the Musical Renaissance was a problematic affair, and
one which was largely determined by the reception of his music. As
already noted, in the 1880s English music critics were deeply divided.
While almost all actively supported and promoted native talent, there
was bitter disagreement about the future course of national music.
Older conservative critics were resolved that Wagner would not provide
the model for the nation's musical future, while younger watchmen
were equally determined that the future should be guided by 'progressive' ideas.

In the late-1870s, Parry resolved to make his way as a disciple of
Bayreuth. His first major premiere, that of the overture *Guillem de
Cabestanh* in 1879, was an occasion that most probably resulted from
George Grove's influence. Parry's *Guillem*, inspired by a tale found in
Hueffer's *The Troubadors*, was overtly Wagnerian in its subject-matter
and, considering the conservatism of several of the major critics, it is
unsurprising that its reception was cool. The *Daily Telegraph* and the
*Morning Post* ignored the occasion altogether, while the *Athenaeum*
recommended that *Guillem* should be heard 'as abstract and not programme music at some future period'.[3] Hueffer in *The Times* blew hot
and cold, commenting that while parts of the work revealed the influence of Wagner's *Tristan*, Parry's 'invention' was where 'the chief
weakness of the composition seems to lie'.[4] Only the *Musical Times* was

---

[2] Graves, *Hubert Parry* p. 177.
[3] *Ath* 22 Mar. 1879.
[4] *T* 18 Mar. 1879.

complimentary, commenting that *Guillem* was 'very clever and well-scored'.[5] Parry's correspondence offers a revealing insight into the difficulties facing the 'music of the future' – as when Hugh Montgomery, one of the composer's closest friends, expressed his outrage and disgust at what *Guillem* represented to him:

> [... There is] that quality in your work which makes Wagner so unsatisfactory to me and immoral in the effect he produces on my emotional condition. A tendency to promiscuous intercourse with all sorts of loose keys instead of that faithful cleaving to one only [...] to which one is accustomed in the respectable masters.[6]

For Montgomery 'Wagner' meant sex; to love *der Meister's* music was to embrace the temptations of the flesh. He, like many others, believed Wagnerism to be a moral danger, a debasing and corrupting tendency comparable to the enjoyment of prostitutes. Parry however, was not to be moved and replied to Montgomery stating how strongly he still felt the 'impress' of Wagner's 'warmth and genius'.[7]

After the *Guillem* setback, Parry turned to the concerto form, a move that effectively signalled a change of direction towards Brahms. In the event the *Piano Concerto in F sharp*, first performed at the Crystal Palace under Manns, polarised the watchmen. Whereas the premiere was conspicuously ignored by the *Daily Telegraph*, *Morning Post* and *Musical Times*, *The Times* had no reservations. Hueffer, writing that the concerto marked a new beginning for English music – which had for so long been crippled by 'Mendelssohnian sentiment clad in Mendelssohnian form' – praised Parry for being:

> all but entirely free from such a tendency, [with his] taste leading unmistakably in the direction of the latest phase of German music [...] we cannot but look upon this deviation from the well-beaten track as a hopeful sign'.[8]

In the same vein, Prout in the *Athenaeum* declared that:

> Mr Parry decidedly belongs to the advanced school of musical thought; his style has, perhaps, more affinity with that of Brahms than any other modern composer. His music is pre-eminently intellectual [... and] what he has to say is always his own, and further, it is never trivial or commonplace.[9]

---

[5] *MT* 1 Apr 1879. The *Musical World* reprinted a review from the *Graphic*, *MW* 22 Mar. 1879.

[6] Letter from Hugh Montgomery to Parry (20 April 1879) q. in Dibble, *C. Hubert H. Parry* p. 172.

[7] Letter from Parry to Hugh Montgomery (15 Sept. 1879) q. in Dibble, ibid. p. 175.

[8] *T* 6 Apr. 1880.

[9] *Ath* 10 Apr. 1880.

However, Davison in the *Musical World*, inimitably mocked the concerto with a cartoon and the observation that, although 'very clever', the piece seemed to be in the 'wrong key'.[10] Once again the battle-lines for the future of English music were drawn for all to see.

The watchmen did not have to wait long for Parry's next premiere, *Scenes from Shelley's Prometheus Unbound*. Yet the composer, with this work, once again gave his heart to *der Meister* and *Prometheus* was more 'undone' than 'unbound' at the first performance. The conservative critics were predictably disappointed and gave the composer and *Prometheus* short shrift. Bennett in the *Daily Telegraph* led the way in condemning the composer for trying 'to out-Wagner Wagner', asserting that only when he had abjured this infatuation would he be capable of 'greater work'.[11] The *Morning Post* also took a hard line on the work, castigating its creator for choosing 'to disdain the Mendelssohnian model' in favour of the 'mannerism' of Wagner and 'the expression of aesthetic emotion'; Barrett even went on to compare Parry with Shakepeare's Macbeth:

> it may therefore be hoped that in his next attempt he may be induced to abandon a borrowed garb which sits but badly upon him and only too clearly betrays the shape of the former wearer'.[12]

The *Musical Times* could not have been more dismissive of *Prometheus*, commenting that, although it had moments of real beauty, 'the dullness which gradually spread itself over the large audience was made even more apparent by these transient gleams of light'. The journal went on to doubt whether the composer was 'a real creator' or simply another deluded 'admirer of the 'music of the future".[13] Even Hueffer in *The Times* found little to enthuse about in the new work, confining himself to such generalities as the music was 'very difficult'.[14] Only the *Athenaeum* had a good word for *Prometheus*, judging it as having 'much real poetic feeling' and 'much really original and beautiful thought'.[15] As far as the watchmen were concerned, Parry's *Prometheus* was clearly fated to remain bound to his rock for quite some time. It was to be two years before the composer (once again) ventured forth with a major new work. In the event, the critics, it seems, had their way, as Parry (temporarily at least) abjured Bayreuth and turned back towards Brahmsian classicism.

---

[10] *MW* 10 Apr. 1880.

[11] *DTel* 9 Sep. 1880. The *Musical World* carried the same review *verbatim*, *MW* 11 Sept. 1880.

[12] *MP* 9 Sept. 1880.

[13] *MT* 1 Oct. 1880.

[14] *T* 8 Sept. 1880.

[15] *Ath* 11 Sept. 1880.

By 1882, Parry was ready to bring forward his *Symphony No. 1* at the Birmingham Festival, a work which proved a spectacular success with both conservative and progressive critics. Just as importantly for the long-term reception of Parry's music, the symphony converted the all-powerful Joseph Bennett to his cause. The latter's notice of the premiere of the *Symphony No. 1* was epoch-making, since it was the review in which the term 'renaissance' was first attached to the national music project. Bennett's report was suffused with a new spirit of forgiveness towards the composer:

> Mr Parry's *Symphony in G* [... is] capital proof that English music has arrived at a Renaissance period. On some former occasions I have had to say hard things of Mr Parry's works, protesting against them as strongly marked by the pretentious crudeness and incoherence distinctive of a certain school which masks its feebleness under a pretence of progress. The symphony belongs to a different category, and distinctly encourages the idea that Mr Parry, having sown his 'wild oats', has returned to the ways of pleasantness and paths of peace.[16]

The reception of this symphony in the *Telegraph* has more than a suggestion of the parable of the prodigal son about it. He that was 'lost' is found again; the folly and dissipation of youth is redeemed by a 'return' to a father's forgiveness. Here the composer is welcomed home to 'classical' form and procedure, having sown his 'wild oats' with the scarlet woman of Bayreuth. For Bennett another vital aspect was that the new work was modern in spirit, belonging 'to our own time, but has, all the same, intimate relations with the past'.[17] It was not only Parry's *Symphony No. 1* that was launched at the Birmingham Festival, but it was also Bennett's campaign to project its composer as the coming man of English music – as a master and helmsman under whose command the Renaissance would be safe.

The other watchmen too were enthusiastic about the *First Symphony*. Hueffer in *The Times* shared the view that it represented a watershed in English music, and admired it for its 'intrinsic merits' and 'for the stage it marks in the history of the English school since that school has freed itself from the leading-strings of Mendelssohn'.[18] In the *Athenaeum* Prout, although was not convinced of the historic significance of the symphony, described it as 'characterised by a loftiness of aim and by a devotion to art for its own sake'.[19] As for Lunn's *Musical Times*, it

---

[16] *DTel* 4 Sept. 1882. See also Chapter 2 above.
[17] Ibid. This review was reprinted *verbatim* in the *Musical World* 9 Sept. 1882.
[18] *T* 2 Sept. 1882.
[19] *Ath* 9 Sept. 1882.

favourably noticed the symphony's premiere in two separate issues.[20] The one dissenter among the watchmen was Barrett of the *Morning Post* who, while acknowledging the importance of the premiere, thought the symphony simply too foreign:

> If he had been less German and more English [...] art would have been better served and his own aspirations more reasonably fulfilled. Native talent is on trial, and it is necessary that all our rising musicians should be loyal and true to themselves and to the cause. Unity is strength, not only physically, but morally. With a definite purpose supported by all who wish well to the art they profess, English genius must come to the front and hold the position again it once occupied so proudly.[21]

Here Barrett presents the cause of English music as a national crusade, a time of 'trial' in which the stakes were of the highest. English composers must have the courage to be 'English', since only then could they be truly original. Here too, in this review, the Grove line on the music history of England can be detected: a land once musically great could retrieve her greatness.[22]

Although Parry's *Symphony No. 1* was never published during the composer's lifetime, according to Jeremy Dibble 'it did much to consolidate Parry's reputation both publicly and professionally'.[23] It did more than that: it began Parry's rise through the ranks of native composers, a process which would eventually lead him to the helm of musical life. The strong promotion of Parry's *Symphony No. 1* by the watchmen began that process whereby the composer was eventually presented to the musical nation as the 'English master'. On the day of the Birmingham premiere, it all looked very different to Parry, who depressingly noted that:

> the greater part of the audience were absolutely cold throughout, and the applause at the end I suppose to have been evoked by the good nature of the stewards and my friends.[24]

However, the reception that really mattered was not that of the 'cold' Birmingham public but rather that of the watchmen of England's music.

Parry's second essay in symphonic form was ignored the critics because of the rather singular circumstances of its premiere. The so-called *'Cambridge'* (or *'University'*) *Symphony* was commissioned by Stanford for the Cambridge University Musical Society (CUMS) to mark Parry's

[20] *MT* 1 Sept. 1882 and 1 Oct. 1882.
[21] *MP* 2 Sept. 1882.
[22] See Hughes and Stradling, pp. 25–6.
[23] Dibble, p. 202.
[24] Parry q. in Graves, p. 235.

honorary doctorate from the university (1883). This piece, conceived as a programme work, was inspired by 'the life of an undergraduate' and the 'jollity of university life'.[25] However, its esoteric subject matter and the fact that it was premiered at CUMS meant it was not covered by the London critics. The *Second Symphony* therefore added nothing to Parry's reputation either with the watchmen or the musical public.[26]

During 1884–86 Parry turned away from the symphony to devote time and energy to an opera project, *Guenever*. Jeremy Dibble in his biography of Parry suggests that the composer's decision to concentrate on opera was largely due to the intense interest in establishing an English national opera tradition at this time.[27] Parry wanted to make his contribution to the quest for an English opera alongside Mackenzie, Stanford and Goring Thomas – all of whom had had new operas staged by the Carl Rosa Company. *Guenever*, however, never came to performance, Rosa declining to have anything to do with it. Despite Dannreuther's lobbying, both the Mannheim Theatre and the Munich Opera also rejected it. The result was that its composer, after 1886, turned against opera; as he wrote later in life:

> Opera is the shallowest fraud man ever achieved in the name of art. Its invariable associates are dirt and tinsel. Its history is falseness, intrigue, shallowness, levity and pretension. It is the appanage of wastrels, the home of humbugs. No composer who is worthy of any reverence at all ever wrote an Opera.[28]

*Guenever* marked the end of Parry's flirtation with Wagner.

The mid-1880s were difficult years for Parry. Although he had gained recognition as a distinguished music historian and academic, he had yet to build upon the success of his *Symphony No. 1* and find his true *métier* as a composer. Although his problems stemmed partly from his own personal and stylistic insecurities, there is little doubt that he blamed the press for some of his troubles and found it difficult to ignore the watchmen's often barbed criticisms of his works. He was intimidated and anguished by the press and its power, as he pointedly wrote in his diary: 'I know it is stupid!, but it is cruel to struggle wearily on, and to have endure the vile sneers of these curs'.[29] Parry never learned to get on with the watchmen and rarely solicited their support or good offices. Of all the 'curs', Parry found Hueffer the

---

[25] Programme-note q. in Dibble, p. 210.

[26] Of the publications surveyed, only the *Athenaeum* (23 Jun. 1883) and the *Musical Times* (1 Jul. 1883) bothered to cover the concert.

[27] Dibble, pp. 225–6.

[28] Parry q. in ibid. p. 243.

[29] Diary entry for 22 Feb. 1885, q. in ibid. p. 232.

most objectionable. When, for example, he discovered that Hueffer had pressurised Dannreuther to perform some of his own songs, he poured his contempt for the critic and the venality of the press into his diary: 'Hueffer is beginning to put pressure on singers and others to perform his wretched productions, under pain of being suppressed by *The Times*'.[30] Parry was always hyper-sensitive about the watchmen, so that in later years even a supportive critic like Fuller Maitland could attract censure for making mildly critical remarks on *The Lotos-Eaters*.[31]

Having wasted two years on *Guenever*, Parry sought to build on his reputation as a symphonist. Only a few months after *Guenever* had disappeared into the mists of time, a performance of Brahms's *Fourth Symphony* conducted by Richter so inspired Parry, that he decided to approach the conductor for a premiere of a revised version of his *Symphony No. 2 'Cambridge'*. When the altered work was eventually given during the 1887 season, the critics gave it a mixed, though broadly favourable, reception. Bennett's reaction in the *Daily Telegraph* was typical: although he believed that the 'programme' would simply create 'a condition of mental confusion bordering on bewilderment', he re-garded the work was 'another proof' that there was in England a growing and 'noble school of composition'. The critic went on to reiterate his conversion to Parry's music:

> We cannot recall a better instance of modern expression kept within 'ancient lines', and the effect of the entire work goes to establish our conviction that within these lines, elastic as they are, there is room enough for any development, such as contemporary taste demands.[32]

Hueffer in *The Times* was ambivalent, and although unhappy about the symphony's programme, he was complimentary about the music:

> A subject of this kind might perhaps serve as an adequate basis for an operetta [...] but it is scarcely fit for embodiment in one of the most ideal forms of the most ideal of arts. Fortunately Mr Parry's music is as unlike its supposed original motive as can well be imagined [... and] qua music [...] fully sustains Mr Parry's reputa-tion as a serious writer of elevated aim.[33]

Hueffer repeated his views in the *Musical World*, commenting that although the symphony opened 'quite well' and 'contained many pas-sages of real beauty', there was much that seemed 'purposeless and

---

[30] Diary entry for 24 Feb. 1885, q. in ibid. p. 232.
[31] Diary entry for 13 Jun. 1892, q. in ibid. p. 298.
[32] *DTel* 8 Jun. 1887.
[33] *T* 10 Jun. 1887.

diffuse'.[34] The *Musical Times* decided to give the symphony a good press, with a review that exuded relief that Parry had eschewed the crudities of Bayreuth and had managed to 'progress' away from that ideal. In this review, we find the first reference to Parry's 'mastery' by a critic:

> Dr Parry is a musician who makes progress, in the sense that time and experience are modifying whatever once was crude in his music. [...] We can heartily praise much of the new symphony [...] the whole work shows fertility of idea, uncommon mastery of detail [...] and a knowledge of how to obtain noble effects of figure and colour.[35]

The epithet 'masterly' was henceforth attached to Parry and his music with increasing frequency. Its connotations are many and include: class relationships (squire-servant); the guild of musicianship (maestro-amateur); male sexuality (master-mistress); musical life (maestro-audience); and notions of naval command (master-crew). The overall effect of the premiere of the revised *Second Symphony* was that Parry's reputation once again began to climb with the critics.[36]

However, only a major work for the choral festival circuit could really radically transform Parry's reputation with both the musical public and critics. The composer eventually grasped this fact and seized the opportunity when the Birmingham Festival committee, at the prompting of his friend, Hans Richter, commissioned a new oratorio for the 1888 festival. Yet there was a fundamental problem: Parry despised orthodox religion believing that 'the theological part of Christianity and all dogmas connected with it are a mistake'.[37] The fact that the composer was prepared to accept an oratorio commission represents the extent to which he was prepared to compromise with the conservative tastes of both the festival public and the critics. Parry's desperation to make a major impact can be detected in a letter to Dannreuther on the *Judith* commission:

> I think that I ought not to let such a chance slip if I can do it. But it's a very short time to find a subject, and to get it into shape and write the stuff. Moreover, I don't like the Oratorio notion [...] Do you think there is anything to be made of the of the poetical material in the same neighbourhood as *Parsifal*?[38]

---

[34] *MW* 11 Jun. 1887.

[35] *MT* 1 Jul. 1887. Barrett in a short review in the *Morning Post*, judged the symphony 'important' and 'scholarly', *MP* 8 Jun. 1887.

[36] A pointer to Parry's still modest standing with the critics in 1887 was the reception of *At a Solemn Music*, an occasion which was virtually ignored by the press.

[37] Letter from Parry to his father (15 Dec. 1873), q. in Dibble, p. 112.

[38] Letter from Parry to Dannreuther (2 Sept. 1887), Bod.Eng. Letters e.117 f. 151–2.

In the event, the Birmingham committee was not to be beguiled by a Wagnerian substitute and Parry had to deliver a conventional oratorio. He wrote to Dannreuther bewailing the fact:

> The Birmingham people stood out for a regular oratorio. I hope you won't swear! After some correspondence in which they declined my alternative proposals, I caved in. But with the mental reservation that there shouldn't be much of religion or biblical oratorio beyond the name.[39]

The tone and content of the above comment confirms the vital status of this work and how anxious Parry was to secure a major festival commission. Having accepted the Birmingham invitation, the composer's work on *Judith* proved vexing and unsatisfactory, as a diary entry reveals:

> stuck fast in the middle of a stupid chorus in the 2nd half 'The God of our Fathers'. Wrote it over and over again – working morning, afternoon, after tea and night and always find it beastly.[40]

Despite having to wrestle with much that was 'beastly', Parry was utterly resolved to achieve both personal success and to do his duty for England's national music.

With the premiere of *Judith* Parry began to take command of the English Musical Renaissance. On the day the watchmen were in Birmingham to ensure *Judith*'s ultimate triumph, with Bennett, once again, to the fore in the *Daily Telegraph*:

> I am disposed to cry 'Welcome Home!' [...] There was a time not so far distant, when the composer of *Judith* appeared to me as a wanderer in the wilderness, roaming aimlessly over a pathless waste. He was however only sowing his wild oats, and it is said of those who perform that feat with energy and determination that they often come back to the pursuit of more legitimate husbandry, [...] Out of darkness into light he has steadily advanced, till now, on the evidence of *Judith* , he stands in the full blaze of orthodoxy, and has 'found salvation'.[41]

Bennett was clearly triumphant and must have felt that his faith in Parry had been fully justified: the sinner had repented, the apostate had indeed returned to the true faith. Bennett was not about to stint on the fatted calf. Other critics too were prepared to welcome *Judith* as a masterpiece of English music: Barrett in the *Morning Post* was at his most generous, judging Parry to have displayed 'invention and scholar-

---

[39] Letter from Parry to Dannreuther (20 Oct. 1887), Bod.Eng. Letters e.117 f.153.
[40] Diary entry for 1 Jan. 1888, q. in Dibble, p. 267.
[41] *DTel* 30 Aug. 1888.

ship and a large sympathy with dramatic needs';[42] while the *Athenaeum* declared of *Judith* that 'no finer oratorio music [had been written] for many years'.[43] Even the *Musical Times* purred with approval (in two successive issues) and paid Parry the highest compliment by suggesting that the 'resemblance' between *Judith* and *Elijah* was 'quite marked'.[44] Only Hueffer, in his last months of life, stood out against the tide of praise in a candid review in which he accused Parry of hack-work:

> The truth is, that Dr Parry has scarcely looked upon his subject in a purely or even in a principally dramatic light. [...] it appeared as if there were a great many instances in which the composer had not been moved by the situation at all; [...] it is not without danger to give counterpoint and scholarly devices to an audience thirsting for emotion [...][45]

In this, his final review of a Parry work, Hueffer made clear his disappointment with the way the composer had turned his back on Wagnerian 'emotion' in favour of 'scholarly' academicism. It was a prescient assessment of Parry's mature style and one that was to be heard with increasing frequency from other watchmen over the years.

One of the most important reviews of *Judith* came from within the RCM itself, penned by Stanford in the *Fortnightly Review*.[46] In it South Kensington may be seen at its most partisan, the article being eulogistic towards Parry and condemnatory of the (perceived) enemies of English music. Most especially, Stanford blamed musical critics for their lack of support for so much that was good and new in contemporary English music. Stanford thundered that *Judith* was a 'source of pride' for which 'art is the better and England the richer'.[47] The fact that Parry was neglected Stanford blamed on the 'principal portion' of the musical press which, 'instead of seeking for merit, more often hunts for faults and not infrequently manufactures them'.[48] Addressing the watchmen directly, Stanford stressed that Parry's music should be appreciated for its 'distinctly English, national atmosphere which gives it a value to this country far greater than the present generation need be expected to admit'.[49] Effectively, the critics were put on notice that to criticise this new 'English' Parry would be to imperil the future of the national music. This identification with English values was fundamental to his

---

[42] *MP* 30 Aug. 1888.
[43] *Ath* 1 Sept. 1888.
[44] *MT* 1 Oct. 1888. See also a lengthy report on *Judith* in *MT* 1 Sept. 1888.
[45] *T* 30 Aug. 1888.
[46] Stanford, 'Mr Hubert Parry's *Judith*'.
[47] Ibid. p. 545.
[48] Ibid. p. 537.
[49] Ibid. p. 539.

elevation to the status of national composer. Up to the premiere of *Judith* Parry had been stigmatised as a composer whose stylistic orientation was at times unclear and confused. Stanford's article changed that perception by inventing the notion of Parry's essential 'Englishness'. It was an idea (as we shall see) that was quickly appropriated by the watchmen themselves. Stanford's piece showed just how successfully (and ruthlessly) the Musical Renaissance could inscribe itself when required.[50]

In 1888 therefore, Parry began to emerge as *the* major figure in the nation's musical life with *Judith*. And it was the watchmen that 'made' *Judith*. One index of Parry's increasing eminence was his election to London's most distinguished club, the Athenaeum that year, being proposed for membership by Grove and the painter, Millais. The price of critical acceptance and national fame was obedience to the demands of the festival public and the conservative forces in musical press.

## 2.   'Legitimate Husbandry'

Hard on the heels of *Judith* came the *Symphony No 3, 'English'*, a work which confirmed Parry as the new captain of the Musical Renaissance. The real key to the symphony's successful premiere (at the Philharmonic Society) lay in the programme notes provided for the concert by Joseph Bennett which placed great stress on the quintessential 'English' quality of the work. Bennett reinforced Parry's new-found 'Englishness' in his review of the occasion in the *Daily Telegraph*, when he ascribed to the symphony 'vigour and general masterfulness', and went on:

> It has been urged in these columns and elsewhere, that English composers, instead of being copyists, as they mostly are, of German models, should study the character and absorb the spirit of our own national music, [...] the typical English melody is simple in structure, marked by rhythmic force, moves with solidity, is well-balanced [... and is] above all, natural. [...] We do not know that he [Parry] sat down with the deliberate purpose of writing an "English Symphony". [...] although the themes of the symphony

---

[50] There was one critic, G. B. Shaw, who was not prepared to toe the South Kensington line on *Judith*. Later that year, Shaw reviewed the London performances of *Judith* in the *Star* (18 Dec. 1888). Here, in a direct riposte to Stanford, Shaw derided Parry's decision to write an oratorio as the 'most gratuitous exploit open to a XIX century Englishman'. Shaw, 'Parry's *Judith*', q. in D. H. Laurence, *Shaw's Music* vol. i pp. 536–40.

are, as themes, absolutely new, an Englishman cannot hear them without an inward sense of familiarity and, so to speak, a feeling of proprietorship.[51]

For Bennett the quest for the 'great English symphony' had ended. Here then, for him, was a work that spoke with the authentic voice of national music, containing within itself the essential characteristics of the race. In his reception of the *Third Symphony* Bennett decreed that Parry was almost biologically 'English', a master musician of whom the nation could be proud. The critic reveals again the kind of Renaissance to which he was committed, one characterised by English pride and English spirit. At the end of his review Bennett returned to his favourite linkage between music and male sexuality; in his symphony Parry is in the 'full vigour of his manhood', while disdaining the feminine 'mystic' and 'sensational'.[52]

The other watchmen were mostly delighted to follow the lead that Bennett had given in his programme-note. Fuller Maitland, in one of his earliest reviews in *The Times*, wrote of the *'English' Symphony*'s 'beauty, vigour and strongly-marked individuality' and its 'unmistakable English character'.[53] Henry Frost, in the *Athenaeum*, also followed the Bennett line by commenting on the 'national colouring' of the symphony's themes – although he did observe the work's title was 'not so designated by the composer'.[54] Finally, in the *Musical Times* review, that might also have been written by Bennett, there was nothing but praise for the new work's purported 'national' characteristics:

> The English spirit of the work is a very interesting feature. It shows that our national music has a character into the spirit of which composers to the manner born can so far enter that their works shall have a distinctly English *cachet*.[55]

In these notices can be heard echoes of Bennett's insistent nationalism, the bourdon of 'little England' with a Gloucestershire burr. Puzzlingly, Barrett in the *Morning Post* virtually ignored the *'English' Symphony*.[56]

In fact, Parry had had no thought of writing an 'English' symphony. During its composition the composer referred to it as a 'Short Symphony', and the autograph score bears the title 'Symphony for Small Orchestra'.[57] The *'English' Symphony*, and all that flowed from it, was

[51] *DTel* 25 May 1889.
[52] Ibid.
[53] *T* 27 May 1889.
[54] *Ath* 1 Jun. 1889.
[55] *MT* 1 Jun. 1889.
[56] *MP* 27 May 1889.
[57] Letter from Parry to the honorary secretary of the Philharmonic Society, Francesco

a Joseph Bennett construction, a piece of brilliant marketing and one
which is still current well over a century later. The *Musical World*
seemed to sum up what many leading critics came to believe after the
*'English' Symphony*'s premiere:

> it is along the path in which [Parry] is now walking that our
> composers must go, if they would lead us to that haven, so much
> desired by many – of a national style.[58]

Parry, the captain and master, entrusted with leading the national music
to a safe anchorage. Although this work was not published until 1907,
it proved to be *the* turning-point, eclipsing even the success of *Judith*.
Thenceforth, Parry's music was inextricably linked to 'Englishness';
after the *'English' Symphony*, it was plain sailing, with the composer
firmly in command of the Musical Renaissance.

Parry premiered two other major works in 1889 which reinforced his
pre-eminent status in English music. With the *Symphony No. 4* he
underlined his credentials as a symphonist, while with the *Ode on St
Cecilia's Day* he affirmed his newly acquired stature on the choral
festival circuit. The premiere of his *Symphony No. 4*, under Richter,
secured the leading watchmen's virtually unanimous approval, with
Fuller Maitland giving the work powerful endorsement that prefigured
his reception of Parry's music in the years ahead:

> a work of vigorous beauty, and no whit less original than any of
> the composer's previous works. [...] It is doubtful whether Dr
> Parry's fourth symphony will attain the wide popularity which may
> be safely predicted for his third; but in any case English musicians
> may be proud of both.[59]

The *Morning Post* judged the work to be 'a decided success', while
Frost in the *Athenaeum* opined that it was the 'first among his [Parry's]
efforts of this kind'.[60] Meanwhile in the *Daily Telegraph*, Bennett as
ever with an eye on the bigger picture (and the biblical allusion), thought
the symphony a work 'out of which will be made the crown of glory of
our reviving English art'.[61] The *Musical World* drew attention to the

---

Berger (25 Nov. 1888), q. in Dibble, p. 276. In this letter Parry referred to his new work
as 'quite a small and unimposing kind of symphony'. A century after its premiere,
Bernard Benoliel, in a CD liner-note for the work, declared: '[Parry] achieves perfectly
what he sets out to do: to create an exuberant English equivalent to the Mendelssohn
'Italian' and the Schumann 'Rhenish' Symphonies. [...] the themes are all thoroughly
English in their rhythmic cut'. Chandos 8896/1990.

[58] *MW* 1 Jun. 1889.
[59] *T* 3 Jul. 1889.
[60] *MP* 3 Jul. 1889 and *Ath* 6 Jul. 1889.
[61] *DTel* 6 Jul. 1889.

*Fourth Symphony*'s 'dignity' and 'loftiness of design', and welcomed it as 'a work of which English artists have every reason to congratulate themselves'.[62] Parry acknowledged his debt to Richter in establishing his reputation by referring to the *Fourth Symphony* as his 'Richter' symphony.

Parry's third big premiere of 1889 was a secular choral work, the *Ode on St Cecilia's Day*, commissioned by the Leeds Festival. Although its composition proved more congenial than *Judith* , Parry was still deeply uneasy about various 'vulgar' aspects of ode's text. Such were the needs of the hour, however, that duty to the nation and its Musical Renaissance took priority; for Parry artistic conviction always came second. Whatever the composer's own reservations about the *Ode on St Cecilia's Day* the watchmen were delighted with it. Fuller Maitland in *The Times* was effusive in promoting the new work as 'a composition to which very high rank among modern English works will be readily accorded'.[63] Bennett too did sterling service in promoting the 'English Parry' in his review; writing of it as 'a masterpiece of our English school', he went on:

> [it] sustains through every number the interest of charming and powerful music – interest certainly not lessened to English ears by the unmistakable English flavour which is perceptible. [...] There are passages everywhere in the work [...] which show that Dr Parry has drunk freely at the fountain of English art – a fountain the waters of which are now more abundant and a great deal purer than many people suppose.[64]

Bennett is here seen projecting Parry's 'Englishness' with an insistence that can only be compared to twentieth-century subliminal advertising. In his *Morning Post* review William Barrett chose to remind his readers of Parry's previous Wagnerite affiliations and of his conversion to a more 'elevated' style of composition:

> He had bound himself like his own "Prometheus", with chains [...] wearing these fetters voluntarily, he misinterpreted the voice of his genius. [...] in his later works he has gained popularity as a composer [...] because he speaks his elevated thoughts in a tongue best understood by the people. [The *Ode* ...] is a further illustration of the power he has learned to wield wisely and well.[65]

In their reviews the critics emphasised Parry's new stature as a composer of choral music which was genuinely popular. Taken together,

---

[62] *MW* 6 Jul. 1889.
[63] *T* 12 Oct. 1889.
[64] *DTel* 12 Oct. 1889.
[65] *MP* 12 Oct. 1889.

*Judith* and the *Ode on St Cecilia's Day*, as Jeremy Dibble argues, 'placed Parry's name at the top of every festival committee's list of 'modern' composers'.[66]

In the 1890s Parry wrote further works which confirmed his willingness to compromise with the festival public's appetite for choral works on biblical subjects. The most significant among these were the oratorios *Job* (1892) and *King Saul* (1894). With *Job*, Parry once again bowed the knee to convention in order to maintain public and critical interest in his work and to advance the cause of the Renaissance. Yet it was never easy; as the composition of *Job* progressed, so did the composer's doubts about the work increase, as he confided in his diary: 'it's flabby [...] and wanting in real vitality'.[67] However the critics judged things differently when *Job* was premiered in home waters of the Gloucester Festival. Joseph Bennett's notice, penned 'on the night', was ecstatic:

> Parry is ...] our brilliant English composer [...]Whatever Dr Parry does has a stamp of its own, and that stamp [...] is that of genius [... *Job* ] made today a profound impression upon an audience which included a host of musicians drawn from all parts by the reputation of our 'English Bach'.[68]

For the *Morning Post*, *Job* marked the newspaper's conversion to Parry's cause, helped perhaps by the arrival of Arthur Hervey as its new critic. In a whole-column review, the paper chose to dwell on Parry's 'prominent position in the world of English music' and on *Job*'s 'dignity' and 'grandeur'.[69] Fuller Maitland in *The Times*, not to be outdone, declared that *Job* proved that 'the oratorio form can still inspire works of the highest genius'; while the *Athenaeum* asserted that *Job* was Parry's 'finest work to date'.[70] Among the music journals, the *Musical Times* was uninhibited in its praise writing of Parry's 'single eye to the glory of his art' and of *Job*'s 'masterfulness'.[71] Perhaps the only critic who was prepared to condemn Parry's capitulation to the forces of conservatism with *Job* was G. B. Shaw, who in the *World* (3 May 1893) criticised the composer for having capitulated to the choral festival committees with a work that amounted to 'the most utter failure ever achieved by a thoroughly respectworthy musician'. Shaw went on:

[66] Dibble, p. 281.
[67] Diary entry for 18 Apr. 1892, q. in Dibble, p. 298.
[68] *DTel* 9 Sept. 1892.
[69] *MP* 9 Sept. 1892.
[70] *T* 9 Sept. 1892 and *Ath* 17 Sept. 1892.
[71] *MT* 1 Oct. 1892. The *Musical Times* might also have had a 'single eye' on Novello's balance sheet since the firm had already agreed to publish *Job*.

> For some time past I have been carefully dodging Dr Hubert
> Parry's *Job*. I had presentiments about it from the first. I foresaw
> that all the other critics would cleverly imply that they thought it
> the greatest oratorio of ancient or modern times [...]And I was
> right: they did.[...] I hope he will burn the score, and throw
> *Judith* in when the blaze begins to flag.[72]

It was the Irish critic's most withering onslaught on the captain of the
English Musical Renaissance. There was however no going back for
Parry; the expectations of both the musical public and the critics were
too high. His choral works had entered the festival mainstream and the
demand for more of the same was growing.

*King Saul* was another monument to Parry's spirit of artistic compromise, since the composer 'had no conviction in the work'.[73] Yet the new
oratorio was a success with the critics. Fuller Maitland, complimenting
Parry for his 'daring' in following Handel in choice of subject, was
moved by both the 'grandeur and dramatic force of the conception'.
While the *Morning Post*, impressed by the work's 'masterly workmanship', thought it to be 'an achievement of great magnitude'.[74] The *Daily
Telegraph*, although not convinced by *King Saul*'s blend of 'modernity'
in an older form, welcomed the new work as 'a noble addition to the
English oratorio concerning which we shall not be afraid to speak with
our enemies at the gate'.[75] Clearly Bennett felt that English composers
and critics still had work to do in defending the citadel of England's
music from the real modernisers on the continent.

Alongside his triumphs on the festival circuit, Parry was fêted with
new honours and burdened with new responsibilities. In 1895 he was
appointed to the Directorship of the RCM (as Grove's successor) and,
in 1899, he became the Heatherian Professor of Music at Oxford
University. Beyond academe further honours flowed; most notably, a
knighthood in 1898 and a baronetcy in the 1902 coronation honours
list. In a contemporary culture obsessed with the sea and sea-power, it
is irresistible to apply naval metaphors to Parry's career as composer,
academic and music administrator. But Parry[76] was a complex personality: on the one hand he was a patrician who loathed jingoism, while
on the other, he was a man of his time whose cultural patriotism
impelled him 'to promote the cause of music as an essential facet of

---

[72] Shaw, 'The Most Utter Failure Ever Achieved' q. in D. H. Laurence, ibid. vol. ii pp.
869–76.

[73] Dibble, p. 315.

[74] *T* 4 Oct. 1894 and *MP* 4 Oct. 1894.

[75] *DTel* 4 Oct. 1894.

[76] Dibble, p. 318. Despite the fact that Parry was Grove's clear choice to take over the
RCM, the retiring Director had reservations: 'he is the best, but O my dear – in many

the nation's strength'. And when Sir Hubert was not commanding the Musical Renaissance, he spent much of his time skippering his yacht, 'Wanderer'.

Parry's attitude to the press did not change with his rise to prominence and he continued to treat critics with suspicion and sometimes hostility. Even when the press was trying to be helpful the composer found it difficult to conceal his irritation and disdain. The flavour of his relationship with the watchmen can be picked up from his correspondence with F. G. Edwards, editor of the *Musical Times*.[77] Of particular interest are Parry's letters to Edwards on the occasion of the composer's address to the first General Meeting of the Folk Song Society (as Vice-President) in 1899. Edwards felt that his journal should carry a full report and contacted Parry for a preview of his speech. The composer could hardly be bothered to reply, and although he eventually relented and sent Edwards a draft, he could scarcely hide his annoyance at the approach.[78] In the event, a journalist was dispatched to cover the meeting with his report being sent to Parry for comment. The composer was not impressed and insisted on correcting the proofs, commenting to Edwards 'the worthy reporter left out half of what I said [...] I think the occasion requires an artistic piece of work, and as it stood in the proof it was extremely ragged'.[79]

Parry's reputation with both musical public and critics had certainly peaked by 1900. The composer's last unambiguous success was probably the *Magnificat* which, with the press still at his feet, had a triumphant reception at the Hereford (Three Choirs) Festival of 1898. In the *Daily Telegraph* Bennett, once again, compared Parry to J. S. Bach:

> The distance is greater in point of time than in musical character, for theirs are important lights in which the living master appears as a legitimate successor of him who died a century and a half ago. [...] This is high praise, and if I knew of words which would make it higher I would use them.[80]

Fuller Maitland in *The Times*, while noting that Parry seemed at several points to use the opening theme of Mendelssohn's *Lobgesang* in the *Magnificat*, commented that:

---

things he will be very poor – no backbone, no power of saying no, or of resisting those whom he likes'. Grove q. in Young, *Grove* p. 241.

[77] British Library, 'Edwards Papers' vol. vi (Egerton 3090) ff.96–177.

[78] Parry to F. G. Edwards, 24 Jan. 1899, 'Edwards Papers' vol. vi f.100.

[79] Parry to F. G. Edwards, 21 Feb. 1899, 'Edwards Papers' vol. vi f.103. Parry's correspondence with Edwards was mostly about RCM news and events. The Folk Song Society report appeared in the March 1899 issue under 'Sir Hubert Parry on Folk-Music'.

[80] *DTel* 16 Sept. 1897.

> the treatment of the two phrases by the two composers is wholly
> different, for Mendelssohn treats his almost exclusively as a motto
> [...] while the English master works it into the inmost texture of
> his fabric, treating it moreover with a grandeur of conception, a
> certainty and power, which were entirely beyond Mendelssohn's
> reach.[81]

No watchman had ever paid such a compliment to a living English
composer. This review also confirms that the epithet 'English master'
had entered the bloodstream of the press reception of Parry. Henry
Frost, in the *Athenaeum* was equally insistent that Parry was firmly
ensconced in the pantheon, asserting that he could 'claim equality with
any musician now living'.[82] The *Musical Times* summed it up, remarking that for once, the 'entire press' was in accord to welcome a work
which deserved 'to rank among the greatest of recent achievements'.[83]

After the turn of the century Parry's reputation suffered a steady
decline with both the critics and musical public. There were several
reasons for this deterioration. On a personal level, as he approached
sixty, the composer's music for the choral circuit became more esoteric
(in a non-Christian, 'ethical' way) and showed signs of faltering inspiration.[84] Of equal importance, however, was the fact that some of his
supporters among the older watchmen had retired and the rising generation was much less sympathetic to his music. Many of these younger
critics held that those composers who had dominated the Renaissance
in the 1880s and 1890s were out of touch with contemporary audiences, their music being too conservative and academic to retain a
broad appeal. Arthur Johnstone of the *Manchester Guardian*, typical of
this new generation, considered Sir Hubert's music 'gritty, the flavour
somewhat acrid and inky, the bouquet artificial'.[85] The younger watchmen had in fact already found a new hero in Edward Elgar, a composer
who to them seemed much more attuned to their generation and a new
century. As always, where the critics led, the musical public was sure to
follow; and Parry was well aware of the situation, fully acknowledging
that Elgar 'had captured the hearts of the people'.[86]

---

[81] *T* 16 Sept. 1897.
[82] *Ath* 25 Sept. 1897.
[83] *MT* 1 Oct. 1897.
[84] Dibble, pp. 420–1.
[85] Arthur Johnstone q. in Reece and Elton, *Musical Criticisms of Arthur Johnstone* pp.
184–6. August Jaeger, critic and music editor at Novello, was no Parry supporter.
Irritated by the popularity of Parry's music, Jaeger wrote to Elgar (12 July 1900) of the
tediouness of having to prepare Parry scores for publication: 'Parry!, Oh, Parry!! very
much Parry!!! Toujours Parry!!!! Fiddles sawing all the time!!! Dear old Parry!!!!!!', q. in
Young, *Letters to Nimrod* p. 98.
[86] Dibble, p. 420.

In this changing climate, Parry's later music had a lukewarm reception from the watchmen. For example, his cantata *Beyond These Voices There is Peace*, commissioned for the Worcester (Three Choirs) Festival of 1908, met with widespread indifference in the press. Robin Legge in the *Daily Telegraph* seemed rather bored by the premiere, preferring instead to dwell on the composer's past glories: 'the work is worthy of consideration if only for the high distinction of the composer who has contributed almost a library to the wealth of England's music'.[87] Even Fuller Maitland *The Times* had limited enthusiasm for the cantata, elusively commenting that 'it is on the same lines as several earlier works, [... but] it must not be supposed that it repeats them'.[88] The *Athenaeum*'s notice was all indifference, remarking that 'in spite of its skill, the music lacks spontaneity'; and while the *Musical Times* did its best to put a gloss on the new work, its reviewer too seemed somewhat at a loss:

> Whatever may be said for or against Parry's creative gifts, no one can deny that there is a personality in all that comes from his pen. The man is reflected in his music, not only his geniality, but his earnestness of purpose, and his high artistic ideals.[89]

Sir Hubert's reputation had been finally reduced to 'personality', reflecting the reality that the Edwardian watchmen had precious little time for a Victorian survivor. By 1912 and the premiere of Parry's new *Symphony No. 5*, the music press had become openly apathetic towards his music. Henry Colles's review of the new symphony in *The Times* was typical for its *ennui*: 'the appearance of a new symphony by Sir Hubert Parry [...] must be an event of the highest interest to serious musical people, because everything he writes is an expression of himself'.[90] In the *Daily Telegraph* Legge wrote that although the symphony contained 'much that is lovely', its 'modernity' was of a 'decade or more ago'.[91] While in a short review, the *Musical Times* recorded that the symphony 'made a great impression' and that the journal would give it 'full consideration' in its next issue – but failed to do so.[92]

Despite the increasingly problematical reception of his music in the new century, Parry had already been anointed as 'master' of the English Musical Renaissance. This state of affairs was enshrined in the musicological scholarship of the Edwardian decade; most notably, in seminal

---

[87] *DTel* 10 Sept. 1908.
[88] *T* 10 Sept. 1908.
[89] *Ath* 12 Sept. 1908 and *MT* 1 Sept. 1908.
[90] *T* 6 Dec. 1912.
[91] *DTel* 6 Dec. 1912.
[92] *MT* 1 Jan. 1913.

works by Fuller Maitland and the Oxford-based historian, Ernest Walker.[93] Yet why did Fuller Maitland and Walker, two of Parry's closest allies, both choose *Prometheus Unbound* as (what Walker called) the 'definite birthday of English music' – as the *Urtext* of the Renaissance? The view from the Edwardian end of the telescope certainly makes for a strange sight. As these two eminences pointed out, *Prometheus* flopped with both critics and public and, although published by Novello shortly after its premiere, it was rarely brought to performance thereafter. Could they seriously have believed that *Prometheus* marked the point when English music was launched into the modern era? (This work was never recorded in the twentieth century and was only ever once broadcast by the BBC – on its centenary in 1980).

The reason why both Fuller Maitland and Walker nominated *Prometheus* as a 'birthday' for English Music surely lies in the musical politics of the early 1900s. By that time, Elgar was acknowledged as the leading light of national music both at home and abroad – a modern 'progressive' in the mould of Richard Strauss. In contrast, Parry's music already seemed dated, a canon that clearly belonged to a different era. The Musical Renaissance, despite the continuing advocacy of its loyal friends among the critics, was in trouble, having lost touch with contemporary developments. For Fuller Maitland and Walker the problem was to present Parry in a modern light which could only be done by associating their hero with the progressive trends he had turned his back on in a quarter of a century earlier. Parry the 'Wagnerian' had to be re-invented and this they did with the 're-discovery' of his *Prometheus Unbound*.

The advent of Elgar therefore was the essential element in the re-discovery of Parry's *Prometheus*. The Worcester composer and the RCM professors had failed to develop a strong and enduring relationship. Elgar was a self-made musician whose career had developed outside the ambit of the music academies and universities. With his sensational successes at home and abroad during 1898–1904, he had propelled himself to the leadership of the national music owing no debt or allegiance to the Grove-Parry Renaissance. Although relations between the Worcester composer and the South Kensington professors remained cordial enough for a while, in 1904 Elgar and Stanford quarrelled and a complete breach occurred between them. Thereafter, Elgar would have little to do with Parry's RCM. By 1906–07, Elgar was widely under-

---

[93] Fuller Maitland, *English Music in the Nineteenth Century* (see especially Chapter 9) and Fuller Maitland, entry on 'Sir Charles Hubert Hastings Parry' in *Grove 2* vol. iii pp. 224–7. See also Walker, *A History of Music in England* p. 300.

stood to be at work on a symphony. Where then might that leave the achievements of Grove-Parry branch of the Renaissance? Might the successes of the RCM professors in the 1880s and 1890s become mere footnotes to the 'true' Elgarian renaissance? A 'birthday' had to be found for the Musical Renaissance remote enough from the earliest Elgar triumphs. It had to be a work by Parry, the 'English master', but which one? Was it to be *Guillem*, the *Piano Concerto*, the unpublished symphonies? Hardly. What then of *Judith*, *Job* or *King Saul* – despised by the composer even in their own time? *Prometheus* therfore had to be unbound so that the notion of Parry as founder and 'master' of the Renaissance could be promoted. And strenuously promoted it was up to, and far beyond, the composer's death.[94]

Parry died on 7 October 1918. Appropriately for a national captain, he was buried in St Paul's Cathedral, that garrison church of England and of the British Empire. Sir Hubert's final resting-place was not to be Westminster Abbey, the necropolis of artists and musicians. Not for him the company in death of Purcell and Handel and (in due course) Stanford and Vaughan Williams. In St Paul's he was put to rest next to the royal family's favourite composer, Sir Arthur Sullivan; but perhaps, more appropriately, close to Admiral Lord Nelson, the Sea-Lord Rodney and the Duke of Wellington, captains all in England's cause. The great and the good were at his funeral: King George V was represented, as were Queen Alexandra and the Prince of Wales. In most other respects the service was very much a Renaissance affair with the watchmen there in force, the *Sunday Times* critic Hermann Klein representing the Institute of Journalists. The newspapers, full of the news of impending military victory in the Great War, did their best to mark Parry's passing. *The Times*, faithful ally of the composer for thirty years, led the way by reminding its readers of the importance of *Prometheus* and of the composer's vital role in the construction of English national music. As the 'Thunderer' observed:

> we [the English] like a thing that is big but unostentatious, solid but articulate, and strong because united. [...] English musical life is full of this spirit, and it was on this that Parry seized.[95]

---

[94] Stuart Jeffries, 'Beyond Jerusalem'. This article reiterates the line that *Prometheus Unbound* was the canonic starting-point of the English Musical Renaissance; of its premiere it declares: 'one of the greatest nights for English music, an evening when the cobwebs of Victoriana were blown away by a remarkable new voice [...] There had hardly been any great music since Purcell. That changed in 1880 [...]'. Jeffries's article however had to admit that *Prometheus* did not feature in the programmes planned to commemorate the 150th anniversary of the composer's birth at the Gloucester (Three Choirs) Festival of 1998.

[95] 'An English Composer: Some Thoughts on Parry', *T* 12 Oct. 1918.

Parry was the 'English master' then to the last. His 'Englishness' was a complex construction and one that in essence originated with the watchmen. The critics sought to mould and direct the composer and, to an astonishing degree, they succeeded. In the end, Parry, out of duty, did what the 'curs' of the press bid him do. In this respect the 'English master' seems rather less than masterful, appearing more like a servant of the needs and interests of his time.

# CHAPTER SEVEN

# Elgar: 'Self-Made' Composer

> The Malvern uplands are to be seen, not described. No apprecia-
> tive mind can fail to be impressed with the bold outline, the imposing
> abruptness, and the verdant loveliness of these everlasting hills.
> [...] The enjoyment of a quiet stroll along these grassy heights is
> greatly enhanced by the companionship of one who habitually
> thinks his thoughts and draws his inspirations from these elevated
> surroundings. [...] Here, in the midst of these delightful Malvern
> surroundings – how welcome their tranquillity – is located the
> home of him who forms the subject of this biographical sketch.[1]

As a shopkeeper's son without capital, Edward Elgar had to make
music pay. Whether it was teaching the violin in the young ladies'
academies of Malvern or recording for the Gramophone Company in
old age, the composer had to work for a living. Elgar needed patronage
and, in winning support for his work, he proved himself a matchless
lobbyist of supporters. At the outset of his career, he enjoyed the
patronage of committee chairmen, conductors and church-organists who
ran the provincial choral festival circuit. These were joined later on by
court officials, composers and members of the Royal Family. Yet Elgar
realised early on that, above all, he needed the support of music journalists for his career to succeed. The watchmen were crucial to him, and
he used them with subtlety and resource in two ways: first, to dissemi-
nate positive information about himself and his work; and second to
voice his opinions about life and musical matters. Elgar was ahead of
his time in using the press to market his 'persona' and to construct an
image of himself which was both flattering and profitable.

Elgar established an productive relationship with most of the watchmen of his era. No other composer of the day took such an interest in
the reception of his music nor went to the same lengths to influence the
way journalists reported his life and music. For evidence of this one
needs to look no further than the fifteen volumes of press clippings held
at the Elgar Birthplace Museum in Broadheath. These substantial tomes
contain hundreds of reviews, biographical sketches and concert programmes, collected by the composer and his circle over the years. The
volumes themselves upon closer inspection have the appearance, to all
intents and purposes, of accounting ledgers, a similarity which vividly

---

[1] Anon. [F. G. Edwards], 'Edward Elgar'.

underscores the powerful fusion of art and business in the composer's life. In these pages is found a balance-sheet of the successes and failures of the composer's career, the profit and loss account of a 'self-made' musician.[2] The range of the material is breathtaking: the *Walsall Observer*, the *Civil & Military Gazette*, the *Irish Sunday Special*, the *Ladies Pictorial*, the *Düsseldorf General-Anziger* , the *New York Times* and *the Chicago Inter-Ocea*n all here rub shoulders with the entire gamut of British national dailies and the musical press. The responsibility for compiling this ever-expanding collection rested with the women in Elgar's life: with his mother; his wife; with Dora Penny, the 'Dorabella' of the *Enigma Variations*, who was 'keeper of the archives' for many years; and finally with his daughter, Carice.[3]


## 1.   'Local Musician'

Elgar's management of the press began with his first choral festival premiere, the overture *Froissart*. No sooner had the Worcester committee commissioned the work for the 1890 event, than he wrote to the most influential critic of the day, Joseph Bennett, explaining that he was a 'young Worcester musician' and that the new commission marked a 'crucial time' in his career.[4] Elgar recognised in Bennett a musical patriot and a champion of the Musical Renaissance. The composer was also aware of the critic's 'local' Severnside roots and unrivalled knowledge of the festival circuit and its networks of patronage. Bennett moreover wrote for the quality daily with the widest circulation, the *Daily Telegraph*. This approach marks the beginning of Elgar's campaign to use the press to promote his music and project his image. He was not to be disappointed with the critic's response:

> Another leading feature of the concert was an overture *Froissart*, specially composed by a local musician [...] The work, which properly aims at a tone of chivalry, is one of considerable interest, arising rather from promise than actual achievement. [...]. But Mr Elgar has ideas and feeling and should be encouraged to persevere. [...] Let him go on, one day he will 'arrive'.[5]

At the first attempt therefore, Elgar had secured a powerful ally in the press, especially significant since this review marked the beginning of the *Daily Telegraph*'s long advocacy of his music in its columns.

---

[2] Ibid. p. 643.
[3] Powell, *Edward Elgar* p. 57.
[4] 'Elgar and Joseph Bennett', *DTel* 4 Sept. 1937.
[5] *DTel* 11 Sept. 1890.

*Froissart* won support from other watchmen too, even if the reviews were generally brief. The *Morning Post* was in no doubt that Elgar was a 'local musician of considerable talent', with an ability which 'with more experience, will place the composer high among the ranks of native musicians'.[6] Henry Frost in the *Athenaeum* congratulated the composer on 'a musicianly and effective piece'; while the *Musical Times* scored *Froissart* as a 'commendable' effort.[7] The one slightly sour note was struck in Fuller Maitland's notice in *The Times* which, tinged with typical patrician condescension, stressed that Elgar was merely a 'young local composer' while fussily remarking:

> the scoring is decidedly clever, although, like most young composers, Mr Elgar is too fond of the brass instruments The depth of his attack, the double bassoon, reaches the limit of absurdity'.[8]

Although Maitland sought to gloss over this review years later, he was never to be reconciled either to Elgar's social background in 'trade', or to his music which he despised for its Wagnerite affiliations and 'vulgar' sensibilities.[9]

Thus began the reception of Elgar at the hands of the watchmen. It is significant how from this first premiere the notion of a 'local', 'Worcester' Elgar, became fixed with the critics. It was an identity that the composer welcomed at the time because he realised that the 'local Elgar' was an image which he could exploit. For a decade thereafter notions that his was a 'native' talent, both national and regional, dominated his reception in the press. This construction of a 'local' Elgar reached out towards the broad revival of English cultural regionalism of the late-nineteenth century. Thomas Hardy, of course, had been singing this song for twenty years: of the inspiration of home and neighbourhood; the comfort of an (imagined) history; and the certainties of well-beloved landscapes. Elgar too embraced his own regionalism as a source of pride, and with not a little self-interest, since his chosen profile as a 'Worcester musician' helped him conquer the festival circuit of the 1890s.

Following on the modest successes of *Froissart* and *The Black Knight* (1893), it was eventually *The Light of Life* which made Elgar into a major force in provincial choral music. Commissioned by the Worcester (Three Choirs) Festival Committee for 1896, this work at its premiere

---

[6] *MP* 11 Sept. 1890.

[7] *Ath* 20 Sept. 1890 and *MT* 1 Oct. 1890.

[8] *T* 11 Sept. 1890.

[9] In a letter to Elgar (17 Jan. 1898), Fuller Maitland tried to blame 'misprints' in 'country telegrammes' for the disparaging remarks in the *Froissart* review. (HWRO:705: 445:7423).

excited intense interest among the watchmen. Bennett, allocating the
oratorio both a preview and a lengthy review in the *Daily Telegraph*,
gave the new work and its composer the strongest endorsement:

> Mr Elgar is a composer with whom we shall all have to reckon [...]
> the work under notice bears the unmistakable stamp of distinction,
> and affords proof of exceptional resources [...] we see the promise
> of higher results [and ...] it is an achievement that makes promise
> well nigh as good as assurance.[10]

Arthur Hervey in the *Morning Post*, having snootily observed that the
festival programme offered 'nothing very tempting to the palate of the
more sophisticated London music lover', went on to commend Elgar for
his 'boldness' and 'sense of orchestral colour'.[11] While in *The Times*,
Fuller Maitland, having informed his readers that the composer was a
'very gifted local musician', then misinformed them that his talents
resulted from 'studies in Germany'. It was on this basis that *The Light
of Life* was endorsed by the 'Thunderer':

> It is undeniably the work of a composer not only well-cultivated
> and trained in his art but also gifted in no small degree. [... Elgar's]
> future will be watched with the greatest interest by all British
> musicians, if only for his unquestionable skill in handling the or-
> chestra.[12]

This review goes to the heart of Fuller Maitland's problem with Elgar:
how could a self-taught provincial possibly aspire to the pantheon of
music? For its part, the musical press was delighted with *The Light of
Life*. Although the *Musical Times* evinced surprise that the new oratorio
did not secure a larger audience on its home turf, the reviewer hoped
that the composer knew how to 'labour and wait'.[13] While S. S. Stratton,
a Birmingham critic who regularly reviewed for the *Monthly Musical
Record*, was only too happy to project his fellow-Midlander in glowing
terms: 'Mr Elgar is a thorough master of orchestral writing, and has
decided dramatic power. The whole work affords evidence of high
culture and natural genius'.[14]

The second Elgar premiere of 1896, the cantata *Scenes from the Saga
of King Olaf*, took place at the North Staffordshire Festival at Hanley, a
triennial venue which had only been in existence since 1888 which had
still to make a name. This premiere in the depths of the Potteries only
served to reinforce Elgar's reputation as a provincial musician. Predict-

---

[10] *DTel* 9 Sept. 1896 and 10 Sept. 1896.
[11] *MP* 9 Sept. 1896 and 10 Sept. 1896.
[12] *T* 9 Sept. 1896.
[13] *MT* 1 Oct. 1896.
[14] *MR* 1 Oct. 1896.

ably perhaps, the premiere was ignored by both *The Times* and the *Morning Post*. It was left to Bennett in the *Daily Telegraph* to give *King Olaf* a truly remarkable review (covering nearly half a page) in which he described the composer as 'an earnest and able musician' who was making his way in the world 'without organised puffery or the aid of any clique'. Although Bennett went on to say that he did not 'on every point of musical faith and practice see eye to eye with the Malvern musician', he thought that in the music:

> lies the power of living talent, the charm of an individuality in art, and the pathos of one who, in utter simplicity, pours forth that which he feels constrained to say, and leaves the issue to fate'.[15]

Henry Frost of the *Athenaeum* also trekked to Hanley and found the town 'dingy' and the area 'grimy'; still, he wrote of Elgar as a 'light of life' in darkest industrial England, a 'musician of great ability' whose *King Olaf* was 'a score of extraordinary merit, full of rich device of every sort'.[16] Thanks to *The Light of Life* and *Olaf*, by the end of 1896, the composer had the provincial festivals at his feet, even if London audiences had heard virtually none of his music.

At this point in his career, Elgar became the object of more intense press coverage, because of the success of his music and for his increasing interest as a musical personality. It was a development to which the composer eagerly responded and he took every opportunity that came his way to promote and project himself in the press. He was clearly in tune with the 'New Journalism', which had recently arrived from across the Atlantic with its insatiable appetite for celebrity stories and personality features.

Hard on the heels of Elgar's festival triumphs of 1896, the first major biographical sketch of the composer appeared in the *Musical Standard* (21 November 1896), a journal edited by the composer's friend, Edward Baughan.[17] In this piece, which was clearly written with the composer's co-operation, Elgar is found plying journalists with press-bites about his life and music. He clearly wanted to project himself to a national readership in three ways. First, he wanted to convey the idea that he was a composer proud of his roots in Worcester, an artist who stood disdainfully outside the networks of London musical life. At the same time, he was keen to stress that relaxing 'country pursuits' did not imply a lack of social or intellectual sophistication; on the contrary, he presented himself

---

[15] *DTel* 31 Oct. 1896.

[16] *Ath* 7 Nov. 1896.

[17] 'Musicians of the Day: Edward Elgar', *Musical Standard* 21 Nov. 1896 vol. vi p. 317. All references are to this article.

as a musician who effortlessly kept up with the 'modern musical world'. Second, great emphasis was placed on Elgar the autodidact, on the young man who had served in his father's shop, on the 'self-made' musician who had achieved his festival triumphs by dint of solitary study and hard work; as Baughan explained: 'Mr Elgar is no man's pupil either for harmony, counterpoint, or orchestration. All that he has achieved in music has been entirely through his own efforts'. Third, the composer was keen to proclaim his social respectability, as evidenced by his marriage to a general's daughter and an easy affluence. Rejecting the stereotype of the musician as permissive bohemian, Elgar projected himself as an artist-gentleman, composer-as-gentry. Taken altogether this was a manly, if rather muddled portrait, reinforced by a specially taken studio-portrait (by May's of Malvern) which consciously evoked a military image redolent of the officers of the Raj. Elgar was to use this photograph again and again in biographical pieces; it was an image of which he was clearly fond. Two days before the appearance of the *Musical Standard* sketch, the *Musical Courier* published what was virtually an identical article (complete with the May portrait), further evidence surely that the composer himself was manipulating his own press coverage.[18] It all worked a treat as Elgar became the object of ever more intense press interest of the following years.

Alongside the gentleman-composer ideal, another increasingly important trope for Elgar by the late 1890s was that of composer as 'bard'. In origin, bards belonged to a Celtic order of minstrel-poets who composed as well as sang and celebrated the achievements of chiefs and warriors. It was a notion which Elgar explored in an interview given to the *Strand Magazine* some years later:

> I like to look on the composer's vocation as the old troubadours or bards did. In those days it was no disgrace to a man to be turned on to step in front of an army and inspire the people with a song. For my own part I know that there are a lot of people who like to celebrate events with music'.[19]

For Elgar the bard trope combined the idea of poet-musician with his local Worcester identity. A bard was a poet-musician of the people, wise

---

[18] 'Mr Edward Elgar', the *Musical Courier* 19 Nov. 1896. This material was given another airing in a short biographical article (with portrait) in the *Windsor Magazine* in its August 1897 issue. In the latter there was a much greater anti-metropolitan slant: 'though they searched for him in London musical circles, at clubs, dinners, receptions and such-like places where lions do congregate, they found him not, for he works away in Malvern, quietly and unostentatiously, and thus keeps his mind all the clearer for music'. The magazine *Spare Moments* (23 Apr. 1898) ran an almost identical article to the one in the *Windsor Magazine*, the above quotation appearing *verbatim*.

[19] de Cordova, 'Dr Edward Elgar' p. 543

and seeing, rooted in history and place, a royal adviser and propagandist of kings: a warrior-hero of art. The bard ideal also connected the composer's modest Severnside background with his professional and social ambitions; as bard he could journey with relative ease from Worcester to Windsor. There is much of the 'bardic' Elgar in *King Olaf* and it is surely significant that he wanted to dedicate the cantata to the King of Norway. In this proposal (which came to nought) his increasing need to affiliate his music with a royal patron becomes apparent. It was a need that was soon to be met with royal recognition and patronage much closer to home.

## 2.   Passing the Rubicon

The cantata *Caractacus*, dedicated to Queen Victoria and commissioned for the 1898 Leeds Festival, was another work of the 'bardic' Elgar. The composer conspicuously set the new piece in his own Malvern backyard with the Severn forests providing the backcloth. Alongside the eponymous hero, much of the action in *Caractacus* centres on the 'warrior bard', Orbin, a confidant of the British king and a musician with a 'golden harp'. Much comes together here with Elgar as Orbin: hero-minstrel, composer-seer, musician-warrior. *Caractacus* is an overtly nationalist work that conveys the aspirations of a provincial composer to become the musical 'bard' of the nation.

The watchmen loved *Caractacus*. The *Daily Telegraph* led the way with Bennett in full flow greeting Elgar as a 'master of the modern musician's resources' and an 'English composer who speaks with so strong and so commanding a voice'.[20] The *Morning Post*, dedicating a column to *Caractacus*, summed up the work's importance in giving the composer a new national profile:

> Mr Elgar has passed the Rubicon. His talent has been exemplified on several previous occasions, and he has proved himself to be a musician fully versed in all the secrets of his art, besides being imbued with a decidedly dramatic temperament. [... *Caractacus* is] the finest work Mr Elgar has yet composed [...].[21]

For his part Fuller Maitland, while snidely remarking that Elgar was relatively unknown, having 'leapt to fame in the west country', could still commend his individuality in a lengthy review in the 'Thunderer'.[22] Even the conservative John Shedlock in the *Athenaeum* was prepared to

---

[20] *DTel* 6 Oct. 1898.
[21] *MP* 6 Oct. 1898.
[22] *T* 6 Oct. 1898.

overlook the composer's Wagnerite affiliations and promoted *Caractacus* as 'a work of great skill, power, and elevated thought'.[23] The *Musical Times*, under its new editor F. G. Edwards, described *Caractacus* as having 'extraordinary freshness, vigour and wealth of colour' and went on: '[Elgar is] a thoroughly original and inspired genius [... and] he is always himself'.[24] The impact of *Caractacus* was indeed huge, being reviewed in such diverse publications as *Lloyd's*, the *Illustrated Church News* and the *Court Journal*. Even the *Ladies Pictorial* ran a review-article, complete with a new Elgar portrait-photograph (by Elliot & Fry of Baker Street) to captivate its readers.[25] Among English composers, not even the stylish and photogenic Sir Arthur Sullivan had enjoyed such adulation. Elgar was indeed 'pin-up' copy.

Elgar's hitherto excellent relationship with the press was, however, about to suffer a minor setback – with the *Enigma Variations*. Although this work, premiered by Richter in 1899, was generally well received, its mysterious programme of 'friends pictured within' annoyed many watchmen. The *Morning Post*'s critic was typical when he grumbled that the meaning of the work's programme would be lost on audiences:

> The point of the joke is lost if no-one can understand it but he who makes it, and as the identities of Mr Elgar's friends are not disclosed it is impossible to say whether their musical portraits do them justice or not. Happily Mr Elgar's music is sufficiently good in itself to be appreciated without paying attention to all these puerilities.[26]

Shedlock in the *Athenaeum*, while hailing the new work's 'charm, variety and character', echoed these reservations:

> the variations stand in no need of a programme; as abstract music they fully satisfy. If the friends recognise their portraits it will, no doubt, please them; but this is altogether a personal matter'.[27]

Meanwhile, *The Times*, while commending the *Variations* for being 'on the surface' a 'clever, original and excellently worked-out' composition, also damned its 'obscure' programme.[28] In the *Daily Telegraph*

---

[23] *Ath* 8 Oct. 1898.

[24] *MT* 1 Nov. 1898.

[25] *Ladies Pictorial* 8 Oct. 1898.

[26] *MP* 20 Jun. 1899.

[27] *Ath* 24 Jun. 1899. Even E. A. Baughan, music critic of the *Daily News* and an enthusiastic Elgarian, referred to the variations as an 'orchestral joke', commenting 'we have no clue as to the identity of the pictures, [we] therefore can offer no opinion as to the fidelity of the portraits'. (*Daily News* 20 Jun. 1899).

[28] *T* 20 Jun. 1899. The anonymous critic of *A Journal for Men and Women* (28 June 1899) pulled ever fewer punches: 'Mr Elgar rather upset my temper by allowing some

Bennett, perhaps anticipating the composer's embarrassment at the hands of the watchmen, settled for a low-key review, describing the work as 'able', being both 'well-wrought and ingenious'.[29]

Elgar had, for once, clearly misjudged the press reaction to one of his works. The embarrassment was palpable and such disapproval of the programme of the *Enigma Variations* might have caused serious damage to the work's long-term prospects and the composer's reputation. However, the *Musical Times*'s review changed the tone of things. Written by August Jaeger (1860–1909), the 'Nimrod' of the ninth variation, this notice pronounced the new work a point of departure for Elgar and for English music:

> Here is an English musician who has something to say and knows how to say it in his own individual and beautiful way. He does not pose as a 'profound' and learned master of his craft; he writes as he feels, there is no affectation or make-believe. Effortless originality – the only true originality – combined with [...] beauty of theme, warmth and feeling are his credentials, and they should open to him the hearts of all who have faith in the future of our English art and appreciate beautiful music wherever it is met.[30]

Here, in Jaeger's defence of the *Enigma Variations*, Elgar is portrayed in the press as a 'natural' talent, a composer without academic side, a sturdy, self-reliant and yet poetic Englishman. How far 'Nimrod' rode to the rescue of the *Enigma Variations* in terms of its canonical status it is impossible to say. Yet there is little doubt that his was a timely intervention which revealed the depth of press support that Elgar could call upon when required.[31]

Elgar's attitude towards the watchmen, and the way in which he was prepared to use them, can be best adduced from his relationship with Frederick G. Edwards, editor of the *Musical Times* (1897–1909). The surviving Elgar-Edwards correspondence, covering a decade, goes far beyond what could be expected between a composer and the editor of

---

nonsense about his clever work to be printed in the programme. [...] A theme and variations, and the composer tells us that the theme "must be left unguessed", and that "through and over the whole set another and larger theme goes but is not played"! This sort of would-be profound and quite unutterable twaddle sets all sensible people against the composer [...] Mr Elgar ought to be above talking such egregious nonsense, and ought to let his brilliant music talk for itself'.

[29] *DTel* 20 Jun. 1899.

[30] *MT* 1 Jul. 1899.

[31] In the wake of the *Enigma Variations*' troubled premiere, a number of flattering portraits of Elgar appeared in the press; they included: 'Sheffield Musical Festival: Interview with Mr Elgar' in the *Sheffield Independent* (18 Jul. 1899); and 'Mr Edward Elgar' in *Ladies Field* (16 Sept. 1899).

his publisher's house-journal.[32] There is nothing to approach this source for the light it sheds on Elgar's relationship with the press and for the way it reveals him as a ruthless manipulator who exploited the *Musical Times* in his own interests.[33] The high point of Elgar's personal and professional relationship with Edwards in fact came when the editor suggested publishing a 'biographical sketch' of Elgar to coincide with the premiere of *The Dream of Gerontius* at the Birmingham Festival of 1900. The events surrounding this article deserve to be examined in some detail.

Although the composer had already been the subject of a many biographical articles, in its scope and prestige the proposed *Musical Times* piece marked an important step in placing Elgar in the front rank of English musicians.[34] When Elgar received the proposal he could not conceal his surprise and delight:

> Dear Edwards if you're sure […] pray put my name down on your list – only you must come here and see how I live – I warn you my life is different to any musician who ever lived, died or did anything. Come and be a weakender [sic] – or a monthender – or a yearender. Gosh! you'll want a new photo – I'll phassen up my phace with an oatmeal bag.[35]

Although Edwards had only a brief visit in mind, the Elgars' insisted he stayed with them at Craeg Lea, their modest home in Malvern. It was there the editor, *en route* to the Three Choirs (Hereford) Festival, researched his sketch, walked the Malvern Hills and became the object of the composer's powerful press management techniques.

The resulting *Musical Times* sketch is pure hagiography. In it Elgar is presented as an artist imbued with the rural grandeur of Worcestershire, who strides proudly through a landscape mottled with history and poetry. In places his angular features seem to be placed in the landscape; with references to 'bold outline' and 'imposing abruptness', Edwards seems to merge composer and countryside.[36] The nub of Edwards's article lies in its portrayal of the composer as ingrained in place, presenting him as artist-countryman rooted in his 'elevated surroundings'. Yet the *Musical Times*'s portrait also stressed Elgar's ordinariness and his reliance on 'his own resources and making the most of his self-made opportunities'.

---

[32] British Library, 'Edwards Papers' vol. vi (Egerton 3090) contains 48 letters from Elgar to F. G. Edwards.

[33] Elgar to Edwards 31 Jan. 1901, ibid. f.51–52.

[34] Edwards' series of musical 'portraits' were important in moving contemporary English composers towards 'celebrity' status.

[35] Elgar to Edwards 17 Nov. 1899, 'Edward Papers' vol. vi f.25.

[36] Anon. [Edwards], 'Edward Elgar'. All references are to this article.

This lack of formal music training was presented as a blessing in disguise since it had freed him from the sterile 'dogmatism of the schools'. The article also reflected on Elgar's bitter experience of living in London. It repeatedly returns to the core idea: Elgar as an artist who remained true to his 'native heath'. Throughout, we hear a *Leitmotiv* of Elgar as countryman-bard, natural aristocrat, man of the people (yet above the masses), composer-gentleman and self-made musician. It had all been printed before, but rarely with such eloquence or authority.

The Edwards Papers reveal just how much the content of the *Musical Times*'s article relied on the composer. Little it seems was left to chance: hospitality at Craeg Lea; rambling on the Malverns; unlimited access to the composer; and a new studio-photograph.[37] When the article was finished, the composer then had the opportunity of correcting the galley-proofs, an arrangement of which both Elgars took full advantage. The Edwards Papers reveal that these 'corrections' were wide-ranging with aspects of the composer's background and social status being treated with exceptional sensitivity. On his roots in 'trade', Elgar bared his soul to Edwards in the letter, which he enclosed with the corrected proofs:

> Now – as to the whole shop episode – I don't care a d—n! I know it had ruined me & made life impossible until I what you call made a name – I only know I was kept out of everything decent 'cos 'his father keeps a shop' [...] but to please my wife do what she wishes [...][38]

And as if poor Edwards had not got the message, Caroline Alice wielded her own blue pencil badgering him with additional amendments.[39] The *Musical Times* 'sketch' is, in every sense, an example of the Elgars' ability to manage the press and provides a unique index as to how much the composer was prepared personally to become in self-presentation and biographical myth-making. When the article had been finalised, it was published with a portrait-photograph of the composer specially taken for the *Musical Times* by Russell & Sons of Bond Street.

---

[37] Elgar to Edwards 23 Aug. 1900, 'Edward Papers', vol. vi ff.30–31.

[38] Elgar to Edwards 19 Sept. 1900, ibid. f.39.

[39] Mrs Elgar, having reminded Edwards that they did not live in a 'villa' (too lower middle-class) or read much Charles Dickens (too radical-liberal), moved on to the thorny issue of the 'shop'. Her concern on the matter is palpable: 'Every word concerning him seems momentous to me [and] I trust that you will agree with my suggestions which to me are very important. [...] Then as E has nothing to do with the business in Worcester would you please leave out details which do not affect him and with which he has nothing to do. His interests being quite unconnected with business. [...] I so immensely appreciate and thank you for your sympathetic sketch'. Caroline Alice Elgar to Edwards 18 Sept. 1900, ibid. ff.35–38. Edwards duly left out of his piece any mention of Elgar Brothers, No. 10 High Street.

The *Musical Times*'s article was a vital part of Elgar's (and Novello's) promotion of *The Dream of Gerontius*, the premiere of which took place in Birmingham that same month. The composer and his supporters expected much from the occasion given the venue, the musical forces involved (Richter and the Hallé), and the solid foundations laid by Elgar's previous festival triumphs. All augured well for the new work and, despite a shaky performance, the watchmen were duly convinced. Although Bennett in the *Daily Telegraph* was concerned about the new work's 'profoundly intimate' subject-matter and Elgar's 'machinery of Wagnerian art', he still judged *Gerontius* to be 'a very striking and brilliant work', stating its composer ranked 'amongst the musicians of whom the country should be proudest'.[40] The *Morning Post* welcomed *Gerontius* as a 'modern' work with 'very great qualities' and remarked upon Elgar's career as:

> extraordinarily rapid, and he has now acquired a position among our leading composers which no one will assuredly be disposed to contest. He is practically a self-taught man, and has succeeded in penetrating the mysteries of composition without extraneous aid'.[41]

Shedlock also voiced approval of *Gerontius* in the *Athenaeum* as a work of 'great skill, power and elevated thought'.[42] Even the *Civil and Military Gazette*, not noted for its interest in musical matters, was excited by *Gerontius*, declaring that:

> unlike Sullivan, Stanford, German, and Taylor, Mr Elgar is absolutely English, and has already been claimed as the greatest Anglo-Saxon composer since Purcell, [...] he may yet create an epoch in the history of English music'.[43]

The reception of *Gerontius* was not however unanimous. Fuller Maitland in *The Times* wrote what was probably the most jaundiced notice of the work; unfavourably comparing it with Stanford's *Eden* and Parry's *Job*, he complained that 'if only he [Elgar] would more often yield to the instinct for melodic beauty [... then] the new composition would merit a very high rank indeed'.[44]

Inevitably perhaps , it was Edwards himself who gave *Gerontius* the strongest reception. In a magisterial *Musical Times* review, he called it 'a work of great originality, beauty, and power; and, above all, of the

---

[40] *DTel* 4 Oct. 1900.
[41] *MP* 4 Oct. 1900.
[42] *Ath* 6 Oct. 1900.
[43] *Civil and Military Gazette* 10 Nov. 1900.
[44] *T* 4 Oct. 1900.

completest sincerity'.[45] Edwards also made the most of the extraordinary endorsement of *Gerontius* by Otto Lessmann, critic of the *Allgemeine Deutsche Musik-Zeitung*, by publishing his review referring to Elgar as a musical 'Messiah':

> the coming man has already risen in the English musical world, an artist who has instinctively freed himself from the scholasticism which, till now, has held English art firmly bound in its fetters.[46]

This review essentially celebrated the triumph of 'instinct' over unfeeling learning, and amounted to an indictment of the achievements of the academics of the Grove-Parry Renaissance. The effect of this notice cannot be overestimated, since it immediately put Elgar on a different plane from his contemporaries by placing him, and England's national music, in the European mainstream.

A few weeks into the new century Queen Victoria died. Beyond the immediate expressions of public grief there was a widely held perception that the Victorian Age had finally passed and a sense of 'new beginnings' was in the air. Elgar, clearly sensing the change in public mood, was determined to turn it to his advantage. As a result, the years 1901–1902 were characterised by the composition of more overtly populist works, such as the *Pomp and Circumstance Marches Nos.1 and 2* and the *Coronation Ode*.

The *Pomp and Circumstance March No. 1* made a sensational impact at its premiere in October 1901 and as result, the press and public alike took an even greater interest in Elgar. The composer, as ever, was pleased to respond. He gave an interview to the *World* newspaper – for its 'Celebrities at Home' series – in which the provincial, 'self-made' Elgar was strongly projected:

> He finds more inspiration in the Malvern Hills than in the streets of Kensington or Clapham. [... He has] never spent any time in the shoppy atmosphere of a conservatoire; not has he owed any of his early successes to friendly backing from Tenterden Street or Prince Consort Road.[47]

At about the same time, two biographical sketches (with portraits) appeared in the German press.[48] Even *Le Guide Musical* ran a feature

---

[45] *MT* 1 Nov. 1900

[46] Lessmann, 'Otto Lessmann on Dr Edward Elgar'.

[47] 'Dr Edward Elgar at Malvern', *The World* 11 Dec. 1901.

[48] *Allgemeine Deutsche Musik-Zeitung* 15 Nov. 1901, and *Düsseldorf General-Anziger* 20 Dec. 1901. Another article on Elgar appeared in the German press a year later: 'Edward Elgar' by Hugo Conrat appeared in *Neue Musik-Zeitung* 24 Dec. 1902. The fact that this piece was over 2,000 words long and appeared with a photograph of the composer, suggests that Elgar gave the London-based journalist an interview.

on Elgar, the first profile of the composer to appear in a French publication.[49]

Nothing better expressed Elgar's new enhanced profile as a national composer than a request from Sir Walter Parratt, Master of the King's Musick, for a *Coronation Ode* to mark the royal accession of 1902. This work, dedicated to Edward VII, marked a new stage in the 'bardic' relationship between Elgar and the Court, to the extent that many thought that that the composer would secure a knighthood in the coronation honours list. The *Coronation Ode*, with its '*Land of Hope and Glory*' finale, was intended by the composer not only to be a public statement of his own patriotic monarchism, but also an act of affiliation to, and identification with, the new sovereign and the Court. In this respect, the *Ode* may be seen as marking Elgar's own 'coronation' as leading composer of the new Edwardian Age. Yet the work did not make the hoped-for impact because the coronation was postponed due to the king's appendectomy. The result that *Coronation Ode*'s premiere in provincial Sheffield was anti-climactic.

Having secured national and international recognition in no small measure with the help of the press, Elgar continued to enhance his prestige by the same means. For him there was to be no respite from the demands of the festival circuit for large-scale choral works. The Birmingham Festival wanted another work for 1903 and, as a result, Elgar set about writing *The Apostles*, an oratorio planned as the first in a trilogy on the early Church. It was a measure of Elgar's new celebrity status that Novello and Co. agreed to pay him £1,000 for its publication rights.[50] With so much at stake Elgar ensured that the premiere of *The Apostles* was accompanied by favourable pre-publicity. The *Daily Dispatch* published a short essay by R. J. Buckley, a Birmingham critic and friend, who was already preparing a biography of the composer.[51] The *Sketch* ran a 'photographic interview' in which Elgar was depicted in twelve poses, intended to express the persona he had so assiduously cultivated in the press over the years.[52] For London readers, the *Pall Mall Gazette*, whose music critic Vernon Blackburn was a loyal Elgarian, ran a long and flattering piece on the very day of the premiere.[53] Even Harmsworth's *Daily Mail*, a newspaper not noted for its coverage of Art-Music, ran a two-page illustrated feature which quoted musical

---

[49] 'Musiciens Anglais: Edward Elgar', *Le Guide Musical* 30 Mar. 1902.

[50] Kennedy, *Portrait of Elgar* p. 189.

[51] Buckley, 'Dr Edward Elgar'. Buckley's book on Elgar appeared in 1905. See 70n below.

[52] 'Photographic Interviews: Dr Edward Elgar', *The Sketch* 7 Oct. 1903.

[53] Anon. [Blackburn], 'Dr Elgar at Home'.

examples from the new oratorio.[54] Elgar and English music were in the news to an unprecedented degree.

The watchmen duly welcomed *The Apostles* on its premiere. Leading the way Joseph Bennett in the *Daily Telegraph* chose to emphasise the international dimension of a 'unique' occasion:

> the whole musical world, not only in this country, but also abroad, has gathered more or less closely around the production of an Englishman. [...] at last a man of our own race and nation has come to the extreme front [...] sturdily independent, courting nobody; he now occupies the position with whom most people are determined to be pleased.[55]

Here Elgar is presented as a 'John Bull' figure with all-important international appeal. The *Morning Post* was in no doubt as to his place in the pantheon:

> the true artist lives in a world of his own. He does not seek success, but devotes himself to the pursuit of the ideal. [...] in his latest score he has made no attempt to gain the suffrages of the masses, [...] *The Apostles* is undoubtedly a work of high import.[56]

*The Times* (probably Robin Legge) concurred in celebrating a major premiere, praising the oratorio for its 'utmost dignity, reverence, and sincerity'.[57] The *Musical Times*, perhaps reflecting the fact that Novello and Co. had stumped up a four-figure sum for the new work, proclaimed that *The Apostles* would soon be rated as the 'most remarkable contribution to sacred art since Brahms's *German Requiem*' and as 'the great Oratorio of the present generation'.[58]

Elgar's carefully constructed network of supporters and patrons extended far beyond the watchmen of the press. There is no better example of the composer's ability to call on impressive connections to promote his career than in the organisation of the Elgar Festival at Covent Garden in 1904. Leo 'Frank' Schuster' took the lead in facilitating this event, deploying his influence at Court to secure the patronage of King Edward and Queen Alexandra (as well as other members of the royal family) for the festival. The occasion attracted enormous press interest. The *Sunday Times* was quick to proclaim its significance:

> the Elgar Festival [...] is the first tribute of the kind that has been paid to an English composer during his lifetime, and in its locale

---

[54] 'Today's Great Musical Event: The Apostles and its Composer', *Daily Mail* 14 Oct. 1903.
[55] *DTel* 15 Oct. 1903.
[56] *MP* 15 Oct. 1903.
[57] *T* 15 Oct. 1903.
[58] *MT* 1 Nov. 1903.

and patronage is an indication that our upper classes are no longer disdainful of any independent movement in native music [...].[59]

Once again, Elgar himself mobilised the watchmen to ensure that a barrage of biographical pieces and interviews would give the festival an even higher profile. As a result a raft of publicity appeared in print during festival-week: the *Graphic* published an interview with prominently featured photographs;[60] while the *Sketch* ran a three-page illustrated feature which stressed the composer's success 'depended largely on the patronage of the Royal Family'.[61] Much more substantial, however, was an 'appreciation' of Elgar (by Baughan) in the *Daily News*, the mouthpiece of the Liberal Party and its middle-class supporters, in which many of the familiar biographical details were enshrined anew:

> Elgar was entirely self-taught [...] it enabled him to keep free from the stunting influence of the schools: he was not enlisted under the banner of Brahms [...] I remember he once told me that if he had not been a musician he would have chosen a career as a soldier.[62]

As if to reinforce his image of 'self-made' warrior-minstrel with the readers of the *Daily News*, Elgar gave Baughan a second interview (after the festival) in which he expressed the hope that the event would 'open the eyes of our governing classes to the importance of music', adding that the 'real supporters of music' were the 'middle-classes'.[63] Although Elgar, as a life-long Conservative, affiliated himself to the 'governing classes', he was clearly not averse to pandering to the Liberal-leaning middle-class when it suited him.[64]

The press duly covered the Elgar Festival with enthusiasm, reporting with glee the attendance of members of the Royal Family at a number of the concerts. However only one new Elgar work was premiered, the overture *In the South*, which the watchmen – perhaps exhausted by their own coverage of the event – reported with some restraint. Bennett in the *Daily Telegraph* gave *In the South* only half a column, pointing out that the whole festival as a whole was the most 'remarkable tribute ever offered to a British-born composer'.[65] *The Times* was equally

---

[59] *The Sunday Times* 13 Mar. 1904.

[60] 'Dr Elgar at Home & at Work', *The Graphic* 19 Mar. 1904.

[61] 'Key Notes', *The Sketch* 23 Mar. 1904. The *Daily Mail* (12 Mar. 1904) joined in with an article by Frank Merry entitled 'Edward Elgar: The New Face of English Music'. Somewhat at the other end of the press spectrum the *Times Literary Supplement* (18 Mar. 1904) published its own (rather grudging) account of the event under the title 'The Elgar Festival'.

[62] Baughan, 'Edward Elgar'.

[63] Anon. [Baughan], 'An Interview with Sir Edward Elgar'.

[64] For a discussion of Elgar's Tory affiliations see Hughes, 'The Duc D'Elgar'.

[65] *DTel* 17 Mar. 1904.

subdued, commenting that *In the South* was a distinguished work mainly because of Elgar's 'masterly treatment of themes'.[66] The *Musical Times*'s notice proclaimed the festival to be a 'triumph for English Music!'[67] Elgar had indeed passed 'his Rubicon', having transformed himself from 'local musician' to England's laureate of music and 'man of the hour' – as he was soon to be hailed by the *Strand Magazine*. It had been a remarkable transition and one achieved with not a little help from the watchmen.[68]

## 3.   'Man of the Hour'

Elgar was knighted on 5 July 1904. The occasion was on one level an intensely 'bardic' moment when the composer finally stood close to throne and court. Elgar's knighthood had the effect of strengthening his relationship with the watchmen and exciting even greater interest in his life and music. Sir Edward's new status was reflected in the publication of two full-scale biographies in 1905–06, both written by music journalists. The first to appear was by Robert Buckley, critic of the *Birmingham Daily Gazette* who involved Elgar personally in the preparation of the volume.[69] In it, the presentation of the composer's life differs substantially from Edwards's sketch of 1900. Although Buckley's Elgar is an artist who plotted his course 'unaided and alone', the Malvern backdrop is played down in order to present the composer as a 'brilliant and cultured talker', an intellectual with international connections.[70] Buckley's 'life' also presents Elgar as a 'progressive' in the continental mould: 'what Wagner did for opera [...] Elgar is doing for oratorio from the point at which it was left by Handel and Mendelssohn'.[71] The second biography, written by the composer's friend Ernest Newman critic at both the *Birmingham Daily Post* and *Manchester Guardian*, targeted a more intellectual readership and emphasised Elgar the 'Great Composer'.[72] For Newman, the 'real' Elgar was not the patriotic peddler of 'pompous

---

[66] *T* 17 Mar. 1904.

[67] *MT* 1 Apr. 1904.

[68] Following the Elgar Festival, an 'illustrated interview' written by Rudolph de Cordova appeared in the *Strand Magazine*. The piece is yet another example of how Elgar 'worked' reporters, talking through them to their readers. The freshest material in this piece centres on Elgar's intellectual hinterland. See de Cordova, 'Dr Edward Elgar' and 20n above.

[69] Buckley, *Sir Edward Elgar*.

[70] Ibid. pp. 4–6 and p. 41.

[71] Ibid. p. 88.

[72] Newman, *Elgar*.

sentiments', but an imaginative and poetic artist whose greatest work, *The Dream of Gerontius*, was 'one of the most remarkable achievements in all music'.[73] These two biographies, the first monographs to be written about a living English composer, provide further proof of Elgar's domination of the nation's music in the Edwardian decade.

Elgar's thoughts on music critics found their expression in a series of public lectures which he delivered as the new Peyton Professor of Music at the University of Birmingham in 1905. The composer's utterances from the Peyton Chair make absorbing reading – of special interest to this book is the fifth lecture in which he focused on 'critics'. At the outset of this lecture he stated his task was: 'to explain to the student the position the critic holds in his artistic life', before bemoaning the haste with which music criticism was written.[74] Sir Edward quickly came to the heart of the matter, the power of the press to arbitrate the destiny of a musical work. As he explained, once a work had been premiered:

> subsequent performances depend in a large measure upon the reports of the papers and anything tending to depreciate the general effect has an influence in deciding committees and conductors who cannot be present, as to their presentation of a work.

He went on to commend those critics who had strongly projected and promoted native composers. Pride of place was understandably reserved for Joseph Bennett, whom he praised for being 'honest, fearless and reasonable' and whom he acknowledged (as we have seen) as the 'patriarch and head of the profession'.[75] Other, more progressive critics came in for special approbation: the late Arthur Johnstone (of the *Manchester Guardian*) for his 'great distinction'; G. B. Shaw, for giving 'new life to musical criticism'; and Ernest Newman, for being a 'champion of the new school'. The composer then turned to the 'shady side of musical criticism' and while not mentioning Fuller Maitland by name, recalled the notorious Sullivan obituary in the *Cornhill Magazine* as being a 'foul, unforgettable episode'. Elgar clearly could not resist taking a very public opportunity of insulting his chief foe among the watchmen. He ended his lecture with an expression of thanks to the watchmen for providing 'guidance and help'. In the broader perspective, however, the Peyton lectures were not a success. There were too many gaffes and rash pronouncements and the series did not have the desired effect of enhancing Elgar's intellectual credentials.

---

[73] Ibid. p. 80.
[74] Young, *A Future for English Music* pp. 163–190. All references are to these pages.
[75] See also Chapter 2 above.

There is some evidence to suggest that Elgar tried to recover from his foray into academe by giving two interviews to the *Musical World*. The first was an impromptu affair given to the Lancastrian critic, Gerald Cumberland, after a concert in Manchester.[76] The composer was so pleased with Cumberland's piece that he invited him to visit him at Hereford in Christmas week 1905 to research a second, more detailed article, for the same journal. Cumberland, like F. G. Edwards before him, was given the Elgar 'treatment': a day at Plas Gwyn; a walk on the banks of the Wye; and generous hospitality at the composer's table.[77] During this encounter Elgar was at pains to stress that he had a life outside music and that months would go by when he would write 'nothing at all'. Although Elgar was evasive on the embarrassment of the Birmingham lectures, Cumberland eventually drew him on the subject of music critics. What he heard was something very different from what had been said to the Peyton audience a few days earlier. Cumberland later recalled Elgar's comments in his memoirs:

> The worst of musical criticism in this country [...] is that there is so much of it and so little that is serviceable. Most of those who are skilled musicians either have not the gift of criticism or they cannot express their ideas in writing, and most of those who can write are deplorably deficient in their knowledge of music. For myself, I never read criticism of my own work; it simply does not interest me. [... Critics] have no standard, no norm, no historical sense.[78]

This interview provides proof positive that Sir Edward's public warmth towards music critics concealed a private contempt. Elgar courted the press and feigned respect for what he could gain. The end-result of the interview was a hagiographic article with a familiar emphasis on the composer as countryman: 'it is when out among the fields and meadows that Elgar is at his best; here his thoughts are free [...] he is at home in the house of both prince and peasant'.[79] Once again, it was all cleverly done and the message was clear: all was well – Sir Edward was unabashed by the grubby carping of critics.

Elgar's first major premiere after the Peyton debacle was that of *The Kingdom*, an event which did nothing to enhance his relationship with the watchmen. The main problem was the oratorio had to be performed in an unfinished state, the composer having persuaded the

[76] Cumberland, 'First Impressions: No. 1 Sir Edward Elgar'.
[77] Cumberland, *Set Down in Malice* pp. 79–87.
[78] Elgar q. in ibid. See Young, *A Future for English Music* for a full account of the furore which followed Elgar's lectures in Birmingham.
[79] Cumberland, 'A Day with Sir Edward Elgar'.

festival committee and his publishers to accept a hastily truncated scheme.[80] The affair was kept secret from both public and critics and, inevitably, the premiere was fraught. In the event, few of the watchmen were taken in. The *Morning Post* judged that much of the music had been 'hurriedly conceived' and that the oratorio's design lacked 'constructive finish'. While *The Times* thought it 'extremely clever', Fuller Maitland also noted an unfortunate 'monotony of treatment' which the work shared with *The Apostles*.[81] The *Athenaeum* gave the premiere a whole page, an opportunity which Shedlock took to deliver a rambling and damning judgement.[82] The recently retired Bennett, however, in a rare signed review in the *Daily Telegraph* had no doubts about the new work:

> Sir Edward Elgar is the man of the hour here now [... who has] by a happy stroke of fortune, captured his countrymen just as they had become in sufficient measure sensible of the modern spirit'.[83]

Bennett had, once again, turned up trumps by tempering the critics' disappointing reception of his protégé's work with his own enthusiasm. But this was Bennett's last notice of an Elgar premiere; he would watch over the composer's camp no more. The *Musical Times* for its part, and perhaps with an eye on Novello's contract to publish the work, blandly declared that Elgar had made the most of his material.[84]

In contrast, Elgar's concert tour of the USA in 1907 was an unambiguous success, a triumph which owed much to his inspired handling of the American press. Having conducted *The Apostles* and *The Kingdom* in New York, the composer went on to Chicago, where he found time to give two interviews to the local press.[85] Miller Ular, the journalist from the *Chicago Sunday Examiner* was favoured with an extended talk about music and America. As always on such occasions, Elgar returned time and time again to his own life-story, depicting himself 'at once as a self-made man, who had supported himself since he was fifteen years old, and an English gentleman'. The American journalist was regaled with a wealth of personal detail underpinned by that Elgar speciality, the telling anecdote, which was ever intended to win over the hearts of critic and readers.[86] Praise for America and its orchestras followed, as did the abjuring of any interest in the reception of music:

---

[80] Moore, Elgar p. 490.

[81] *MP* 4.Oct 1906 and T 4 Oct. 1906.

[82] *Ath* 6 Oct. 1906.

[83] *DTel* 4 Oct. 1906.

[84] *MT* 1 Nov. 1906.

[85] *Chicago Sunday Examiner* 7 Apr. 1907 and *Chicago Inter-Ocean* 7 Apr. 1907.

[86] Ular, 'Sir Edward Elgar Talks of Musical Criticism'.

> I simply write what I want, and go ahead with it and pay no
> attention to criticism. Why, since I wrote *The Dream of Gerontius*
> I have not read a single paragraph in a newspaper or a magazine
> about myself – not a word of criticism. [...] As to fame, I care
> nothing for it.[87]

The ever-expanding number of volumes of news cuttings at home in
Hereford, of course, told a very different tale. Still, the exuberant
articles written by the Chicago journalists bear eloquent witness to the
composer's ability to handle the press – and to his skill in providing
good copy even in a faraway land that he heartily disliked.

The defining challenge for a nineteenth-century composer was the
symphony. Elgar finally approached the genre in 1908 determined to
leave nothing to chance to ensure success. The triumph of his *Symphony No. 1* was to be assured through massive pre-publicity and
extensive promotion. Elgar was not to be disappointed and the new
work, premiered by the Hallé under Richter's baton, had a sensational
premiere – its reception at the hands of the watchmen playing a crucial
role in its success. In the *Daily Telegraph*, Legge was emphatic that the
symphony added 'a masterwork to our national musical literature', and
was so impressed that he wrote a second review in his *Musicus* column
the following day.[88] The *Morning Post*, while reminding its readers that
the composer had always been sceptical of the 'trammels of form', went
on to celebrate the new symphony as:

> a work of the future [that] will stand as a legacy for coming
> generations; in it are the loftiness and nobility that indicate a
> masterpiece [...] we recognise it as a possession of which to be
> proud.[89]

In the *Athenaeum*, Shedlock declared that 'great expectations' had been
raised and 'fully realised', in a work that was 'thoroughly modern'.[90] The
*Musical Times*, in a long preview article, stressed that the occasion was
not only a triumph for Elgar and the Musical Renaissance, but also for
the symphonic form itself.[91] Among the leading critics only Fuller Maitland
refused to join in the fun deigning not to attend the Manchester premiere.

Most of the watchmen heard the *Symphony No. 1* again a few days
later, at its Queen's Hall premiere. Although this time Fuller Maitland
was there, the result was a meagre review of only fifty lines, in which
little praise was laced with much venom; even Elgar's orchestration,

---

[87] Ibid.
[88] *DTel* 4 and 5 Dec. 1908.
[89] *MP* 4 Dec. 1908.
[90] *Ath* 5 Dec. 1908.
[91] *MT* 1 Dec. 1908.

which Maitland had thought his strongest suit, now only excited the desire for 'a little relief from the constant wealth of sonorities'.[92] *The Times* went on to wage a campaign against the symphony in the ensuing weeks in a desperate and futile bid to undermine its popularity and commercial success. It must have been the final straw for the critic, who loathed the mingling of art and 'trade', when the Harrod's store decided to sponsor performances of the *First Symphony* as part of its 60th anniversary celebrations.[93]

Two years later, Elgar once again mobilised his supporters in the press on the occasion of the premiere of his *Violin Concerto*. It was to prove his last big pre-war success with critics and music public alike. The composer, having given Robin Legge a favoured preview of the new work, was not disappointed with the *Daily Telegraph*'s description of the concerto as of 'rare beauty and stupendous skill'.[94] The other watchmen were almost equally ecstatic. Francis Barrett in the *Morning Post* had no doubts as to the concerto's importance:

> The occasion was an expression of musical patriotism of a kind that has long been needed in this country, and it should have a far-reaching effect since it is calculated to eliminate once and for all the indifference to native worth which has for so long kept creative music in England at a standstill.[95]

*The Times*, in the last weeks of Fuller Maitland's tenure as critic, printed a review which was probably by its occasional critic, Laurence Haward: 'it may at once be said that the work is a masterpiece [... and] must surely rank as one of the great concertos of the world'.[96] The *Musical Times* strongly promoted the new work with a powerful preview article from Ernest Newman.[97] Six months after its premiere, Elgar was awarded the Order of Merit in the coronation honours list of 1911; it was the highest accolade yet extended to him by a grateful King and nation. Even with his assured eminence, Sir Edward continued to court the press when he felt his celebrity status needed a boost. A good example of this is the way he gave two interviews in 1912, both clearly intended to publicise his OM and his move to 'Severn House' – the grand mansion which he had bought on the slopes of Hampstead Hill.[98]

[92] *T* 8 Dec. 1908.
[93] Moore, *Elgar* p. 549.
[94] *DTel* 11 Nov. 1910. See also Chapter 2 above.
[95] *MP* 11 Nov. 1910.
[96] *T* 11 Nov. 1910.
[97] Newman, 'Elgar's Violin Concerto'.
[98] 'Musicus' [Legge], 'Sir E. Elgar OM, at Home'. See also 'Celebrities at Home', *The World* 22 Oct. 1912.

In the years immediately preceding the Great War, Elgar's dominance of the national music scene began to slip. There were three fundamental reasons for this decline: changing musical fashion, especially the advent of folk-song; a new younger generation of critics less sympathetic to the composer; and, what could be called 'Elgar fatigue' among watchmen and public alike.[99] Accordingly, the reception of the *Second Symphony* (1911), *The Music Makers* (1912) and the *Symphonic Study Falstaff* (1913), was bitterly disappointing to the composer.

Even so, Elgar's rapport with some of the watchmen extended through the Great War and, in many respects, up to his death in 1934. G. B. Shaw, Edwin Evans, Sammy Langford, as well as older friends, like Ernest Newman, all continued to lend their assistance to Elgar's cause. Robin Legge, until his retirement in 1931, remained among the staunchest of Elgar's supporters by continuing to place the music columns of the *Daily Telegraph* at his disposal. Even from beyond the grave the composer was still be able to command loyalty from elements in the press. A year after his death, the *Daily Telegraph* launched an appeal to secure the Broadheath birthplace cottage as a permanent Elgar museum, so that:

> all may help towards making the cottage at Broadheath as dear to lovers of music as the national monuments at Stratford, Chalfont and Grasmere are to the lovers of poetry.[100]

In the succss of the *Telegraph*'s appeal we can detect the first sign that 'Elgar' would become a national monument, 'our Shakespeare of music', as the composer's friend, Alice Stuart-Wortley, put it.[101] Ever since the 'Shakespearisation' of Elgar has continued apace and is surely nearing completion now, at the beginning of a new century. There is no better index of this process than the Bank of England's decision in 1999 to issue a new-design £20 note with the composer's portrait on the reverse. This move was presumably intended to honour the composer in the centenary year of the *Enigma Variations*. On the coinage of the realm, Elgar is literally the 'face' of English music, his portrait being

---

[99] Francis Toye, critic at *Vanity Fair*, was a young music journalist who was not prepared to toe the Elgarian line. A few days after the premiere of the *Violin Concerto*, Toye wrote a withering article entitled 'Velgarity' in which he lampooned the reception of the new work by critics and public: he [Elgar] is likely to be overwhelmed by the torrents of snobbery, advertisement, and flattery [...] 'master and hero' though he may be, the time has not yet come for his deification [...]'. *Vanity Fair* 16 Nov. 1910.

[100] *DTel* 29 Aug. 1935. The paper ran the appeal for two months (29 Aug.-26 Oct. 1935) first on a daily, then on a weekly, basis. £2,200 was eventually raised.

[101] Letter of condolence from Alice Stuart-Wortley to Carice Elgar (23 Feb. 1934), q. in Moore, *Edward Elgar: The Windflower Letters* p. 339.

presented alongside images of St. Cecilia and his beloved Worcester Cathedral to complete an iconic statement. Here, on Britain's currency, is the final apotheosis of the 'local musician' and 'self-made' composer. What more convincing index could there be of the success of Elgar, and the English Musical Renaissance, than to join Shakespeare, the national bard, and several eminent Victorians – Darwin, Faraday and Dickens – on the coinage of everyday transactions. Immortality indeed, and a development for which the composer himself carefully prepared the ground – not least in his very special relationship with the press.

# Conclusion

> There was never a time when Criticism was more needed than now.[...] It is Criticism, as Arnold points out, that creates the intellectual atmosphere of the age.[...] It is Criticism [that] makes culture possible [...] It is Criticism that leads us.[1]

Despite Oscar Wilde's stricture of 1891, critics and criticism had come a long way in the Victorian age. As the second half of the nineteenth century unfolded critics were increasingly seen as cultural curators and high priests. The critic in turn elevated art to the status of a religion making the artist into the new god of an increasingly sceptical age. The educated classes experienced culture through the prism of criticism. In this respect, the watchmen of music were just as important as composers and performers. In a very real sense they were the arbitrators of the future of English music.

The period between the Great Exhibition and the Great War witnessed enormous change in British culture and society. Traditional Christianity, that central pillar of Victorianism, came under attack from the secularising forces of Darwinian science and post-Christian philosophy. As Charles Kingsley pointed out in 1863: 'Darwin is conquering everywhere [...] by the mere force of truth and fact'.[2] The other pillar of Victorian belief, faith in the new industrial society, also came under severe scrutiny. As Herbert Sussman has commented on the literature of the era, 'the decade of the Great Exhibition marks the end of hope in the blessings of the machine'.[3]

Art gained an enhanced value as Victorian piety faltered. The Aesthetic Movement championed the notion that 'art mattered', that life should be lived through the senses and that beauty was nourishment for the human spirit.[4] Within the new aestheticism, there was a conviction that culture and commerce were incompatible, and that the critic should embrace an active role in changing an aggressively materialist society. As the new century approached, culture increasingly became a site of struggle between conservatives and progressives, modernisers and reac-

---

[1] Wilde, 'The Critic as Artist' pp. 205–6 and p. 212.

[2] Kingsley q. in Reardon, *Religious Thought* p. 217. See also Chadwick, *Secularization of the European Mind*.

[3] Sussman q. in Wiener, *English Culture* p. 30.

[4] For a discussion of Walter Pater's challenge to the Victorian cultural order, see Hughes and Stradling, pp. 21–2. For an account of the impact of Lord Frederick Leighton (1830–96) on Victorian painting , see Jones, 'Attic Attitudes'.

tionaries.[5] Music had long-since been accepted as a civilising, educative force and, for the middle-classes, a means of differentiating themselves from the masses.

Many English composers and critics found it hard to keep up with the pace of change in music and society. As far as the watchmen were concerned, most regarded the English Musical Renaissance as a delicate child who should not be exposed too early to the rigours of life. English music criticism therefore remained largely defensive towards national music. Yet there were a few radical, iconoclastic voices among the watchmen who were prepared to challenge orthodoxy and posit a different Renaissance from the one dominated by the London academies and the ancient universities.

The conjunction of art and politics in the nineteenth century led many watchmen to approach their craft in a 'political' spirit. The first generation of critics was conservative, horrified by the political and musical upheavals of the 1840s. Later critics too were haunted by the spectre of Wagner and it was not until the 1890s that there was a broad acceptance of his legacy. Many more critics found their music conservatism and patriotism reinforced by a rapidly changing international situation after 1870. The newly unified Germany and Italy presented new challenges to England's political and cultural security. Meanwhile other, lesser, nationalisms (Czech, Hungarian, Norwegian) drew further unwelcome attention to English inferiority in music.

The national press experienced an unprecedented transformation in the second half of the nineteenth century. The Education Act of 1870 was certainly the key factor in increasing literacy in the general population and newspapers were not slow to reach out to an expanding readership. The 'new journalism' in turn effected a profound change in the national press. Despite accusations of vulgarity and Americanisation, this phenomenon helped to clear the ground for the wave of mass-circulation dailies that were to appear before the end of the century.[6] The market for periodicals also experienced a tremendous expansion in the later decades of the nineteenth century. Even so, several of the older literary journals did not move with the times and experienced a decline in circulation and profitability. The music press for its part continued to thrive with the launch of several successful new

---

[5] Many late-Victorians and Edwardians looked to art for solace and escape from their industrial society in mythologies of 'Englishness'. See Rich, 'Quest for Englishness'; Colls and Dodd, *Englishness*; and Boyes, *Imagined Village*.

[6] A King's Cross newspaper vendor of the 1890s commented that the *Daily Mail* was bought by: 'thousands of working men who had never bought a newspaper before'. Q. in Koss, *Rise and Fall* vol. ii p. 369.

titles, including the *Strad* (1890) and the *Musical News* (1891).[7] None of the new journals could, however, dislodge the *Musical Times* from its pre-eminent position.

Alongside the expansion of the press went the 'professionalisation' of journalism, a development that culminated in the foundation of the Institute of Journalists in 1886. Journalism by the end of the century was not only respectable, but also regarded as glamorous and fun, with one contemporary referring to it as 'the youngest and freest of the professions'.[8] Music critics were bound to benefit from this change in status; so that even an upper middle-class patrician like Fuller Maitland could enter journalism without danger of social taint. The cult of the critic added greatly to the new power and social acceptability of arts journalism.

The music profession experienced profound change after 1850 with the demand for music and musicians increasing dramatically.[9] Music, however, still had to prosper in a difficult social and cultural climate. The English Musical Renaissance was largely achieved without the support of either the royal court (after Prince Albert's death in 1861) or the political class, by whom 'neither music nor musicians were taken seriously'.[10] Rather music relied mostly on the effort and initiative of individuals for its progress, seen at its best in the development of the concert-life of the Crystal Palace. The success and profitability of the latter depended greatly on the watchmen since 'neither Manns not the Directors could take an audience for granted and relied on a relatively small core of informed critics and musicians in building an audience and keeping it'.[11]

The construction of national music was dogged by many vicissitudes. As we have seen, the watchmen settled on several English composers as champions of the Renaissance but only in Elgar did they eventually find a suitable hero. His success at home and, eventually, in Germany ensured a consensus that the search for a 'great' English composer was over. After all, in the quest for a definitive English oratorio, it was not until Elgar's *Gerontius* that the watchmen celebrated a work that secured both national and international acclaim. Likewise, in the search for an English symphony, although the critics greeted several efforts as

---

[7] Streatfeild, entry on 'Musical Periodicals – England' in *Grove 2* vol. iii pp. 680–4.

[8] Q. in Jones, *Powers of the Press* p. 129.

[9] Ehrlich, *Music Profession* pp. 51–75.

[10] Ibid. p. 73.

[11] *Musical Life*, p. 122. The Crystal Palace management was under no illusions about the importance of the watchmen since it reserved the private 'end gallery' for 'critics, directors and their guests'. Both Davison and Bennett were very close to the Crystal Palace authorities, ibid. p. 67 and p. 118.

definitive, it was not until Elgar's *Symphony No. 1* that a native symphony went immediately into the repertoire and stayed there. The quest for a sustainable national opera however remained unfulfilled by 1914.[12]

The press in 1914 remained the most important medium for the transmission of ideas just as it had been in 1850. Music reviews were to be found in an enormous range of newspapers and other publications. The quantity of music coverage was simply vast. Elgar's personal collection of press notices bear eloquent testimony to the sheer range of publications that were routinely covering music by the end of the century. Although daily newspapers retained their reportage of music in the period before the Great War, the space allocated relative to other content experienced a significant decline.

In any event, by 1914, it was incontrovertible that England had experienced a 'musical renaissance'. It had been a joint effort: composers, critics, administrators, patrons, impresarios, publishers and the musical public, all had played a part. The force that bound them together was pride in nation and a desire to construct a national music as part of a vibrant cultural life. It is, of course, impossible to quantify the impact of music journalism. We can only go by the high importance and respect accorded to the watchmen by composers and public alike. The musical public could experience new music only through live performance and the review columns of newspapers and journals.[13] The evidence presented in this study demonstrates that the critics' influence on the canon formation of English music cannot be overestimated.

By the end of the century there was a growing perception that the role of the critic was shifting. As Oscar Wilde implored, the critic should cease to be the lofty eminence that the Victorians created and aspire to a more radical, more heroic ideal. For him the critic, in his ability to interpret art, had transcended the artist in importance.[14] Criticism, according to Wilde, should be a liberating force, a means to question everything, most especially authority and reverence for the past. To be a true modern was to be a critic.[15]

---

[12] The most successful English opera ever, Rutland Boughton's *The Immortal Hour* was premiered on 26 Aug. 1914 at the first Glastonbury Festival in an amateur performance. The press reaction was effectively non-existent. However, the opera enjoyed a record-breaking London run (of 216 consecutive performances) during 1922–23. It had a further long run in the capital during 1923–24 and major revivals in 1926 and 1932. Hurd, 'The Immortal'.

[13] Elgar signed his first contract with the Gramophone Company in Dec. 1913. Moore, *Elgar* p. 657. The gramophone revolution was still at an early stage in 1913 and it was not a factor in the reception history of English music before the Great War.

[14] Wilde, 'The Critic as Artist' p. 125 and pp. 136–7.

[15] Ibid. p. 169.

By 1914, English cultural life was being buffeted by winds of change blowing from the continent and there was a widely held view that the cultural 'establishment' was on the run. The world of painting was shocked in 1910 by Roger Fry's 'Manet & the Post-Impressionists' exhibition in London, a show which was attacked by many art critics as a rejection of western civilisation. As *The Times* commented on Fry's exhibition: 'like anarchism in politics, it is a rejection of all civilisation has done'.[16] English composers and critics too were forced to confront, in Robert Hughes's celebrated phrase, the 'shock of the new'. The sensuality of Debussy, the controversial operas of Richard Strauss, and the sexually charged ballets of Stravinsky all provided challenges which many feared English music would find difficult to meet.

Yet as war came in 1914, English music had already made a fundamental choice as to its future direction. The Pastoral School was to be England's version of modernism, a pre-war consensus having already formed around this development among musicians and critics alike. Although there were a handful of composers, like Josef Holbrooke and Cyril Scott, who were prepared to explore continental modernism, Vaughan Williams and his fellow pastoralists had already mapped out the route. Theirs however, was not to be a trek 'toward the unknown region', but rather a journey back to a (largely imagined) English past. The Great War only had the effect of reinforcing this decision. As a result, 'Little England' survived the trenches in better shape than 'Great Britain'.

The period 1850–1914 marked the high noon of music journalism in the press. Never again were the watchmen to wield quite so much clout. In this period a unique series of developments came together in the English Musical Renaissance, shifts which dimensionally increased the impact of music critics and the importance of music criticism. Yet, already in 1914, change was (almost literally) in the air as the impact of radio broadcasting was about transform the way in which an expanding population accessed music. Although the critics would continue to serve the nation's music, they would not again enjoy the same dominance and dignity that once secured them routine invitations to the Directors Gallery at Grove's Crystal Palace. Nevertheless, in the post Great War world of the BBC and sound recording, music journalists still wielded great influence over the nation's musical destiny. The new broadcasting media simply created new 'doorkeepers' to guard the citadel and new 'watchmen' to patrol the walls of England's music.

---

[16] *The Times* q. in Stansky, *On or About* p. 1.

# Appendix A

**Chief music critics and editors of journals.**

The Times

J. W. Davison – Music Critic (1846–78).
Francis Hueffer – Music Critic (1878–89).
J. A. Fuller Maitland – Music Critic (1889–1911)
H. C. Colles – Music Critic (1911–43)

*The* Daily Telegraph

Campbell Clarke – Music Critic (1855?-70)
Joseph Bennett – Music Critic (1870–1906)
Robin Legge – Music Critic (1906–31)

*The* Morning Post

C. L. Gruneisen – Music Critic (1844–67)
W. A. Barrett – Music Critic (1867–91)
Arthur Hervey – Music Critic (1892–1908)

*The* Athenaeum

Henry F. Chorley – Music Critic (1833–68)
Campbell Clarke – Music Critic (1868–70)
Charles L. Gruneisen – Music Critic (1870–79)
Ebenezer Prout – Music Critic (1879–89)
Henry Frost – Music Critic (1889–98)
J. S. Shedlock – Music Critic (1898–1916)

*The* Musical Times

Alfred J. Novello – Editor (1844–63)
Henry Lunn – Editor (1863–87)
William A. Barrett – Editor (1887–91)
Edgar Jacques – Editor (1891–97)
F. G. Edwards – Editor (1897–1909)
W. G. McNaught – Editor (1909–18)

*The* Musical World

J. W. Davison – Editor (1843–85)
Francis Hueffer – Editor (1886–88)
Edgar F. Jacques – Editor (1888–91).


**Critics and Journalists: Biographical Notes**

Barrett, William A. (1834–91): music critic on the *Morning Post* (1866–91) and editor of the *Musical Times* (1887–91), he was also critic on the *Monthly Musical Record*. Barrett was a freemason and organist of the Grand Lodge (after Sullivan) and wrote books on English glees, madrigals and Balfe.

Barry, Charles A. (b 1830): musician, critic and editor of the *Monthly Musical Record* (1874–76) in succession to Prout. Barry was a 'progressive' and an early convert to Bruckner.

Baughan, Edward A: Music critic of the *Daily News* (c. 1904–10). Baughan projected Elgar strongly in his columns. He published a biography of Paderewski (1906).

Bennett, Joseph (1831–1911): music journalist and librettist, who spent much of his long career as critic on the *Daily Telegraph* (1870–1906). Bennett was a regular contributor to the *Musical Times*, the *Musical World* as well other publications. He was founder-editor of *Concordia* (1875–76) and editor of *The Lute* (1883–88). He also acted as editor of *Musical World* during J. W. Davison's last illness. A biographer of Mendelssohn, Bennett provided libretti (or 'books') for Sullivan, Mackenzie, Cowen and MacCunn.

Blackburn, Vernon (1866–1907): music critic on the *Fortnightly Review* and *Pall Mall Gazette* (1893–1907).

Chorley, Henry F. (1808–72): friend of Charles Dickens and (with J. W. Davison) one of the founding-fathers of English music criticism. Chief critic on the *Athenaeum* (1833–68), Chorley was also a librettist.

Clarke, Sir Campbell (1830–1902): critic of the *Daily Telegraph* (1855?-1870) and the *Athenaeum* (1868–70), he also served as secretary of the Philharmonic Society (1864–66).

Colles, H. C. (1879–1943): a protégé of Fuller Maitland, he served as assistant music-critic of *The Times* (1906–11) and the chief critic (1911–43). Colles was editor of *Grove 3* (1927) and *Grove 4* (1940). Colles worked the RCM (1919–43), where he was Professor of Music History.

Corder, Frederick (1852–1932): a frequent contributor to *Musical Times*, Corder was also co-founder of the 'Society of British Composers'

(1905) and fellow of the Philharmonic Society. Educated at the RAM and Cologne Conservatorium, Corder was appointed Professor of Composition at the RAM (1888) and RAM Curator (1889).

Dannreuther, Edward (1844–1906): German musician and writer, he was one of Grove's contributors to the *Dictionary* and *Macmillan's Magazine*. He was also the Professor of Piano at the RCM (1895–1906).

Davison, James W. (1813–1885): one of the founders of English music criticism, Davison wielded enormous influence as music critic of *The Times* (1846–78) and editor of the *Musical World* (1843–85).

Edwards, H. Sutherland (1827–1906): long-serving critic on the *St James's Gazette*, and contributor to the *Morning Post* and *Concordia*. Sutherland Edwards was a close friend of J. W. Davison and left a memoir, *Personal Recollections* (1900).

Edwards, Frederick G. (1853–1909): editor of the *Musical Times* (1897–1909) was educated at the RAM. He was a close friend of George Grove.

Engel, Carl (1818–82): German-born scholar and spiritual ancestor of the folk-song revival. In 1866, Engel wrote *An Introduction to the Study of National Music* and, in 1878–79, he published an important series of articles in the *Musical Times* on 'The Literature of National Music'.

Fremantle, George (d. 1895): critic of the *Manchester Guardian* (1867–95) and a close friend of Sir Charles Hallé. He was a 'progressive' in his columns.

Frost, Henry (1848–1901): organist, music critic, and early supporter of Wagner in England. Professor of Piano at the Guildhall School of Music (1880–88), he worked as second critic (under Prout) on the *Athenaeum* and, after 1879, and as its chief critic (1889–98). Frost was also critic on the *Standard* (1888–1901) and a contributor to the *Musical Times* in the 1880s.

Fuller Maitland, John A. (1856–1936): served as critic of the *Pall Mall Gazette* (1880–84), and London critic of the *Manchester Guardian* (1884–89), before becoming chief critic at *The Times* (1889–1911). Author of many books on music, he was editor of *Grove 2* and music editor for the *Encyclopaedia Britannica*. A friend of Stanford's, he was a major figure in the music journalism of the English Musical Renaissance. Fuller Maitland was co-founder of the Folk Song Society (1899).

Glover, Howard (d. 1876): music critic of the *Morning Post* in the 1850s and 1860s.

Graves, Charles L. (1856 and-1944): Irish-born music journalist on *The Spectator*, *Pall Mall Gazette*, the *Musical Times* and *Punch*). Graves was also the biographer Grove (1903) and Parry (1926) as well as the author of *Post-Victorian Music* (1911).

Grove, Sir George (1820–1900): lighthouse-builder turned writer on music, Grove was editor of *Macmillan's Magazine* (1868–83) as well as of *Grove 1*. He also served as Director of the RCM (1883–94).

Gruneisen, Charles L. (1806–79): music critic of the *Morning Post* (1844–1867) and the *Athenaeum* (1870–79), he was also a biographer of Meyerbeer (1848) and author of *The Opera and the Press* (1869).

Hervey, Arthur (1855–1922): chief critic on the *Morning Post* (1892–1908), he was an authority on French music. Unusually for a music critic, Hervey was also a composer.

Hueffer, Francis [Franz] (1843–89): German-born music writer and journalist, critic on *The Times* (1878–89) and editor of the *Musical World* (1887–1888). He was also editor of 'The Great Musicians' series and as the librettist of Mackenzie's two operas, *Columba* (1883) and *The Troubadour* (1886).

Hogarth, George (1783–1870): music critic of the *Daily News* (1846–66) and author of several major works on music: *Musical History* (1835), *Memoirs of the Opera in Italy, France, Germany & England* (1851) and *The Philharmonic Society of London* (1862).

Jacques, Edgar F. (1850–1906): editor-proprietor of the *Musical World* (1888–91) and editor of the *Musical Times* (1892–97). Jacques was chief critic on the *Observer* (1894–1906) and *Sunday Times* (c. 1901–06). He also wrote programme notes for the Queen's Hall Promenade Concerts (1895–1902).

Johnstone, Arthur (1861–1904): music critic of the *Manchester Guardian* (1896–1904).

Kalisch, Alfred (1863–1933): critic of the *World* (1899–1912) and the *Daily News* (1912–?33).

Klein, Hermann (1856–1934): music critic on the *Sunday Times* (1881–1901), Klein wrote a valuable memoir *Thirty Years of Musical Life in London 1870–1900.* (1903).

Langford, Samuel 'Sammy' (1863–1927): music critic on the *Manchester Guardian* (1906–22?).

Legge, Robin (1862–1933): assistant-critic on *The Times* (1891–1906), and then chief critic on the *Daily Telegraph* (1908–31).

Lunn, Henry C. (1817–94): editor of the *Musical Times* (1863–87).

McNaught, William G. (1849–1918): editor of both Novello's *School Music Review* (1892–1918) and the *Musical Times* (1909–18).

Newman, Ernest (1868–1959): music critic on the *Birmingham Daily Post* (1906–19), the *Manchester Guardian* (1905–06) and the *Sunday Times* (1920–58).

Prout, Ebenezer (1835–1909): critic of the *Athenaeum* (1879–89) and founding-editor of the *Monthly Musical Record* (1871–74). Prout also held professorial posts at the National Training School (1876–82), RAM (1879–1909), Guildhall School of Music (1894–1909) and Dublin University (1894–1909).

Runciman, John F. (1866–1916): music critic on the *Saturday Review* (1894–1916), he also wrote biographies of Purcell (1909) and Wagner (1913)

Shaw, George B. (1856–1950): playwright and music critic on the *World* (1888–89) and the *Star* (1890–94).

Shedlock, John S. (1843–1919): chief critic of the *Athenaeum* (1898–1916) and editor of the *Monthly Musical Record* (in the 1900s). Shedlock also translated Riemann's *Dictionary of Music* (1893).

Southgate, T. L.: editor of the *Musical Standard* (c. 1868–73) and co-founder and editor of the *Musical News* (1891).

Squire, William Barclay (1855–1927): critic on the *Saturday Review* (1888–94) and the *Globe* (1894–1901), he was the librettist of Stanford's opera, *The Veiled Prophet*.

Streatfeild, Richard (1866–1919): critic of the *Daily Graphic* (1898–1912).

Stratton, Steven S. (1840–1906): critic of the *Birmingham Daily Post* (1877–1906) and contributor to the *Monthly Musical Record*, he was the *Musical Times*'s correspondent in Birmingham 'for many years'. He also the co-compiler of the Brown & Stratton *Biographical Dictionary of Musicians* (1897).

Turpin, E. H. (1835–1907): editor of the *Musical Standard* (1880–86) and co-founder and editor of the *Musical News*.

# Appendix B:
# Premieres of English Music reviewed in Newspapers and Journals

**Bantock, Granville (1868–1946)**

*Symphonic Poem: Jaga-Naut*
Philharmonic Society: 21 March 1900

*DTel*: [No review]
*T*: 'Philharmonic Society' (22 Mar. 1900)
*Ath*: [No review]
*MT*: 'Philharmonic Concerts' (1 Apr. 1900, vol. xli pp. 255–6)

*Orchestral Poem: The Witch of Atlas*
Worcester Festival: 10 September 1902

*DTel*: [No review]
*T*: 'The Three Choirs Festival' (11 Sept. 1902)
*Ath*: 'Festival of the Three Choirs' (20 Sept. 1902, No. 3908 pp. 390–1)
*MT*: 'Worcester Musical Festival' (1 Oct. 1902, vol. xliii pp. 675–6).

*Cantata: Omar Khayyam* [Part 1]
Birmingham Festival: 4 October 1906

*DTel*: 'Birmingham Festival: Bantock's Omar Khayyam' (5 Oct. 1906)
*T*: 'Birmingham Musical Festival' (6 Oct. 1906)
*Ath*: 'The Birmingham Festival' (13 Oct. 1906, No. 4120 pp. 450–1)
*MT*: 'The Birmingham Musical Festival' (1 Nov. 1906, vol. xlvii pp. 757–9).

*Orchestral Drama: Fifine at the Fair*
Birmingham Festival: 2 October 1912

*DTel*: 'Birmingham Festival: Two New Works' (4 Oct. 1912)
*T*: 'Birmingham Musical Festival' (3 Oct. 1912)
*Ath*: [No review]
*MT*: 'The Birmingham Musical Festival' (1 Nov. 1912, vol. liii)

## Bennett, W. Sterndale (1816–75)

*Cantata: The May Queen*
Leeds Festival: 8 September 1858

*DTel*: 'The Leeds Musical Festival' (10 Sept. 1858)
*T*: 'Leeds Musical Festival' (10 Sept. 1858)
*Ath*: 'Leeds Festival' (11 Sept. 1858 No. 1611 pp. 337–8)
*MT*: 'The Leeds Musical Festival' (1 Oct. 1858, vol. viii p. 323).

*Fantasia-Overture: Paradise and the Peri Op. 42*
Philharmonic Society: 14 July 1862

*DTel*: 'Philharmonic Society' (16 Jul. 1862)
*T*: [No review]
*Ath*: 'Philharmonic Jubilee Concert' (19 Jul. 1862 No. 1712 p. 89)
*MT*: [No review].

*Symphony in G minor Op. 43*
Philharmonic Society: 27 June 1864

*DTel*: 'Philharmonic Society' (29 Jun. 1864)
*T*: [No review]
*Ath*: 'Music and the Drama' (2 Jul. 1864 No. 1914 pp. 24–5)
*MT*: [No review]

*Oratorio: The Woman of Samaria Op. 44*
Birmingham Festival: 28 August 1867

*DTel*: 'Birmingham Musical Festival' (29 Aug. 1867)
*T*: 'Birmingham Musical Festival' (29 Aug. 1867)
*Ath*: 'The Birmingham Festival' (7 Sept. 1867, No. 2080 pp. 312–13)
*MT*: 'The Birmingham Festival' (1 Oct. 1867, vol. xiii pp. 165–9).

*Orchestral Prelude: Ajax*
Philharmonic Society: 8 July 1872

*DTel*: 'Philharmonic Concerts' (11 Jul. 1872)
*T*: [No review]
*Ath*: [No review]
*MT*: 'Philharmonic Society' (1 Aug. 1872, vol. xv p. 564).

## Bexfield, William R. (1824–53)

*Oratorio: Israel Restored*
Norwich Festival: 22 September 1852

*T*: 'The Norwich Musical Festival' (23 Sept. 1852)
*Ath*: 'The Norwich Festival' (25 Sept. 1852, No. 1300 pp. 1038–9)
*MT*: 'The Norwich Festival' (1 Oct. 1852, vol. v pp. 75–6).

## Boughton, Rutland (1878–1960)

*Symphonic Poem: Midnight*
Birmingham Festival: 5 October 1909

*DTel*: 'Birmingham Festival' (6 Oct. 1909)
*T*: 'Birmingham Musical Festival' (7 Oct. 1909)
*Ath*: 'The Birmingham Triennial Musical Festival' (9 Oct. 1909, No. 4276 p. 435)
*MT*: 'Birmingham Musical Festival' (1 Nov. 1909, vol. l pp. 735–7).

## Cliffe, Frederick (1857–1931)

*Symphony No. 1 in C minor*
Crystal Palace: 20 April 1889

*DTel*: 'Crystal Palace' (22 Apr. 1889)
*T*: Mr Manns's Benefit Concert' (22 Apr. 1889)
*Ath*: 'Crystal Palace – Mr Manns's Benefit Concert' (27 Apr. 1889, No. 3209 p. 545)
*MT*: 'Crystal Palace Concerts' (1 May 1889, vol. xxx pp. 278–9).

*Symphony No. 2 in E minor*
Leeds Festival: 6 October 1892

*DTel*: 'Leeds Festival' (8 Oct. 1892)
*T*: 'Leeds Musical Festival' (7 Oct. 1892)
*Ath*: 'Music: The Week' (15 Oct. 1892, No. 3390 pp. 523–5)
*MT*: 'Leeds Musical Festival' (1 Nov. 1892, vol. xxxiii pp. 662–4)

*Violin Concerto in D minor*
Norwich Festival: 7 October 1896

*DTel*: 'Norwich Musical Festival' (9 Oct. 1896)
*T*: 'The Norwich Festival' (8 Oct. 1896)
*Ath*: 'Music: The Week' (10 Oct. 1896, No. 3598 pp. 492–3)
*MT*: 'Norwich Musical Festival' (1 Nov. 1896, vol. xxxvii pp. 734–6).


**Coleridge-Taylor, Samuel (1875–1912)**

*Ballade for Orchestra*
Gloucester Festival: 15 September 1898

*DTel*: 'Three Choirs Festival' (16 Sept. 1898)
*T*: 'Gloucester Music Festival' (15 Sept. 1898)
*Ath*: 'Festival of the Three Choirs' (17 Sept. 1898, No. 3699 pp. 394–5)
*MT*: 'Gloucester Musical Festival' (1 Oct. 1898, vol. xxxix pp. 666–8).

*Scenes from the Song of Hiawatha*
Royal Albert Hall: 22 March 1900

*DTel*: 'Royal Choral Society' (23 Mar. 1900)
T: 'Royal Choral Society' (23 Mar. 1900)
*Ath*: 'Albert Hall: Royal Choral Society' (31 Mar. 1900, No. 3779 p. 409)
*MT*: 'Mr S Coleridge-Taylor's Hiawatha' (1 Apr. 1900, vol. xli pp. 246–7).

*Toussaint l'Ouverture*
Queen's Hall: 26 October 1901

*DTel*: 'Queen's Hall' (28 Oct. 1901)
*T*: 'Newman's Symphonic Concerts' (28 Oct. 1901)
*Ath*: 'Music: The Week' (2 Nov. 1901, No. 3862 pp. 602–3)
*MT*: 'London Concerts' (1 Dec. 1901, vol. xlii p. 819).

*Orchestral Variations on an African Theme*
Philharmonic Society: 14 June 1906

*DTel*: 'Philharmonic Society' (15 Jun. 1906)
*T*: 'Philharmonic Society' (15 Jun. 1906)
*Ath*: 'Musical Gossip' (23 Jun. 1906, No. 4104 pp. 774–5)
*MT*: 'Philharmonic Society' (1 Jul. 1906, vol. xlvii p. 485).

## Corder, Frederick (1852–1932)

*Orchestral Suite: Im Schwarzwald*
Crystal Palace: 20 March 1880

*DTel*: [No review]
*T*: 'Two English Composers' (6 Apr. 1880)
*Ath*: 'Music: The Week' (27 Mar. 1880, No. 2735 pp. 418–19)
*MT*: 'Crystal Palace' (1 Apr. 1880, vol. xxi pp. 173–4)

*Opera: Nordisa*
Liverpool Royal Court Theatre: 26 January 1887

*DTel*: [No review]
*T*: 'Nordisa' (27 Jan. 1887)
*Ath*: 'Music This Week' (5 Feb. 1887, No. 3093 pp. 199–201)
*MT*: 'Production of Nordisa' (1 Feb. 1887, vol. xxviii p. 100).


## Cowen, Frederick Hymen (1852–1935)

*Cantata: The Corsair*
Birmingham Festival: 29 August 1876

*DTel*: 'Birmingham Musical Festival' (30 and 31 Aug. 1876)
*T*: 'Birmingham Musical Festival' (1 Sept. 1876)
*Ath*: 'Birmingham Musical Festival' (2 Sept. 1876, No. 2549 pp. 313–
    14)
*MT*: 'The Birmingham and Hereford Musical Festivals' (1 Oct. 1876,
    vol. xvii pp. 615–21).

*Opera: Pauline*
Carl Rosa Co. [Lyceum Theatre]: 22 November 1876

*DTel*: 'Carl Rosa Opera Company' (25 Nov. 1876)
*T:* [No review]
*Ath*: 'Mr Cowen's Opera – Pauline' (25 Nov. 1876, No. 2561 p. 696)
*MT*: 'Carl Rosa Company' (1 Dec. 1876, vol. xvii p. 696).

*Symphony No. 3 in C minor, 'Scandinavian'*
St James's Hall: 18 December 1880

*DTel*: 'Saturday Orchestral Concerts' (20 Dec. 1880)
*T*: 'Mr Cowen's New Symphony' (21 Dec. 1880)
*Ath*: 'Music' (25 Dec. 1880, No. 2774 pp. 873–4)
*MT*: 'Saturday Orchestral Concerts' (1 Jan. 1881, vol. xxii pp. 22–3).

*Cantata: St Ursula*
Norwich Festival: 13 October 1881

*DTel*: 'Norwich Musical Festival (15 Oct. 1881)
*T*: 'The Norwich Musical Festival' (14 Oct. 1881)
*Ath*: 'Norwich Musical Festival' (22 Oct. 1881, No. 2817 pp. 535–6)
*MT*: 'Norwich Musical Festival' (1 Nov. 1881, vol. xxii pp. 566–8).

*Symphony No. 4 in B flat minor, 'Cambrian'*
Philharmonic Society: 28 May 1884

*DTel*: 'Mr Cowen's 'Welsh' Symphony' (29 May 1884)
*T*: 'Philharmonic Society' (29 May 1884)
*Ath*: 'Music: The Week' (31 May 1884, No. 2953 pp. 704–5)
*MT*: 'Philharmonic Society' (1 Jun. 1884, vol. xxv pp. 334–5).

*Symphony No. 5 in F major*
Cambridge University Musical Society: 9 June 1887 and Richter Concert (London) 13 June 1887.

*DTel*: 'Richter Concerts' (15 Jul. 1887)
*T*: 'Mr Cowen's New Symphony' (14 Jun. 1887).
*Ath*: 'Cambridge University Musical Society' (18 Jun. 1887, No. 3112 p. 807)
*MT*: 'Cambridge University Musical Society' (1 Jul. 1887, vol. xxviii p. 411).

*Oratorio: Ruth*
Three Choirs Festival: 8 September 1887

*DTel*: 'Festival of the Three Choirs' (10 Sept. 1887)
*T*: 'The Worcester Musical Festival' (9 Sept. 1887)
*Ath*: 'Worcester Musical Festival' (17 Sept. 1887, No. 3125 pp. 380–1)
*MT*: 'Worcester Musical Festival' (1 Oct. 1887, vol. xxviii pp. 599–601).

*Opera: Thorgrim*
Drury Lane: 22 April 1890

*DTel*: 'Carl Rosa Opera Company' (23 Apr. 1890)
*T*: 'Mr Cowen's New Opera' (23 Apr. 1890)
*Ath*: 'Carl Rosa Company' (26 Apr. 1890, No. 3261 pp. 539–40)
*MT*: 'Carl Rosa Company' (1 May 1890, vol. xxxi pp. 277–9).

*Oratorio: The Transfiguration*
Gloucester Festival: 12 September 1895

*DTel*: 'Festival of the Three Choirs' (13 Sept. 1895)
*T*: 'The Three Choirs Festival' (13 Sept. 1895)
*Ath*: 'The Gloucester Festival' (21 Sept. 1895, No. 3543 pp. 394–5)
*MT*: 'Gloucester Musical Festival' (1 Oct. 1895, vol. xxxvi pp. 670–2).

## Davies, Henry Walford (1869–1941)

*Cantata: Everyman*
Leeds Festival: 6 October 1904

*DTel*: 'Leeds Festival: Dr Davies's Everyman' (7 and 8 Oct. 1904)
*T*: 'The Leeds Festival' (10 Oct. 1904)
*Ath*: 'Leeds Musical Festival' (15 Oct. 1904, No. 4016 pp. 521–3)
*MT*: 'Leeds Musical Festival' (1 Nov. 1904, vol. xlv pp. 730–2).

*Noble Numbers*
Hereford Festival: 8 September 1909

*DTel*: 'Three Choirs Festival' (9 Sept. 1909)
*T*: 'Music: The Three Choirs Festival' (9 Sept. 1909)
*Ath*: 'Hereford Musical Festival' (11 Sept. 1911, No. 4272 p. 306)
*MT*: 'Hereford Musical Festival' (1 Oct. 1909, vol. l pp. 663–5).

*Song of St Francis*
Birmingham Festival: 2 October 1912

*DTel*: 'Birmingham Festival: Two New Works' (4 Oct. 1912)
*T*: 'Birmingham Musical Festival' (3 Oct. 1912)
*Ath*: 'The Birmingham Festival' (5 Oct. 1912, No. 4432 p. 386)
*MT*: 'The Birmingham Musical Festival' (1 Nov. 1912, vol. liii pp. 722–7).

**Delius, Frederick (1862–1934)**

*Legende for Violin and Orchestra*
St James's Hall: 30 May 1899

*DTel*: 'A New Composer' (1 Jun. 1899)
*T*: 'The Delius Orchestral Concert' (31 May 1899)
*Ath*: 'Musical Gossip' (3 Jun. 1899, No. 3736 pp. 698–9)
*MT*: 'Mr Fritz Delius' (1 Jul. 1899, vol. xl p. 472).

*Piano Concerto*
Queen's Hall: 22 October 1907

*DTel*: 'An English Concerto' (23 Oct. 1907)
*T*: 'Concerts' (23 Oct. 1907)
*Ath*: [No review]
*MT*: 'Mr Delius's Piano Concerto' (1 Nov. 1907, vol. xlviii p. 739).

*Sea Drift*
Sheffield Festival: 7 October 1908

*DTel*: [No review]
*T*: 'Sheffield Musical Festival' (8 Oct. 1908)
*Ath*: 'The Sheffield Festival' (10 Oct. 1908, No. 4224 pp. 445–6)
*MT*: 'Sheffield Musical Festival' (1 Nov. 1908, vol. xlix pp. 726–7).

*Mass of Life*
Queen's Hall: 7 June 1909

*DTel*: 'The Beecham Concerts: A Mass of Life' (8 Jun. 1909)
*T*: 'Queen's Hall Concert' (8 Jun. 1909)
*Ath*: 'Queen's Hall' (12 Jun. 1909, No. 4259 pp. 709–10)
*MT*: 'A Mass of Life' (1 Jul. 1909, vol. l pp. 465–6).

*A Dance Rhapsody*
Hereford Festival: 9 September 1909

*DTel*: 'Three Choirs Festival' (10 Sept. 1909)
*T*: 'Music: The Three Choirs Festival' (10 Sept. 1909)
*Ath*: 'The Hereford Festival' (18 Sept. 1909, No. 4273 p. 338)
*MT*: 'Hereford Musical Festival' (1 Oct. 1909, vol. l pp. 663–5).

**Elgar, Edward (1857–1934)**

*Concert Overture: Froissart*
Worcester Festival: 9 September 1890

*DTel*: 'Festival of the Three Choirs' (11 Sept. 1890)
*MP*: 'Festival of the Three Choirs' (11 Sept. 1890)
*T*: 'Worcester Musical Festival' (11 Sept. 1890)
*Ath*: 'The Worcester Festival' (20 Sept. 1890, No. 3282 pp. 393–4)
*MT*: 'Worcester Musical Festival' (1 Oct. 1890, vol. xxxi pp. 596–9).

*Oratorio: The Light of Life*
Worcester Festival: 8 September 1896

*DTel*: 'Festival of the Three Choirs' (9 Sept. 1896)
*MP*: 'The Worcester Musical Festival' (9 Sept. 1896) and 'The Worcester Festival' (10 Sept. 1896)
*T*: 'The Festival of the Three Choirs' (9 Sept. 1896)
*Ath*: 'The Worcester Musical Festival' (12 Sept. 1896, No. 3594 p. 363)
*MT*: 'Worcester Musical Festival' (1 Oct. 1896, vol. xxxvii pp. 665–7).

*Cantata: Scenes from the Saga of King Olaf*
North Staffordshire Festival: 30 October 1896

*DTel*: 'North Staffordshire Festival' (31 Oct. 1896)
*MP*: [No review]
*T*: [No review]
*Ath*: 'The North Staffordshire Festival (7 Nov. 1896, No. 3602 p. 644)
*MT*: 'More Festival Novelties' (1 Oct. 1896, vol. xxxvii pp. 667–9) and 'North Staffordshire Musical Festival' (1 Dec. 1896, vol. xxxvii pp. 805–6).

*Cantata: Caractacus*
Leeds Festival: 5 October 1898

*DTel*: 'Leeds Musical Festival: The New Works' (5 Oct. 1898) and 'Leeds Musical Festival' (6 Oct. 1898)
*MP*: 'Leeds Musical Festival' (6 Oct. 1898)
*T*: 'Leeds Musical Festival' (6 Oct. 1898)
*Ath*: 'The Leeds Festival' (8 Oct. 1898, No. 3702 p. 496)
*MT*: 'The Leeds Musical Festival' (1 Nov. 1898, vol. xxxix pp. 730–2).

*Variations on an Original Theme, 'Enigma'*
St James's Hall: 19 June 1899

*DTel*: 'Richter Concerts' (20 Jun. 1899)
*MP*: 'Concerts: New Works at the Richter Concert' (20 Jun. 1899)
*T*: 'Richter Concerts' (20 Jun. 1899)
*Ath*: 'St James's Hall – Richter Concert' (24 Jun. 1899, No. 3739 p. 793)
*MT*: 'Richter Concerts' (1 Jul. 1899, vol. xl pp. 464–71).

*Song-Cycle: Sea Pictures*
Norwich Festival: 5 October 1899

*DTel*: 'Norwich Festival' (6 Oct. 1899)
*MP*: 'Norwich Musical Festival' (6 Oct. 1899)
*T*: 'Norwich Musical Festival' (6 Oct. 1899)
*Ath*: 'Musical Gossip' (14 Oct. 1899, No. 3755 pp. 530–1)
*MT*: 'Norwich Musical Festival' (1 Nov. 1899, vol. xl pp. 747–8).

*Oratorio: The Dream of Gerontius*
Birmingham Festival: 3 October 1900

*DTel*: 'Birmingham Festival' (4 Oct. 1900)
*MP*: 'Birmingham Musical Festival' (4 Oct. 1900)
*T*: 'Birmingham Musical Festival' (4 Oct. 1900)
*Ath*: 'The Birmingham Festival' (6 Oct. 1900, No. 3806 pp. 449–50)
*MT*: 'The Birmingham Musical Festival' (1 Nov. 1900, vol. xli pp. 730–4).

*Concert Overture: Cockaigne (In London Town)*
Philharmonic Society (Queen's Hall): 20 June 1901

*DTel*: 'Philharmonic Society' (21 Jun. 1901)
*MP*: [No review]
*T*: 'Philharmonic Society' (21 Jun. 1901)
*Ath*: 'Queen's Hall – Philharmonic Concert' (29 Jun. 1901, No. 3844 p. 830)
*MT*: 'The Philharmonic Society' (1 Jul. 1901, vol. xlii pp. 464–72).

*Coronation Ode*
Sheffield Festival: 2 October 1902

*DTel*: [No review]
*MP*: 'Sheffield Musical Festival' (3 Oct. 1902)
*T*: 'The Sheffield Musical Festival' (3 Oct. 1902)
*Ath*: 'The Sheffield Triennial Musical Festival' (11 Oct. 1902, No. 3911 pp. 493–4)
*MT*: 'The Sheffield Musical Festival' (1 Nov. 1902, vol. xliii pp. 729–31).

*Oratorio: The Apostles*
Birmingham Festival: 14 October 1903

*DTel*: 'Birmingham Festival' (15 Oct. 1903)
*MP*: 'Birmingham Musical Festival: Dr Elgar's The Apostles' (15 Oct. 1903)
*T*: 'Birmingham Musical Festival' (15 Oct. 1903)
*Ath*: 'The Birmingham Musical Festival' (17 Oct. 1903, No. 3964 pp. 522–3)
*MT*: 'The Birmingham Musical Festival' (1 Nov. 1903, vol. xliv pp. 725–8).

*Concert Overture: In the South*
Elgar Festival, Royal Opera House Covent Garden: 16 March 1904

*DTel*: 'Elgar Festival: The Queen Present' (17 Mar. 1904)
*MP*: 'The Elgar Festival: Closing Performance' (17 Mar. 1904)
*T*: 'The Elgar Festival' (17 Mar. 1904)
*Ath*: 'The Elgar Festival' (19 Mar. 1904, No. 3986 pp. 378–9)
*MT*: 'The Elgar Festival' (1 Apr. 1904, vol. xlv pp. 241–3).

*Oratorio: The Kingdom*
Birmingham Festival: 3 October 1906

*DTel*: 'Birmingham Festival: Elgar's The Kingdom' (4 Oct. 1906)
*MP*: 'Birmingham Musical Festival' (4 Oct. 1906)
*T*: 'Birmingham Musical Festival' (4 Oct. 1906)
*Ath*: 'The Birmingham Festival' (6 Oct. 1906, No. 4119 pp. 412–13)
*MT*: 'The Birmingham Musical Festival' (1 Nov. 1906, vol. xlvii pp. 757–9).

*Symphony No. 1 in A flat*
Free Trade Hall, Manchester: 3 December 1908

*DTel*: 'Sir Edward Elgar's New Symphony: Master Work in English Music' (4 Dec. 1908) and 'Elgar's Symphony' (5 Dec. 1908)
*MP*: 'Dr Elgar's New Symphony: Production in Manchester' (4 Dec. 1908)
*T*: [No review]
*Ath*: 'Sir Edward Elgar's Symphony in E flat' (5 Dec. 1908, No. 4232 p. 729)
*MT*: 'Sir Edward Elgar's Symphony' (1 Dec. 1908, vol. xlix pp. 778–780) and 'Elgar's Symphony' (1 Jan. 1909, vol. l pp. 24–5).

*Violin Concerto in B minor*
Philharmonic Society (Queen's Hall): 10 November 1910

*DTel*: 'Sir E. Elgar's Concerto: Triumhant Success' (11 Nov. 1910)
*MP*: 'Sir Edward Elgar's New Violin Concerto: Musical Masterpiece' (11 Nov. 1910)
*T*: 'Philharmonic Society: Sir E Elgar's New Work' (11 Nov. 1910)
*Ath*: 'Queen's Hall – Sir Edward Elgar's Violin Concerto' (19 Nov. 1910, No. 4334 p. 634)
*MT*: 'Elgar's Violin Concerto' (1 Oct. 1910, vol. li pp. 631–4) and 'The Philharmonic Society: Sir Edward Elgar's New Violin Concerto' (1 Dec. 1910, vol. li pp. 781–2).

*Symphony No. 2 in E flat*
Queen's Hall: 24 May 1911

*DTel*: 'London Musical Festival: Elgar's New Symphony' (25 May 1911)
*MP*: 'London Musical Festival' (25 May 1911)
*T*: 'Elgar's New Symphony' (25 May 1911)
*Ath*: 'The London Musical Festival' (27 May 1911, No. 4361 pp. 609–10)
*MT*: 'Elgar's Second Symphony' (1 May 1911, vol. lii pp. 295–300).

555

*Ode: The Music Makers*
Birmingham Festival: 1 October 1912

*DTel*: 'Birmingham Festival: Elgar's New Ode' (3 Oct. 1912)
*MP*: 'Birmingham Festival' (2 Oct. 1912)
*T*: 'Birmingham Musical Festival: Sir Edward Elgar's New Cantata' (2 Oct. 1912) and 'Birmingham Musical Festival: Four New Works' (3 Oct. 1912)
*Ath*: 'The Birmingham Festival' (5 Oct. 1912, No. 4432 p. 386)
*MT*: 'The Birmingham Musical Festival' (1 Nov. 1912, vol. liii pp. 722–7).

*Symphonic Study: Falstaff*
Leeds Festival: 2 October 1913

*DTel*: 'Leeds Festival: Falstaff of Elgar' (4 Oct. 1913)
*MP*: 'Leeds Musical Festival' (3 Oct. 1913)
*T*: 'Leeds Musical Festival: Sir Edward Elgar's New Work Falstaff (3 Oct. 1913)
*Ath*: 'Musical Gossip' (4 Oct. 1913, No. 4484 p. 354)
*MT*: 'Falstaff by Edward Elgar' (1 Sept. 1913, vol. liv pp. 575–9) and 'Leeds Triennial Festival' (1 Nov. 1913, vol. liv pp. 735–45).

**German, Edward (1862–1936)**

*Symphony No. 2 in A minor, 'Norwich'*
Norwich Festival: 4 October 1893

*DTel*: 'Norwich Musical Festival' (5 Oct. 1893)
*T*: 'Norwich Musical Festival' (5 Oct. 1893)
*Ath*: 'The Norwich Festival' (7 Oct. 1893, No. 3441 p. 497)
*MT*: 'Norwich Festival' (1 Nov. 1893, vol. xxxiv pp. 656–8).

**Harty, Hamilton (1879–1941)**

*Tone Poem: With the Wild Geese*
Cardiff Festival: 23 September 1910

*DTel*: 'Cardiff Festival: Notable New Work' (26 Sept. 1910)
*T*: 'Music: Cardiff Festival' (24 Sept. 1910)
*Ath*: 'Cardiff Triennial Festival' (1 Oct. 1910, No. 4327 p. 398)
*MT*: 'The Cardiff Festival' (1 Nov. 1910, vol. li p. 719).

## Holbrooke, Josef (1878–1958)

*Symphonic Poem: The Raven*
Crystal Palace: 3 March 1900

*DTel*: 'Crystal Palace Concerts' (5 Mar. 1900)
*T*: [No review]
*Ath*: 'Crystal Palace Concerts' (17 Mar. 1900, No. 3777 p. 344)
*MT*: 'Crystal Palace Concerts' (1 Apr. 1900, vol. xli pp. 256–7).

*Symphonic Poem: The Bells*
Birmingham Festival: 4 October 1906

*DTel*: 'Birmingham Festival' (5 Oct. 1906)
*T*: 'Birmingham Musical Festival' (5 Oct. 1906)
*Ath*: 'The Birmingham Festival' (6 Oct. 1906, No. 4119 pp. 412–13)
*MT*: 'The Birmingham Musical Festival' (1 Nov. 1906, vol. xlvii pp. 757–9).

*Opera: Pierrot and Pierrette*
His Majesty's Theatre: 11 November 1909

*DTel*: 'Afternoon Theatre: Pierrot and Pierrette' (12 Nov. 1909)
*T*: 'The Afternoon Theatre' (12 Nov. 1909)
*Ath*: [No review]
*MT*: 'Mr Holbrooke's Opera' (1 Dec. 1909, vol. l p. 795).

## Holst, Gustav (1874–1934)

*The Mystic Trumpeter*
Queen's Hall: 29 June 1905

*DTel*: [No review]
*T*: 'Concerts' (1 Jul. 1905)
*Ath*: 'Musical Gossip' (8 Jul. 1905, No. 4954 p. 59)
*MT*: [No review].

*Suite: Beni Mora*
Queen's Hall: 1 May 1912

*DTel*: 'English Music at the Queen's Hall' (2 May 1912)
*T*: 'Mr Balfour Gardiner's Concert' (2 May 1912)
*Ath*: 'Musical Gossip' (11 May 1912, No. 4411 p. 543)
*MT*: 'Mr Balfour Gardiner Concerts' (1 Jun. 1912, vol. liii p. 390).

*Suite: 'Phantastes'*
Queen's Hall: 23 July 1912

*DTel*: 'Patron's Fund Concert' (24 Jul. 1912)
*T*: [No review]
*Ath*: 'Musical Gossip' (27 Jul. 1912, No. 4422 p. 100)
*MT*: 'The Patron's Fund Concert' (1 Aug. 1912, vol. liii p. 532).

*The Cloud Messenger*
Queen's Hall: 4 March 1913

*DTel*: 'Queen's Hall' (5 Mar. 1913)
*T*: 'Mr Balfour Gardiner's Concert' (5 Mar. 1913)
*Ath*: 'Musical Gossip' (8 Mar. 1913, No. 4454 p. 292)
*MT*: 'The Balfour Gardiner Concerts (Queen's Hall)' (1 Apr. 1913, vol. liv p. 255).


**Horsley, Charles E. (1822–76)**

*Oratorio: David*
Liverpool Philharmonic Society: 11 November 1850

*T*: [No review]
*Ath*: 'Liverpool Philharmonic Society' (16 Nov. 1850, No. 1203 pp. 1194–5)
*MT*: [No review].

**Leslie, Henry D. (1822–96)**

*Oratorio: Immanuel*
St Martin's Hall, London: 2 March 1854

*T*: 'Mr Leslie's "Immanuel"' (6 Mar. 1854)
*Ath*: 'St Martin's Hall' (4 Mar. 1854, No. 1375 p. 285)
*MT*: 'Brief Chronicle of the Last Fortnight' (15 Mar. 1854, vol. v p. 403).

*Cantata: Judith*
Birmingham Festival: 3 September 1858

*DTel*: 'The Birmingham Triennial Musical Festival' (4 Sept. 1858)
*T*: 'The Birmingham Musical Festival' (4 Sept. 1858)
*Ath*: 'Birmingham Festival' (4 Sept. 1858, No. 1610 pp. 305–6)
*MT*: 'Birmingham Musical Festival' (1 Oct. 1858, vol. viii pp. 318–23).

**MacFarren, George A. (1813–87)**

*Violin Concerto in G minor*
Philharmonic Society: 12 May 1873

*DTel*: [No review]
*T*: [No review]
*Ath*: 'Concerts' (17 May 1873, No. 2377 p. 640)
*MT*: 'Philharmonic Society' (1 Jun. 1873, vol. xvi p. 107).

*Oratorio: The Resurrection*
Birmingham Festival: 30 August 1876

*DTel*: 'Birmingham Musical Festival' (1 Sept. 1876)
*T*: 'Birmingham Musical Festival' (31 Aug. 1876)
*Ath*: 'Birmingham Musical Festival' (2 Sept. 1876, No. 2549 pp. 313–14)
*MT*: 'The Birmingham and Hereford Musical Festivals' (1 Oct. 1876, vol. xvii pp. 615–17).

*Oratorio: King David*
Leeds Festival: 12 October 1883

*DTel*: 'Leeds Musical Festival' (13 Oct. 1883)
*T*: 'The Leeds Musical Festival' (13 Oct. 1883)
*Ath*: 'Leeds Musical Festival' (20 Oct. 1883, No. 2921 pp. 503–5)
*MT*: 'Leeds Musical Festival' (1 Nov. 1883, vol. xxiv pp. 602–6).


**Mackenzie, Alexander C. (1847–1935)**

*Cantata: The Bride*
Worcester Festival: 6 September 1881

*DTel*: 'Worcester Musical Festival' (8 Sept. 1881)
*T*: 'The Worcester Musical Festival' (10 Sept. 1881)
*Ath*: 'Worcester: Festival of the Three Choirs' (10 Sept. 1881, No. 2811
    pp. 346–7)
*MT*: 'The Worcester Musical Festival' (1 Oct. 1881, vol. xxii pp. 509–
    12)

*Opera: Columba*
Drury Lane Theatre: 9 April 1883

*DTel*: 'Drury-Lane Theatre' (11 Apr. 1883)
*T*: 'Columba' (11 Apr. 1883)
*Ath*: 'Carl Rosa Opera Season' (31 Mar. 1883, No. 2892 pp. 417–18)
    and 'Drury Lane Theatre' (14 Apr. 1883, No. 2894 pp. 484–6)
*MT*: 'Drury Lane Theatre' (1 May 1883, vol. xxiv pp. 261–3).

*Oratorio: The Rose of Sharon*
Norwich Festival: 16 October 1884

*DTel*: 'Norwich Musical Festival' (17 Oct. 1884)
*T*: 'Norwich Musical Festival' (17 Oct. 1884)
*Ath*: 'Norwich Musical Festival' (25 Oct. 1884, No. 2974 pp. 535–6)
*MT*: 'Norwich Musical Festival' (1 Nov. 1884, vol. xxv pp. 633–5).

*Violin Concerto in E major*
Birmingham Festival: 26 August 1885

*DTel*: 'Birmingham Musical Festival' (28 Aug. 1885)
*T*: 'Birmingham Musical Festival' (27 Aug. 1885 and 28 Aug. 1885)
*Ath*: 'Birmingham Musical Festival' (29 Aug. 1885, No. 3018 pp. 280–81)
*MT*: 'The Birmingham Musical Festival' (1 Sept. 1885, vol. xxvi pp. 530–46).

*Opera: The Troubadour*
Carl Rosa Co., Drury Lane: 8 June 1886

*DTel*: 'The Troubadour' (10 Jun. 1886)
*T*: 'The Troubadour' (9 Jun. 1886)
*Ath*: 'Drury Lane: The Troubadour' (12 Jun. 1886, No. 3059 p. 789)
*MT*: 'The Carl Rosa Opera Season' (1 Jul. 1886, vol. xxvii pp. 397–401).

*Piano Concerto in G major, 'Scottish'*
Philharmonic Society: 24 March 1897

*DTel*: 'Philharmonic Concerts' (25 Mar. 1897)
*T*: 'Philharmonic Society' (25 Mar. 1897)
*Ath*: 'Queen's Hall: Philharmonic Concerts' (27 Mar. 1897, No. 3622 p. 424)
*MT*: 'Philharmonic Society' (1 Apr. 1897, vol. xxxviii pp. 239–40).

*Suite for Orchestra: London Day by Day*
Norwich Festival: 22 October 1902

*DTel*: 'Norwich Musical Festival' (24 Oct. 1902)
*T*: 'Norwich Musical Festival' (24 Oct. 1902)
*Ath*: 'Norwich and Norfolk Triennial Musical Festival' (25 Oct. 1902, No. 3913 pp. 558–9)
*MT*: 'The Norwich Musical Festival' (1 Nov. 1902, vol. xliii pp. 747–8).

**Parry, C. H. Hubert (1848–1918)**

*Overture: Guillem de Cabestanh*
Crystal Palace: 15 March 1879

*DTel*: [No review]
*MP*: [No review]
*T*: 'Crystal Palace' (18 Mar. 1879)
*Ath*: 'Crystal Palace Concerts' (22 Mar. 1879, No. 2682 p. 387)
*MT*: 'Crystal Palace' (1 Apr. 1879, vol. xx p. 206)
*MW*: 'Crystal Palace' (22 Mar. 1879, vol. lvii p. 189). [*The Graphic*]

*Piano Concerto in F sharp*
Crystal Palace: 3 April 1880

*DTel*: [No review]
*MP*: [No review]
*T*: 'Two English Composers' (6 Apr. 1880)
*Ath*: 'Crystal Palace – Saturday Concerts' (10 Apr. 1880, No. 2737 p. 479)
*MT*: [No review]
*MW*: 'F Sharp or F Natural' (10 Apr. 1880, vol. lviii p. 231).

*Scenes from Shelley's 'Prometheus Unbound'*
Gloucester Festival: 7 September 1880

*DTel*: 'Festival of the Three Choirs' (8 Sept. 1880)
*MP*: 'Gloucester Musical Festival' (9 Sept. 1880)
*T*: 'The Gloucester Musical Festival' (8 Sept. 1880)
*Ath*: 'The Gloucester Musical Festival' (11 Sept. 1880, No. 2759 pp. 346–7).
*MT*: 'The Gloucester Musical Festival' (1 Oct. 1880, vol. xxi pp. 498–507)
*MW*: 'Festival of the Three Choirs' (11 Sept. 1880, vol. lviii pp. 575–8).

*Symphony No. 1 in G*
Birmingham Festival: 31 August 1882

*DTel*: 'Birmingham Musical Festival' (1 and 4 Sept. 1882)
*MP*: 'Birmingham Triennial Festival' (2 Sept. 1882)
*T*: 'Birmingham Musical Festival' (1 and 2 Sept. 1882)
*Ath*: 'The Birmingham Musical Festival' (9 Sept. 1882, No. 2863 pp. 346–8)
*MT*: 'Birmingham Musical Festival' (1 Sept. 1882, vol. xxiii p. 484)
*MW*: 'Birmingham Musical Festival' (9 Sept. 1882, vol. lx pp. 555–7 and pp. 561–3).

*Symphony No. 2 in F 'Cambridge'*
Cambridge University Musical Society: 12 June 1883

*DTel*: [No review]
*MP*: [No review]
*T*: [No review]
*Ath*: 'Cambridge University Musical Society' (23 Jun. 1883, No. 2904 pp. 806–7)
*MT*: 'Cambridge University Musical Society' (1 Jul. 1883, vol. xxiv p. 383)
*MW*: [No review].

*Ode: 'At a Solemn Music'*
The Bach Choir: 17 May 1887

*DT*: [No review]
*MP*: [No review]
*T*: 'Berlioz's Te Deum' (19 May 1887)
*Ath*: 'St James's Hall – The Bach Choir' (21 May 1887, No. 3108 pp. 680–1)
*MT*: 'The Bach Choir' (1 Jun. 1887, vol. xxviii pp. 343–4)
*MW*: [No review].

*Symphony No. 2 in F 'Cambridge' (Revised)*
Richter Concerts: 6 June 1887

*DTel*: 'Richter Concerts' (8 Jun. 1887)
*MP*: 'Richter Concerts' (8 Jun. 1887)
*T*: 'Recent Concerts' (10 Jun. 1887)
*Ath*: 'Richter Concerts' (11 Jun. 1887, No. 3111 pp. 776–7)
*MT*: 'Richter Concerts' (1 Jul. 1887, vol. xxviii p. 409)
*MW*: 'Richter Concerts' (11 Jun. 1887, vol. lxv p. 457).

*Oratorio: Judith*
Birmingham Festival: 29 August 1888

*DTel*: 'Birmingham Musical Festival' (30 Aug. 1888)
*MP*: 'Birmingham Musical Festival' (30 Aug. 1888)
*T*: 'Birmingham Musical Festival' (30 Aug. 1888)
*Ath*: 'Birmingham Musical Festival' (1 Cep. 1888, No. 3175 pp. 298–9)
*MT*: 'New Works at Birmingham' (1 Sept. 1888, vol. xxix pp. 521–4)
   and 'Birmingham Musical Festival' (Oct. 1888, vol. xxix pp. 600–3)
*MW*: 'Birmingham Musical Festival' (1 Sept. 1888, vol. lxvii pp. 689–
   92).

*Symphony No. 3, 'English'*
Philharmonic Society: 23 May 1889

*DTel*: 'Philharmonic Society' (25 May 1889)
*MP*: 'Philharmonic Society' (27 May 1889)
*T*: 'Philharmonic Society' (27 May 1889)
*Ath*: 'Philharmonic Concerts' (1 Jun. 1889, No. 3214 pp. 703–4)
*MT*: 'Philharmonic Society' (1 Jun. 1889, vol. xxx p. 342)
*MW*: 'Philharmonic Society' (1 Jun. 1889, vol. lxix p. 351).

*Symphony No. 4 in E minor*
Richter Concerts: 1 July 1889

*DTel*: 'Concerts' (6 Jul. 1889)
*MP*: 'Richter Concert' (3 Jul. 1889)
*T*: 'Recent Concerts' (3 Jul. 1889)
*Ath*: 'St James's Hall – The Richter Concerts' (6 Jul. 1889, No. 3219 p.
   41)
*MT*: 'Richter Concerts' (1 Aug. 1889, vol. xxx pp. 473–4)
*MW*: 'The Richter Concerts' (6 Jul. 1889, vol. lxix p. 436).

*Ode on St Cecilia's Day*
Leeds Festival: 11 October 1889

*DTel*: 'Leeds Musical Festival' (12 Oct. 1889)
*MP*: 'The Leeds Musical Festival' (12 Oct. 1889)
*T*: 'Leeds Musical Festival' (12 Oct. 1889)
*Ath*: 'The Leeds Festival' (19 Oct. 1889, No. 3234 pp. 529–31)
*MT*: 'Leeds Musical Festival' (1 Nov. 1889, vol. xxx pp. 658–61)
*MW*: 'Leeds Musical Festival' (19 Oct. 1889, vol. lxix pp. 726–8).

*Oratorio: Job*
Gloucester Festival: 8 September 1892

*DTel*: 'Festival of the Three Choirs' (9 Sept. 1892)
*MP*: 'The Gloucester Musical Festival' (9 Sept. 1892)
*T*: 'Gloucester Musical Festival' (9 Sept. 1892)
*Ath*: 'The Gloucester Festival' (17 Sept. 1892, No. 3386 pp. 395–6)
*MT*: 'Gloucester Musical Festival' (1 Oct. 1892, vol. xxxiii pp. 598–600).

*Overture: To an Unwritten Tragedy*
Worcester Festival: 13 September 1893

*DTel*: 'Festival of the Three Choirs' (14 Sept. 1893)
*MP*: 'Festival of the Three Choirs' (14 Sept. 1893)
*T*: 'Worcester Musical Festival' (14 Sept. 1893)
*Ath*: 'The Worcester Festival' (23 Sept. 1893, No. 3439 pp. 425–6)
*MT*: 'Worcester Musical Festival' (1 Oct. 1893, vol. xxxiv pp. 598–9).

*Oratorio: King Saul*
Birmingham Festival: 3 October 1894

*DTel*: 'Birmingham Festival' (4 Oct. 1894)
*MP*: 'Birmingham Musical Festival' (4 Oct. 1894)
*T*: 'Birmingham Musical Festival' (4 Oct. 1894)
*Ath*: 'The Birmingham Festival' (6 Oct. 1894, No. 3493 pp. 462–3) and 'Birmingham – The Triennial Musical Festival' (13 Oct. 1894, No. 3494 pp. 499–500)
*MT*: 'Birmingham Festival' (1 Nov. 1894, vol. xxxv pp. 743–5).

*Invocation to Music (An Ode in Honour of Purcell)*
Leeds Festival: 2 October 1895

*DTel*: 'Leeds Musical Festival: Visit of the Prince of Wales' (3 Oct. 1895)
*MP*: 'Leeds Musical Festival' (3 Oct. 1895)
*T*: 'The Leeds Festival' (3 Oct. 1895)
*Ath*: 'The Leeds Festival' (12 Oct. 1895, No. 3546 pp. 500–1)
*MT*: 'Leeds Musical Festival' (1 Nov. 1895, vol. xxxvi pp. 742–3).

*Magnificat*
Hereford Festival: 15 September 1897

*DTel*: 'Three Choirs Festival: A New Magnificat' (16 Sept. 1897)
*MP*: 'Festival of the Three Choirs' (16 Sept. 1897)
*T*: 'Hereford Musical Festival' (16 Sept. 1897)
*Ath*: 'The Festival of the Three Choirs' (25 Sept. 1897, No. 3648 pp. 426–7)
*MT*: 'Festival of the Three Choirs' (1 Oct. 1897, vol. xxxviii pp. 677–8).

*Song of Darkness and Light*
Gloucester Festival: 15 September 1898

*DTel*: 'Three Choirs Festival' (16 Sept. 1898)
*MP*: 'Festival of the Three Choirs' (16 Sept. 1898)
*T*: 'Gloucester Musical Festival' (16 Sept. 1898)
*Ath*: 'Festival of the Three Choirs' (24 Sept. 1898, No. 3700 pp. 425–6)
*MT*: 'Gloucester Musical Festival' (1 Oct. 1898, vol. xxxix pp. 666–8).

*The Soul's Ransom (A Psalm for the Poor)*
Hereford Festival: 12 September 1906

*DTel*: 'Hereford Festival' (13 Sept. 1906)
*MP*: 'Three Choirs Festival: Sir Hubert Parry's New Work' (13 Sept. 1906)
*T*: 'Hereford Musical Festival' (13 Sept. 1906)
*Ath*: 'Hereford Musical Festival' (15 Sept. 1906, No. 4116 pp. 310–11)
*MT*: 'Hereford Musical Festival' (1 Oct. 1906, vol. xlvii pp. 688–9).

*Cantata: Beyond These Voices there is Peace*
Worcester Festival: 9 September 1908

*DTel*: 'Worcester Festival' (10 Sept. 1908)
*MP*: 'Three Choirs Festival: Parry's New Work and Elgar's The Kingdom' (10 Sept. 1908)
*T*: 'Worcester Musical Festival' (10 Sept. 1908)
*Ath*: 'The Worcester Festival' (12 Sept. 1908, No. 4220 p. 310)
*MT*: 'Worcester Musical Festival' (1 Oct. 1908, vol. xlix pp. 645–7).

*Symphony No. 5 in B minor*
Royal Philharmonic Society: 5 December 1912

*DTel*: 'Royal Philharmonic Society: A Fine Symphony' (6 Dec. 1912)
*MP*: 'Royal Philharmonic Society' (6 Dec. 1912)
*T*: 'Royal Philharmonic Society' (6 Dec. 1912)
*Ath*: 'Philharmonic Society' (14 Dec. 1912, No. 4442 p. 738)
*MT*: 'The Royal Philharmonic Society' (1 Jan. 1913, vol. liv p. 38).

*From Death to Life*
Brighton Festival: 12 November 1914

*DTel*: 'Brighton Musical Festival' (13 Nov. 1914)
*MP*: 'Brighton Musical Festival' (13 Nov. 1914)
*T*: 'Brighton Musical Festival: British Works conducted by their Composers' (13 Nov. 1914)
*Ath*: 'Brighton Musical Festival' (21 Nov. 1914, No. 4543 p. 539)
*MT*: 'Brighton Musical Festival' (1 Dec. 1914, vol. lv p. 701).


**Pierson, Hugo Henry (1815–73)**

*Oratorio: Jerusalem*
Norwich Festival: 23 September 1852

*T*: 'Norwich Musical Festival' (24 and 25 Sept. 1852)
*Ath*: 'The Norwich Festival' (25 Sept. 1852, No. 1300 pp. 1038–9).
*MT*: 'Norwich Musical Festival' (1 Sept. 1852, vol. v pp. 51–9) and (1 Jun. 1853, vol. v pp. 198–203).

*Oratorio: Hezekiah [Extracts]*
Norwich Festival: 1 September 1869

*DTel*: 'Norwich Musical Festival' (2 Sept. 1869)
*T*: 'Norwich Musical Festival' (2 Sept. 1869)
*Ath*: 'Norwich Musical Festival' (4 Sept. 1869, No. 2184 pp. 314–15)
*MT*: 'The Norwich and Worcester Musical Festivals' (1 Oct. 1869, vol. xiv pp. 231–7).

**Prout, Ebenezer (1835–1909)**

*Cantata: Hereward*
St James's Hall: 4 June 1879

*DTel*: 'Hackney Choral Association' (6 Jun. 1879)
*T*: 'Mr Prout's "Hereward"' (5 Jun. 1879)
*Ath*: 'Concerts' (14 Jun. 1879, No. 2694 pp. 769–70)
*MT*: 'Borough of Hackney Choral Association' (1 Jul. 1879, vol. xx pp.
366–8).

*Symphony No. 3 in F major*
Birmingham Festival: 26 August 1885

*DTel*: 'Birmingham Musical Festival' (27 Aug. 1885)
*T*: 'Birmingham Musical Festival' (27 Aug. 1885)
*Ath*: 'Birmingham Musical Festival' (5 Sept. 1885, No. 3019 pp. 311–
12)
*MT*: 'The Birmingham Musical Festival' (1 Sept. 1885, vol. xxvi pp.
530–46).

**Smyth, Ethel M. (1858–1944)**

*Mass in D*
Albert Hall: 18 January 1893

*DTel*: 'Royal Choral Association' (19 Jan. 1893)
*T*: 'Royal Choral Society' (19 Jan. 1893)
*Ath*: 'Albert Hall – Royal Choral Society: Miss E. M. Smyth's Solemn
Mass' (21 Jan. 1893, No. 3404 p. 94)
*MT*: 'Royal Choral Society' (1 Feb. 1893, vol. xxxiv p. 86).

*Opera: Der Wald*
Royal Opera House, Covent Garden: 18 July 1902

*DTel*: [No review]
*T*: 'The Royal Opera' (19 Jul. 1902)
*Ath*: 'Music: The Week' (26 Jul. 1902, No. 3900 p. 134)
*MT*: 'The Royal Opera' (1 Aug. 1902, vol. xliii p. 539).

*Opera: The Wreckers*
His Majesty's Theatre: 22 June 1906

*DTel*: 'The Wreckers' (22 Jun. 1909)
*T*: 'Music' (23 Jun. 1909)
*Ath*: 'Music: This Week' (26 Jun. 1909, No. 4261 pp. 766–7)
*MT*: 'The Wreckers' (1 Jul. 1909, vol. l p. 467).


**Somervell, Arthur (1863–1937)**

*Orchestral Ballad: Helen of Kirkonnell*
Philharmonic Society: 23 March 1893

*DTel*: 'Philharmonic Society' (24 Mar. 1893)
*T*: 'Philharmonic Society' (25 Mar. 1893)
*Ath*: 'St James's Hall: Philharmonic Concerts' (1 Apr. 1893, No. 3414
   pp. 417–18)
*MT*: 'Philharmonic Society' (1 Apr. 1893, vol. xxxiv p. 215).

*Ode to the Sea*
Birmingham Festival: 7 October 1897

*DTel*: 'Birmingham Festival: An "Ode to the Sea"' (8 Oct. 1897)
*T*: 'The Birmingham Musical Festival' (8 Oct. 1897)
*Ath*: 'Birmingham Festival' (16 Oct. 1897, No. 3651 p. 532)
*MT*: 'Birmingham Musical Festival' (1 Nov. 1897, vol. xxxviii pp. 745–
   7)

*Symphony in D minor, 'Thalassa'*
Queen's Hall: 17 February 1913

*DTel*: 'London Symphony Orchestra: Dr Somervell's New Works' (18
   Feb. 1913)
*T*: 'Dr Somervell's Symphony' (18 Sept. 1913)
*Ath*: 'Musical Gossip' (22 Feb. 1913, No. 4452 p. 227)
*MT*: 'London Symphony Orchestra' (1 Mar. 1913, vol. liv pp. 175–6).

**Stanford, C. V. (1852–1924)**

*Symphony No. 1 in B flat major*
Crystal Palace: 8 March 1879

*DTel*: [No review]
*T*: [No review]
*Ath*: 'Crystal Palace Concerts' (15 Mar. 1879, No. 2681 p. 354)
*MT*: 'Crystal Palace' (1 Apr. 1879, vol. xx p. 206).

*Opera: The Canterbury Pilgrims*
Carl Rosa Co., Drury Lane: 28 April 1884

*DTel*: 'Drury-Lane Theatre' (29 Apr. 1884)
*T*: 'The Canterbury Pilgrims' (29 Apr. 1884)
*Ath*: 'Music: The Week' (3 May 1884, No. 2949 pp. 575–7)
*MT*: 'Drury Lane Theatre' (1 Jun. 1884, vol. xxv pp. 333–4).

*Opera: Savonarola*
Covent Garden: 9 July 1884

*DTel*: 'Covent-Garden Theatre' (10 Jul. 1884)
*T*: 'Mr Stanford's Savonarola' (10 Jul. 1884) and 'Mr Stanford's
   Savonarola' (11 Jul. 1884)
*Ath*: 'Music: The Week' (12 Jul. 1884, No. 2959 p. 59)
*MT*: 'The German Opera Season' (1 Aug. 1884, vol. xxv pp. 456–7).

*Elegiac Ode*
Norwich Festival: 15 October 1884

*DTel*: 'Norwich Musical Festival' (16 Oct. 1884)
*T*: 'Norwich Musical Festival' (16 Oct. 1884)
*Ath*: 'Norwich Musical Festival' (18 Oct. 1884, No. 2973 pp. 504–5)
*MT*: 'Norwich Musical Festival' (1 Nov. 1884, vol. xxv pp. 633–5).

*Choral Ballad: The Revenge*
Leeds Festival: 14 October 1886

*DTel*: 'Leeds Musical Festival' (15 Oct. 1886)
*T*: 'Leeds Musical Festival' (15 Oct. 1886)
*Ath*: 'Leeds Musical Festival' (23 Oct. 1886, No. 3078 pp. 541–3)
*MT*: 'Leeds Musical Festival' (1 Nov. 1886, vol. xxvii pp. 653–7).

*Symphony No. 3 in F minor, 'Irish'*
Richter Concerts: 27 June 1887

*DTel*: [No review]
*T*: [No review]
*Ath*: 'Music: This Week' (2 Jul. 1887, No. 3114 pp. 28–9).
*MT*: [No review]

*Symphony No. 4 in F major*
Crystal Palace: 23 February 1889

*DTel*: [No review]
*T*: 'Crystal Palace Concerts' (25 Feb. 1889)
*Ath*: 'Crystal Palace – Professor Stanford's Symphony No. 4 in F' (2 Mar. 1889, No. 3201 p. 288)
*MT*: 'Crystal Palace Concerts' (1 Mar. 1889, vol. xxx pp. 151–2).

*Oratorio: Eden*
Birmingham Festival: 7 October 1891

*DTel*: 'Birmingham Festival' (8 Oct. 1891) and 'Birmingham Musical Festival' (9 Oct. 1891)
*T*: 'Birmingham Musical Festival' (8 Oct. 1891) and 'Birmingham Musical Festival' (9 Oct. 1891)
*Ath*: 'The Birmingham Festival' (17 Oct. 1891, No. 3338 pp. 523–5)
*MT*: 'Birmingham Musical Festival' (1 Nov. 1891, vol. xxxii pp. 660–1).

*Opera: The Veiled Prophet of Khorassan*
Covent Garden: 26 July 1893

*DTel*: 'Royal Opera, Covent Garden' (27 Jul. 1893)
*T*: 'The Opera' (27 Jul. 1893)
*Ath*: 'Covent Garden Opera' (5 Aug. 1893, No. 3432 p. 201)
*MT*: 'Royal Opera, Covent Garden' (1 Aug. 1893, vol. xxxiv p. 439).

*Opera: Shamus O'Brien*
Paris, Opera Comique: 2 March 1896

*DTel*: '"Shamus O'Brien"' (3 Mar. 1896)
*T*: 'Opera Comique Theatre' (3 Mar. 1893)
*Ath*: 'Production of Professor Villiers Stanford's New Irish Opera – Shamus O'Brien' (7 Mar. 1896, No. 3567 p. 320)
*MT*: 'Shamus O'Brien' (1 Apr. 1896, vol. xxxvii p. 240).

*Requiem*
Birmingham Festival: 6 October 1897

*DTel*: 'Birmingham Festival: Dr Stanford's Requiem' (7 Oct. 1897)
*T*: 'The Birmingham Musical Festival' (7 Oct. 1897)
*Ath*: 'Birmingham Festival' (9 Oct. 1897, No. 3650 p. 496)
*MT*: 'Birmingham Musical Festival' (1 Nov. 1897, vol. xxxviii pp. 745–
   7).

*Symphony No. 6 in E flat major*
Queen's Hall: 18 January 1906

*DTel*: 'London Symphony Orchestra' (19 Jan. 1906)
*T*: 'Concerts' (19 Jan. 1906)
*Ath*: 'Queen's Hall: London Symphony Concert' (27 Jan. 1906, No.
   4083 p. 114)
*MT*: 'London Symphony Orchestra: Sir Charles Stanford's New Sym-
   phony) (1 Feb. 1906, vol. xlvii p. 121).

*Five Songs of the Fleet*
Leeds Festival: 13 October 1910

*DTel*: 'Leeds Festival: Songs of the Fleet' (15 Oct. 1910)
*T*: 'Leeds Musical Festival' (14 Oct. 1910)
*Ath*: 'The Leeds Festival' (22 Oct. 1910, No. 4330 p. 498)
*MT*: 'The Leeds Festival' (1 Nov. 1910, vol. li pp. 719–29).


**Sullivan, Arthur (1842–1900)**

*The Tempest Music*
Crystal Palace: 5 April 1862

*DTel*: 'Crystal Palace' (7 Apr. 1862)
*MP*: 'Crystal Palace Concerts' (7 Apr. 1862)
*T*: 'Crystal Palace Concerts' (7 Apr. 1862)
*Ath*: 'Crystal Palace: The TeMPest Music by Mr A. Sullivan' (12 Apr.
   1862, No. 1798 pp. 504–5)
*MT*: [No review]
*MW*: 'Crystal Palace Concerts' (12 Apr. 1862, vol. xl p. 231).

*Cantata: Kenilworth*
Birmingham Festival: 8 September 1864

*DTel*: 'Birmingham Musical Festival' (10 Sept. 1864)
*MP*: 'Birmingham Musical Festival' (10 Sept. 1864)
*T*: 'Birmingham Musical Festival' (12 Sept. 1864)
*Ath*: 'Birmingham Festival' (17 Sept. 1864, No. 1925 pp. 378–9).
*MT*: 'The Musical Festivals' (1 Oct. 1864, vol. xi pp. 365–75)
*MW*: 'Birmingham Musical Festival' (24 Sept. 1864, vol. xlii pp. 609–
    10).

*Symphony in E major 'Irish'*
Crystal Palace: 10 March 1866

*DTel*: [No review]
*MP*: 'Crystal Palace Concerts' (12 Mar. 1866)
*T*: 'Concerts' (12 Mar. 1866)
*Ath*: 'Crystal Palace Concerts' (17 Mar. 1866, No. 2003 pp. 371–2).
*MT*: 'Crystal Palace' (1 Apr. 1866, vol. xii p. 263)
*MW*: 'A New Symphony' (17 Mar. 1866, vol. xliv p. 166).

*Overture 'In Memoriam'*
Norwich Festival: 30 October 1866

*DTel*: 'Norwich Musical Festival: The Royal Visit' (1 Nov. 1866)
*MP*: 'Norwich Musical Festival' (2 Nov. 1866)
*T*: 'Norwich Musical Festival' (1 Nov. 1866)
*Ath*: 'The Norwich Festival' (3 Nov. 1866, No. 2036 pp. 575–6).
*MT*: 'The Norwich Musical Festival' (1 Dec. 1866, vol. xii pp. 421–4)
*MW*: 'Norwich Musical Festival' (3 Nov. 1866, vol. xliv pp. 695–8).

*Cello Concerto in D*
Crystal Palace: 24 November 1866

*DTel*: 'Crystal Palace' (26 Nov. 1866)
*MP*: [No review]
*T*: [No review]
AT: 'Crystal Palace Concert' (1 Dec. 1866, No. 2040 p. 722)
*MT*: [No review]
*MW*: [No review].

*Operetta: Cox and Box*
Adelphi Theatre: 11 May 1867

*DTel*: 'Adelphi Theatre' (14 May 1867)
*MP*: 'Adelphi Theatre' (13 May 1867)
*T*: 'Adelphi Theatre' (13 May 1867)
*Ath*: 'Musical and Dramatic Gossip' (18 May 1867, No. 2064 p. 669)
*MT*: [No review]
*MW*: [No review].

*Oratorio: The Prodigal Son*
Worcester Festival: 8 September 1869

*DTel*: 'Worcester Musical Festival' (9 and 10 Sept. 1869)
*MP*: 'Worcester Festival' (9 Sept. 1869)
*T*: 'Worcester Musical Festival' (9 and 11 Sept. 1869)
*Ath*: 'Worcester Musical Festival' (18 Sept. 1869, No. 2186 p. 377).
*MT*: 'The Norwich and Worcester Musical Festivals' (1 Oct. 1869, vol.
   xiv pp. 231–7)
*MW*: 'Worcester Musical Festival' (11 Sept. 1869, vol. xlvii pp. 640–2).

*Operetta: Thespis*
Gaiety Theatre: 26 December 1871

*DTel*: 'Gaiety' (27 Dec. 1871)
*MP*: 'Gaiety' (27 Dec. 1871)
*T*: 'Christmas Entertainments – Gaiety' (27 Dec. 1871).
*Ath*: 'Gaiety Theatre' (30 Dec. 1871, No. 2305 p. 893)
*MT*: [No review]
*MW*: [No review].

*Oratorio: The Light of the World*
Birmingham Festival: 27 August 1873

*DTel*: 'Birmingham Musical Festival' (28 Aug. 1873)
*MP*: 'Birmingham Musical Festival' (28 Aug. 1873)
*T*: 'Birmingham Musical Festival' (28 Aug. 1873)
*Ath*: 'Birmingham Festival' (30 Aug. 1873, No. 2392 pp. 280–1).
*MT*: 'The Birmingham and Hereford Musical Festivals' (1 Oct. 1873,
   vol. xvi pp. 235–42)
*MW*: 'Birmingham Musical Festival' (30 Aug. 1873, vol. li pp. 582–4).

*Operetta: HMS 'Pinafore'*
Opera-Comique, London: 25 May 1878

*DTel*: [No review]
*MP*: [No review]
*T*: 'Opera-Comique' (27 May 1878)
*Ath*: 'Strand Opera Comique' (1 Jun. 1878, No. 2640 p. 709).
*MT*: 'Opera-Comique' (1 Jun. 1878, vol. xix p. 329)
*MW*: [No review].

*Operetta: The Pirates of Penzance*
Fifth Avenue Theatre, New York: 31 December 1879 and Opera-
    Comique, London: 3 April 1880

*DTel*: 'Opera-Comique' (5 Apr. 1880)
*MP*: 'Opera Comique' (5 Apr. 1880)
*T*: [No review]
*Ath*: 'Opera-Comique' (10 Apr. 1880, No. 2736 p. 479)
*MT*: 'Opera-Comique' (1 May 1880, vol. xxi pp. 230–1)
*MW*: 'The Pirates of Penzance' (10 Apr. 1880, vol. lviii pp. 223–4).

*Oratorio: The Martyr of Antioch*
Leeds Festival: 15 October 1880

*DTel*: 'Leeds Musical Festival' (16 Oct. 1880)
*MP*: 'Leeds Triennial Musical Festival' (16 Oct. 1880)
*T*: 'The Leeds Festival' (16 Oct. 1880)
*Ath*: 'Leeds Triennial Musical Festival' (23 Oct. 1880, No. 2765 pp.
    538–41)
*MT*: 'Leeds Musical Festival' (1 Nov. 1880, vol. xxi pp. 546–50)
*MW*: 'Mr Sullivan's Martyr of Antioch' (16 Oct. 1880, vol. lviii pp.
    662–3).

*Operetta: The Mikado*
Savoy Theatre, London: 14 March 1885

*DTel*: 'Savoy Theatre' (16 Mar. 1885)
*MP*: 'Savoy Theatre' (16 Mar. 1885)
*T*: 'A Japanese Opera' (16 Mar. 1885)
*Ath*: 'Savoy Theatre: The Mikado, a Japanese Opera in Two Acts'. (21
    Mar. 1885, No. 2995 pp. 384–5)
*MT*: [No review]
*MW*: 'Gilbert and Sullivan's New Opera' (21 Mar. 1885, vol. lxiii p. 185).

*Cantata: The Golden Legend*
Leeds Festival: 16 October 1886

*DTel*: 'Leeds Musical Festival' (18 Oct. 1886)
*MP*: 'The Leeds Musical Festival' (18 Oct. 1886)
*T*: 'Leeds Musical Festival' (18 Oct. 1886)
*Ath*: 'Leeds Musical Festival' (23 Oct. 1886, No. 3078 pp. 541–3)
*MT*: 'Leeds Musical Festival' (1 Nov. 1886, vol. xxvii pp. 653–7)
*MW*: 'Provincial Festivals' (23 Oct. 1886, vol. lxiv pp. 681–2).

*Operetta: The Gondoliers*
Savoy Theatre, London: 7 December 1889

*DTel*: 'The Gondoliers' (9 Dec. 1889)
*MP*: 'Savoy Theatre' (9 Dec. 1889)
*T*: 'Savoy Theatre' (9 Dec. 1889)
*Ath*: 'Savoy Theatre: The Gondoliers, a Comic Opera in Two Acts'. (14
    Dec. 1889, No. 3242 p. 829)
*MT*. [No review]
*MW*: 'The Gondoliers' (14 Dec. 1889, vol. lxix p. 892).

*Grand Opera: Ivanhoe*
Royal English Opera House, London: 31 January 1891

*DTel*: 'Royal English Opera' (2 Feb. 1891)
*MP*: 'Sullivan's New Opera – Ivanhoe' (2 Feb. 1891)
*T*: 'The Royal English Opera House' (2 Feb. 1891)
*Ath*: 'Royal English Opera House – Production of Sir Arthur Sullivan's
    Ivanhoe' (7 Feb. 1891, No. 3302 pp. 193–4) and (14 Feb. 1891, No.
    3303 p. 226)
*MT*: 'Ivanhoe' (1 Mar. 1891, vol. xxxii pp. 149–50).

**Thomas, A. Goring (1850–92)**

*Choral Ode: The Sun-Worshippers*
Norwich Festival 13 October 1881

*DTel*: 'Norwich Musical Festival' (17 Oct. 1881)
*T*: 'Drury Lane Theatre' (14 Oct. 1881)
*Ath*: 'Norwich Triennial Musical Festival' (22 Oct. 1881, No. 2817 pp.
    535–6)
*MT*: 'Norwich Musical Festival' (1 Nov. 1881, vol. xxii pp. 566–8).

*Opera: Esmeralda*
Drury Lane Theatre 26 March 1883

*DTel*: 'Drury Lane Theatre' (29 Mar. 1883)
*T*: 'Drury Lane Theatre' (27 Mar. 1883)
*Ath*: 'Carl Rosa Opera Season' (31 Mar. 1883, No. 2892 pp. 417–18)
*MT*: 'Drury Lane Theatre' (1 Apr. 1883, vol. xxiv pp. 191–2).

*Opera: Nadeshda*
Carl Rosa Co. : 16 April 1885

*DTel*: 'Drury Lane Theatre: Nadeshda' (17 Apr. 1885)
*T*: 'Nadeshda' (17 Apr. 1885)
*Ath*: 'Music: The Week' (25 Apr. 1885, No. 3000 pp. 543–4)
*MT*: 'Drury Lane Theatre' (1 May 1885, vol. xxvi pp. 263–4).

**Vaughan Williams, R. (1872–1958)**

*Toward the Unknown Region*
Leeds Festival: 10 October 1907

*DTel*: 'Leeds Musical Festival: Three New Works' (12 Oct. 1907)
*T*: 'Leeds Musical Festival' (12 Oct. 1907)
*Ath*: 'Leeds Musical Festival' (19 Oct. 1907, No. 4173 pp. 490–1)
*MT*: 'Leeds Musical Festival' (1 Nov. 1907, vol. xlviii pp. 737–8).

*Song-Cycle: On Wenlock Edge*
Aeolian Hall: 15 November 1909

*DTel*: [No review]
*T*: 'Music: Aeolian Hall' (16 Nov. 1909)
*Ath*: [No review]
*MT*: [No review].

*Fantasia on a Theme of Thomas Tallis*
Gloucester Festival: 6 September 1910

*DTel*: 'Gloucester Festival: Sir E. Elgar's Triumph' (8 Sept. 1910)
*T*: 'Gloucester Musical Festival' (7 Sept. 1910)
*Ath*: 'The Gloucester Musical Festival' (10 Sept. 1910, No. 4324 pp. 301–2)
*MT*: 'The Gloucester Festival' (1 Oct. 1910, vol. li p. 650).

*A Sea Symphony*
Leeds Festival: 12 October 1910

*DTel*: 'Leeds Festival' (14 Oct. 1910)
*T*: 'Leeds Musical Festival: A 'Sea Symphony'' (14 Oct. 1910)
*Ath*: 'The Leeds Festival' (15 Oct. 1910, No. 4329 pp. 464–5)
*MT*: 'The Leeds Festival' (1 Nov. 1910, vol. li pp. 719–29).

*Five Mystical Songs*
Worcester Festival: 14 September 1911

*DTel*: 'The Three Choirs' (15 Sept. 1911)
*T*: 'Worcester Musical Festival: The Evening Performance' (15 Sept. 1911)
*Ath*: [No review]
*MT*: 'Worcester Musical Festival' (1 Oct. 1911, vol. lii pp. 665–7).

*Fantasia on Christmas Carols*
Hereford Festival: 12 September 1912

*DTel*: 'Hereford Festival' (14 Sept. 1912)
*T*: 'Three Choirs Festival: More Christmas Music' (13 Sept. 1912)
*Ath*: 'Musical Gossip' (21 Sept. 1912, No. 4430 p. 319)
*MT*: 'Hereford Musical Festival' (1 Oct. 1912, vol. liii pp. 664–6).

*A London Symphony*
Queen's Hall: 27 March 1914

*DTel*: 'A London Symphony: Vaughan Williams' New Work' (30 Mar. 1914)
*T*: [No review]
*Ath*: [No review]
*MT*: 'Dr Vaughan Williams's New Symphony' (1 May 1914, vol. lv pp. 310–11).

# Bibliography

**Section A: Primary Unpublished Sources**

1) The British Library
   Additional 41570–41574 : F. G. Edwards Papers
   —        54793    : The Macmillan Archive
   —        55236    :  —
   Egerton    3090–3097  : F. G. Edwards

2) Daily Telegraph Archive

3) Elgar Birthplace Museum [Broadheath]

4) Hereford and Worcester Record Office [HWRO]

5) The Times Archive


**Section B: Published Contemporary Sources**

*Books*

[Place of publication is London unless otherwise indicated]

Balfour A. J.: *Decadence.* (CUP 1908).
Barnett J. F.: *Musical Reminiscences and Impressions.* (Hodder and Stoughton 1906).
Banister H. C.: *George Alexander Macfarren: His Life, Works and Influence.* (Bell 1891).
Bennett J.: *Forty Years of Music, 1865–1905.* (Methuen 1908).
———. *Leeds Triennial Musical Festivals. Analytical Programmes 1880/83/86.* (No publisher given, 1886).
———. *A Story of Ten Hundred Concerts: being a Short Account of the Origin and Progress of the Monday Popular Concerts.* (Chappell 1887).
Bennett Sterndale J. R.: *The Life of William Sterndale Bennett.* (CUP 1907).
Berger F.: *Reminiscences, Impressions and Anecdotes.* (Sampson Low 1913).

Blaikie Murdoch W. G.: *The Renaissance of the Nineties*. (Moring 1911).

Boughton R. and Buckley R. R.: *Music Drama of the Future*. (Reeves 1911).

Brown J. D. & Stratton S. D.: *British Musical Biography: A Dictionary of Musical Artists, Authors and Composers, Born in Britain and its Colonies*. (Da Capo Press 1897/1977).

Buckley R. J.: *Sir Edward Elgar*. (Lane 1905).

Burkhardt J.: *The Civilisation of the Period of the Renaissance in Italy*. 2 vols (Kegan Paul 1878).

Chorley H.: *Autobiography, Memoirs and Letters*. 2 vols (Bentley 1873). [Compiled by H. G. Hewlett.]

———. *Thirty Years' Musical Recollections*. 2 vols (Hurst & Blackett 1862).

———. *Modern German Music: Recollections and Criticisms*. 2 vols (Smith & Elder 1854).

———. *The National Music of the World*. (Ed.) H. G. Hewlett (Sampson Low 1880).

Colles H. C.: *Grove Dictionary of Music and Musicians*. 3rd edition 5 vols (Macmillan 1927).

———. *The Oxford History of Music* vol vii – Symphony and Drama 1850–1900. (OUP, Oxford 1934).

Crowest F. J: *Phases of Musical England*. (Remington 1881).

Cumberland, Gerald [C. F. Kenyon]: *Set Down in Malice*. (Grant Richards 1919).

Cummings W. H.: *Purcell*. (Sampson Low 1881).

Davison H.: *Music in the Victorian Era: From Mendelssohn to Wagner, Being the Memoirs of J. W. Davison*. (Reeves 1912).

Edwards H. S.: *History of the Opera*. (Allen 1862).

———. *The Life of Rossini*. (Hurst & Blackett 1869).

———. *Personal Recollections*. (Cassell 1900).

Engel C.: *An Introduction to the Study of National Music*. (Longmans 1866).

———. *The Literature of National Music*. (Novello 1879).

Fox Bourne H. R.: *English Newspapers: Chapters in the History of Journalism*. 2 vols (Chatto & Windus 1887).

Findon B. W.: *Sir Arthur Sullivan and his Operas*. (Sisley 1908).

Frost H. F.: *Schubert*. ('The Great Musicians', Sampson Low 1881).

Fuller Maitland, J. A.: *Brahms*. ('New Library of Music' ed. E. Newman, Methuen 1911).

———. *A Door-Keeper of Music*. (Murray 1929).

———. *English Music in the Nineteenth Century*. (Grant Richards 1902).

———. (ed): *Grove's Dictionary of Music and Musicians*. 2nd edition 5 vols (Macmillan 1904–10).

———. *Henry Purcell 1658–96*. (Fratelli Bocca Editori, Torino 1895).

———. *Joseph Joachim*. ('Living Masters of Music' ed. R. Newmarch, Bodley Head 1905).

———. *Masters of German Music*. (Osgood McIlvane 1894).

———. *The Music of Parry and Stanford: An Essay in Comparative Criticism*. (Heffer 1934).

———. *The Musician's Pilgrimage: A Study in Artistic Development*. (Smith, Elder 1899).

———. *The Oxford History of Music vol iv: The Age of Bach and Handel*. (Oxford OUP 1902).

———. *Schumann*. (Sampson Low 1884).

———. *The Spell of Music: An Attempt to Analyse the Enjoyment of Music*. (Murray 1926).

———. 'Sullivan', *Cornhill Magazine* vol. x Jan.–Jun. 1901 pp. 300–309.

Galloway W. J.: *Musical England*. (Christopher 1910).

———. *The Operatic Problem*. (Long 1902).

Goddard J.: *The Deeper Sources of the Beauty and Expression of Music*. (Reeves 1906).

———. *Musical Development*. (Goddard & Co. 1868).

———. *The Philosophy of Music: A Series of Essays*. (Boosey 1862).

———. *Reflections upon Musical Art*. (Goddard & Son 1893).

Graeme E.: *Beethoven: A Memoir*. (Griffin 1870).

Graves C. L.: *All the Papers: A Journalistic Review*. (Pitman 1914).

———. *Hubert Parry: His Life and Works*. 2 vols (Macmillan 1926).

———. *The Life and Letters of Sir George Grove*. (Macmillan 1903).

———. *Post-Victorian Music*. (Macmillan 1911).

Grove G. (ed): *Dictionary of Music and Musicians 1450–1889*. 4 vols (Macmillan 1879–1889).

———. *Music in England. The Proposed Royal College of Music*. (Murray 1882).

———. *The Royal College of Music*. (Clowes 1883).

Gruneisen C. L.: *The Opera & the Press*. (Hardwicke 1869).

Hanslick E.: *The Beautiful in Music*. Translated by G. Cohen. (Novello 1891).

Hatton J.: *Journalistic London*. (Sampson Low 1882).

Haweis H. R.: *Music and Morals*. (Strahan 1871).

Hervey A.: *Masters of French Music*. (Osgood McIvane 1894).

Hogarth G.: *Musical History, Biography & Criticism: A General Survey of Music*. (Parker 1835).

Hueffer F.: *Richard Wagner and the Music of the Future*. (Chapman & Hall 1874).

————. *Musical Studies*. (Adam & Black 1880).

————. *Richard Wagner*. (Sampson Low 1881).

*Half a Century of Music in England 1837–87: Essays Towards a History*. (Chapman & Hall 1889).

Hullah F. R.: *Life of John Hullah*. (Longmans 1886).

Jackson H.: *The Eighteen Nineties*. (Grant Richards 1913).

Johnstone A.: *Musical Criticism*. (Manchester University Press 1905).

Joyce F. W.: *The Life of the Reverend Sir F. A. Gore Ouseley*. (Methuen 1896).

Klein H.: *Thirty Years of Musical Life in London 1870–1900*. (Heinemann 1903).

————. *Musical Notes: An Annual Critical Record of Important Musical Events*. 3 vols 1886/7 (Carson & Comerford 1888); (Novello 1889 & 1890).

Latham M.: *The Renaissance of Music*. (Stott 1890).

Legge R. & Hansell W. E.: *Annals of the Norwich and Norfolk Triennial Music Festivals, 1824–93*. (Jarrold 1896).

Liszt F.: *Pages Romantiques*. (Alcan, Paris 1912).

Lunn H.: *Musings of a Musician*. (Cocks 1854).

Mackenzie A. C.: *A Musician's Narrative*. (Cassell 1927).

Marx A. B.: *The Music of the Nineteenth Century & Its Culture*. Trans A. H. Wehran. (Cocks 1855).

Mitchell C.: *The Newspaper Press Directory*. (Mitchell 1858).

Newman E.: *Elgar* (Bodley Head 1906).

————. (ed): H. F. Chorley: *30 Years' of Musical Recollection*. (Knopf New York/London 1926).

————. *Testament of Music*. (ed) H. van Thal (Putnam 1962).

Parry C. H. H.: *Studies of the Great Composers*. (21st edn Routledge 1887/1950).

————. *The Art of Music*. (Kegan Paul 1893).

————. *The Music of the Seventeenth Century* (The Oxford History of Music vol 3, OUP 1902).

————. *Summary of the History and Development of Medieval and Modern Music*. (Novello 1905).

————. *Johann Sebastian Bach: The Story of the Development of a Great Personality*. (Putnam 1909).

————. *College Addresses delivered to the Students of the Royal College of Music*. (ed) H. C. Colles. (Macmillan 1920)

Pater W.: *Studies in the History of the Renaissance*. (Macmillan 1873).

Peabody C.: *English Journalism*. (Cassell, Petter & Galpin 1882).

Riemann H. & Shedlock J. S. (trans.): *Dictionary of Music*. (Augener 1893).

Runciman J. F.: *Purcell*. (Bell 1909).

Ruskin J.: *Queen of the Air: Being A Study of the Greek Myths of Cloud and Storm.* (Smith & Elder 1869).

Schmitz Oscar A. H. / Herzl H. (trans.): *The Land Without Music.* (1914 – new ed 1918: Jarrolds 1926).

Schumann R.: *Music and Musicians: Essays and Criticisms.* Edited & translated F. R. Ritter (Reeves 1877).

———. *Schumann On Music.* (Dover, Minneola New York 1988. Translated & ed by H. Pleasants.

Sell H.: *Sell's Dictionary of the World's Press.* (Sell's 1883–1914). [In 29 volumes 1883–1914.]

Shaw G. B.: *The Perfect Wagnerite: A Commentary on The Ring of the Niblungs.* (Grant Richards 1898).

———. *Music in London 1890–94.* 3 vols (Constable 1932).

———. *London Music in 1888–89.* (Constable 1937).

Simcoe H. A.: *Sullivan v. Critic, or Practice v. Theory: A Study in Press Phenomena.* (Simpkin, Marshall, Hamilton Kent & Co. 1906).

Smyth E.: *Impressions That Remained.* 2 vols (Longmans 1920).

Smythe-Palmer A.: *The Ideal of a Gentleman.* (Routledge 1908).

Stanford C. V.: *Interludes, Records and Reflections.* (Murray 1922).

———. *Pages from an Unwritten Diary.* (Arnold 1914).

———. *Studies and Memories.* (Constable 1908).

——— & Forsyth C.: *A History of Music.* (Macmillan 1916).

Streatfeild R. A.: *The Case of the Handel Festival.* (No publisher given 1897).

———. *Modern Music and Musicians.* (Methuen 1906).

Sullivan Arthur: *About Music: An Address Delivered in the Town Hall, Birmingham, on the 19th October 1888.* (Birmingham and Midland Institute, Birmingham 1888).

Symon J. D.: *The Press and its Story* (Seeley & Service 1914).

Thibaut A. F. J.: *On Purity in Musical Art.* Translated W. H. Gladstone (Murray 1825/1877).

Wagner R. / Dannreuther E. (trans): *Beethoven.* (Reeves 1880).

— / Ashton Ellis W. (trans): *Prose Works.* 8 vols (Kegan Paul 1892–99).

Wakefield A. M. (ed): *Ruskin on Music.* (Allen 1894).

Walker E.: *A History of Music in England.* (OUP, Oxford 1907).

Walzel O.: *German Romanticism.* (1914 Putnam ed 1932). Translated by E. Lussky.

Weber Carl M. von: *Writings on Music.* (CUP, Cambridge 1981).Translated by M. Cooper and edited by J. Warrac

Weber Max M. von: *Carl Maria von Weber: The Life of an Artist.* 2 vols (Chapman & Hall 1865) Translated by J. P. Simpson.

Wilde O.: *Interludes* (Osgood & McIlvane 1891).

Willeby C.: *Masters of English Music.* (Osgood McIvane 1893).

Wyndham Saxe H.: *Arthur Sullivan*. (Bell 1903).

———. *August Manns and the Saturday Concerts: A Memoir and a Retrospect*. (Walter Scott 1909).

——— & G. L'Epine: *Who's Who in Music*. (Pitman 1913).


*Articles, Chapters & Essays*

Anon. [Baughan E. A.?]: 'An Interview with Sir Edward Elgar', *Daily News* 25 Mar.1904.

———. [Bennett J.?]: 'The Golden Legend in Berlin', *MT* Jun.1887.

———. [Edwards F. G.]: 'Edward Elgar', *MT* Oct.1900.

———. [Lunn H.?]: 'English Opera', *MT* Mar.1873.

———. [Lunn H.?]: 'English Opera', *MT* May 1882.

Baughan E. A.: 'Edward Elgar: An Appreciation', *Daily News* 12 Mar.1904.

Bennett J.: 'Anton Dvorak', *MT* Apr.1884.

———. 'Critics I Have Known', *MT* Jun.1899.

———. 'Critics I Have Known', *MT* Jul.1899.

——— 'Critics I Have Known', *MT* Oct.1899.

———. 'English Music', *DTel* 8.Dec.1908

———. 'English Music in 1884', *MT* Jun.1884.

———. 'Robert Schumann', *Pall Mall Gazette* 30 Nov.1868.

———. 'The Drift of Modern Music', *MT* Jul.1873.

———. 'The Influence of Handel on Music in England', *MT* Jul.1877.

———. 'Victorian Music', *MT* Jan.–Jul. & Sep. –Dec.1897.

———. 'Wagner', *MT* Jan.–Dec.1890, Jan.–May & Jul.–Dec.1891).

Buckley R. J.: 'Dr Edward Elgar', *Daily Dispatch* 22 Sep. 1903.

Corder F.: 'Professor Macfarren on Richard Wagner', *MT* Nov.1883.

Cordova de R.: 'Dr Edward Elgar', *Strand Magazine* May 1904 vol. xxvii pp. 537–44.

Cumberland G.: 'First Impressions No. 1: Sir Edward Elgar', MW 16 Dec.1905.

———. 'A Day with Sir Edward Elgar', *MW* 15 Jan.1906.

Finlay M.: 'The Stradivarius', *Strand Musical Magazine* Apr.1897 vol. v pp. 204–7.

Frost H. F.: 'The Future of Opera', *MT* Oct.1884.

Fuller Maitland J. A.: 'Sullivan', *Cornhill Magazine* vol. x Jan.–Jun.1901 pp. 300–9.

Grove G.: 'The Royal College of Music', *Strand Musical Magazine* Feb.1895 vol. i pp. 83–89.

Hervey A.: 'Music during the Victorian Age', *Strand Musical Magazine* Jun.1897 vol. v pp. 323–336.

Lessmann O.: 'Otto Lessmann on Dr Edward Elgar', *MT* Jan.1901.

Lunn H.: 'A Musical Congress', *MT* Jul.1866.

———. 'A Musical Utopia', *MT* Jan.1879.

———. 'An Autumn Gossip on Music', *MT* Oct.1863.

———. 'Drawing-Room Music', *MT* Nov.1866.

———. 'Free and Cheap Concerts for the Poor', *MT* Jun.1879.

———. 'Musical Grievances', *MT* Mar.1866.

———. 'Musical Ignorance', *MT* Nov.1868.

———. 'Patronage', *MT* Jun.1877.

———. 'Popular Music', *MT* Dec.1878.

———. 'The London Musical Season', *MT* Sep. 1863.

———. 'The London Musical Season', *MT* Aug.1885.

———. 'The Music of the Future', *MT* May 1868.

Mackenzie A. C.: 'The Royal Academy of Music', *Strand Musical Magazine* vol. i Jan.1895 pp. 4–10.

'Musicus' [Legge R.]: "Sir Edward Elgar OM at Home', *DTel* 6 Jan.1912.

Newman E.: "Elgar's Violin Concerto', *MT* Oct.1910.

Runciman J. F.: 'English Music in the Nineteenth Century', *Saturday Review* 13 Jan.1900.

———. 'Musical Criticism and the Critics', *Fortnightly Review* 1894 vol. lvi pp. 170–83.

Stanford C. V.: 'Mr Hubert Parry's Judith', *Fortnightly Review* 1888 vol. xliv pp. 537–45.

———. 'Some Aspects of Musical Criticism in England', *Fortnightly Review* 1894 vol. lv pp. 826–31.

Ular M.: 'Sir Edward Elgar Talks of Musical Criticism', *Chicago Sunday Examiner* 7 Apr.1907.

Wilde O.: 'The Critic as Artist' (In Wilde O.: *Interludes*).

Zedlitz von M. A.: 'Interviews with Eminent Musicians. No. 3 – Sir Arthur Sullivan', *Strand Musical Magazine* Mar.1895 vol. i pp. 169–74.


*Newspapers & Periodicals*

[More specific references are provided for some publications in Appendix B]


The *Athenaeum* 1833–1914

*Concordia* 1875–6

The *Daily Telegraph* 1855–1914

The *Monthly Musical Record* 1871–1914

The *Morning Post* 1850–1914

The *Musical Times* 1844–1914

The *Musical World* 1847–1891 and 1905–6

*The Times* 1850–1914.

## Section C: Secondary Sources

*Books*

Allott M. & Super R. H. (eds): *Mathew Arnold. (*OUP, Oxford 1986).

Anderson R.: *Elgar.* ('The Dent Master Musicians', S. Sadie (ed); Dent 1993).

Ashton R.: *Little Germany: German Refugees in Victorian Britain.* (OUP, Oxford 1989).

Bantock M.: *Granville Bantock: A Personal Portrait.* (Dent 1972).

Bashford C. & Langley L. (eds): *Music and British Culture 1785–1914. Essays in Honour of Cyril Ehrlich.* (OUP 2000).

Belsey C.: *Critical Practice.* ('New Accents' Series, Methuen 1980).

Benoliel, B.: *Parry before Jerusalem.* (Ashgate, Aldershot 1997).

Bledsoe R.: *H. F. Chorley: A Study.* (Ashgate, Aldershot 1998).

Boyes G.: *The Imagined Village: Culture, Ideology and the English Folk Revival.* (Manchester University Press, Manchester 1993).

Brown T. A.: *The Aesthetics of Robert Schumann.* (Owen 1969).

Bujic B. (ed.): *Music and European Thought, 1851–1912.* (CUP, Cambridge 1988).

Chadwick O.: *The Secularization of the European Mind in the Nineteenth Century.* (CUP, Cambridge 1975).

Charlton P. : *John Stainer and the Musical Life of Victorian Britain.* (David & Charles 1984).

Coleridge-Taylor A.: *The Heritage of Samuel Coleridge-Taylor.* (Dobson 1979).

Colls R. & Dodd R. (eds): *Englishness, Politics and Culture 1880–1920.* (Croom Helm, Beckenham 1986).

Dahlhaus C.: *Aesthetics of Music.* (CUP, Cambridge 1982). Translated by W. Austin.

———. *Foundations of Music History.* (CUP, Cambridge 1983).

———. *Realism in Nineteenth-Century Music.* (CUP, Cambridge 1985). Translated by M. Whittall.

Ellis K.: *Music Criticism in Nineteenth-Century France: 'La Revue et Gazette Musicale'.* (CUP, Cambridge 1995).

Engell J.: *The Creative Imagination: Enlightenment to Romanticism.* (Havard University Press, Cambridge Mass. 1981).

Ehrlich C.: *The First Philharmonic: A History of the Royal Philharmonic Society* (Clarendon Press, Oxford 1995).

———. *The Music Profession in England since the Eighteenth-Century: A Social History.*
(Clarendon Press, Oxford 1985).

———. *The Piano: A History.* (Clarendon Press, Oxford 1990).

Fowler R.: *Language in the News: Discourse & Ideology in the Press.* (Routledge 1991).

Fubini E.: *The History of Music Aesthetics.* Translated by M. Hatwell. (Macmillan 1964/90).

Furst L. R.: *Romanticism.* (Methuen 1969/1976).

Girouard M.: *The Return to Camelot: Chivalry and the English Gentleman.* (Yale University Press 1981).

Griffiths D. (ed): *The Encyclopedia of the British Press.* (Macmillan 1992).

Haskell H. (ed.): *The Attentive Listener: Three Centuries of Music Criticism.* (Faber 1995).

Harker D.: *Fakesong: The Manufacture of British 'Folk Song', 1700 to the Present Day.* (Open University Press, Milton Keynes 1985).

Harris M. & T. O'Malley (eds): *Studies in Newspaper and Periodical History.* (Greenwood Press, Westport Mass. 1993, 1994 & 1995).

Hawkes T.: *Structuralism and Semiotics.* (Methuen 1977).

Hobsbawm E. & Ranger T. (eds): *The Invention of Tradition.* (CUP Cambridge 1993).

Holub R. C.: *Reception Theory: A Critical Introduction.* (Methuen, 1984).

Houghton W. E.: *The Victorian Frame of Mind 1830–70.* (Yale University Press, New Haven 1957).

———. (ed) : *The Wellesley Index to Victorian Periodicals, 1824–1900.* 3 vols (University of Toronto Press, Toronto 1966–79).

Howes F.: *The English Musical Renaissance.* (Secker & Warburg 1966).

Hughes M. & Stradling R. A.: *The English Musical Renaissance 1840–1940: Constructing a National Music.* (Manchester University Press, Manchester 2001).

Hurd M.: *Vincent Novello & Company.* (Granada 1981).

Hutchings A.: *Church Music in the Nineteenth Century.* (Jenkins 1967).

Hyatt King A.: *William Barclay Squire 1855–1927. Musical Librarian* (The Bibliographical Society 1957).

Jacobs A.: *Arthur Sullivan: A Victorian Musician.* (OUP 1984 & Ashgate, Aldershot 1992).

Jones A.: *Powers of the Press.* (Scolar, Aldershot 1996).

Karpeles M.: *Cecil Sharp: His Life and Work.* (Routledge 1967).

Kennedy M.: *Portrait of Elgar.* (OUP 1968/82).

Koss S. E.: *The Rise and Fall of the Political Press in Britain.* 2 vols (University of North Carolina Press, 1981/1984).

Kramer L.: *Music as Cultural Practice 1800–1900.* (University of California Press, 1990).

Laurence D. H.: *Shaw's Music: The Complete Musical Criticism of Bernard Shaw.* 3 vols (The Bodley Head).

Lee A. J.: *The Origins of the Popular Press in England, 1855–1914.* (Croom Helm 1976).

Leppert R.: *Music and Image.* (CUP 1988).

Leppert R. & McClary S.: *Music and Society: The Politics of Composition, Performance and Reception.* (CUP, Cambridge 1987).

Longyear R. M.: *Nineteenth-Century Romanticism in Music.* Third Edition (Prentice Hall, Englewood Cliffs NJ 1988).

Macdonald H.: *Berlioz.* (Dent 'The Master Musicians Series', ed S. Sadie 1982).

MacDougall H. A.: *Racial Myth in English History.* (Harvest House, Montreal & University Press of New England 1982).

Machann C. & Burt F. D. (eds): *Matthew Arnold: In His Time and Ours.* (University of Virginia Press, Charlottesville 1988).

Maine B.: *Behold These Daniels: Studies of Contemporary Music Critics.* (Brown 1928).

———. *Elgar, His Life and Works.* 2 vols (Bell 1933).

———. *The Glory of English Music.* (Wilmer 1937).

Marsden G. (ed.): *Victorian Values: Personalities & Perspectives in Nineteenth Century History.* (Longman 1990).

Musgrave M.: *The Musical LIfe of the Crystal Palace.* (CUP, Cambridge 1995).

Monk R. (ed.): *Edward Elgar: Music & Literature.* (Scolar Press, Aldershot 1990).

———. (ed.): *Elgar Studies.* (Ashgate, Aldershot 1993).

Moore J. N.: *Edward Elgar: A Creative Life.* (OUP 1984).

———. *Edward Elgar: The Windflower Letters.* (Clarendon Press, Oxford 1989).

———. *Elgar and His Publishers: Letters of a Creative Life.* 2 vols (OUP 1987).

Newman G.: *The Rise of English Nationalism: A Cultural History 1740–1830.* (Weidenfeld & Nicholson 1987).

Newman V.: *Ernest Newman: A Memoir.* (Putnam 1963).

Norris C.: *Deconstruction: Theory & Practice.* (Methuen 1982).

———. (ed.): *Music and the Politics of Culture.* (Lawrence & Wishart 1989).

Norris G.: *Stanford, the Cambridge Jubilee and Tchaikovsky.* (David & Charles 1980).

Pirie P. : *The English Musical Renaissance.* (Gollancz 1979).

Plunket Greene H.: *Charles Villiers Stanford.* (Arnold 1935).

Porte J. F.: *Sir Charles V. Stanford.* (Kegan Paul 1921).

———. *Sir Edward Elgar.* (Kegan Paul 1921).

Powell R.: *Edward Elgar: Memories of a Variation.* (Ashgate, Aldershot 1994).

Rainbow B.: *The Land Without Music: Music Education in England 1800–60 and its Continental Antecedents.* (Novello 1967).

Reardon B. M. G.: *Religious Thought in the Victorian Age: A Survey from Coleridge to Gore.* Second Edition (Longman 1995).

Reed D.: *The Popular Magazine in Britain and the United States 1880–1960.* (British Library 1997).

Reid C.: *The Music Monster: A Biography of J. W. Davison, Music Critic of 'The Times' of London.* (Quartet Books 1984).

Rowse A. L.: *Matthew Arnold: Poet & Prophet.* (Thames & Hudson 1976).

Schafer R. Murray: *E. T. A. Hoffman and Music.* (University of Toronto Press, Toronto and Buffalo 1975).

Scholes P. A.: *The Mirror of Music 1844–1944: A Century of Musical Life in Britain as reflected in the Pages of 'The Musical Times'.* 2 vols (Novello 1947).

Shannon R.: *The Crisis of Imperialism 1865–1915.* (Paladin 1976).

Shattock J. & Wolff M. (eds): *The Victorian Periodical Press* (Leicester University Press, Leicester 1982).

Stansky P. : *On or About December 1910: Early Bloomsbury and Its Intimate World.* (Harvard University Press 1996).

Stradling R. A. & Hughes M.: *The English Musical Renaissance 1860–1940: Construction and Deconstruction.* (Routledge 1993).

Stradling R. A, Newton S. & Bates D. (eds): *Conflict and Coexistence: Nationalism and Democracy in Modern Europe.* (University of Wales Press, Cardiff 1997).

Sturrock J.: *Structuralism and Since: From Levi Strauss to Derrida.* (OUP 1979).

Sullivan A. (ed.): *British Literary Magazines: The Romantic Age, 1789–1836.* (Greenwood Press, Westport Mass. 1983).

————. *British Literary Magazines: The Victorian & Edwardian Age, 1837–1913.* (Greenwood Press, Westport Conn. 1984).

Taylor R.: *Robert Schumann: His Life & Work.* (Panther 1985).

Temperley N. (ed): *Blackwells History of Music in Britain: The Romantic Age 1800–1914.* (Blackwell 1981).

The Times, The Office of: *The History of the Times.* vol 3 (1947).

Thomas K. (ed): *Victorian Thinkers.* (OUP, Oxford 1993).

Trend M.: *The Music Makers: Heirs and Rebels of the English Musical Renaissance, Elgar to Britten.* (Weidenfeld & Nicholson 1985).

Vann J. D. & Van Arsdel R. T. (eds): *Victorian Periodicals: A Guide to Research.* (Modern Language Association of America, New York 1978).

Vaughan Williams U.: *RVW: A Biography of Ralph Vaughan Williams.* (OUP 1964).

Watson D.: *Liszt*. (Dent 'The Master Musicians' 1985).

Weber W.: *Music and the Middle-Class: The Social Structure of Concert Life in London, Paris and Vienna 1830–48*. (Croom Helm 1975).

Weinstock H.: *Rossini: A Biography*. (Knopf, New York 1968/Limelight, New York 1987).

Wiener J. H.: *Papers for the Millions: The New Journalism in Britain, 1850s to 1914*. (Greenwood Press, Westport, Conn. 1988).

Wiener M.: *English Culture and the Decline of the Industrial Spirit, 1850–1980*. (Penguin 1985).

Williams K.: *The English Newspaper: An Illustrated History to 1900*. (Springwood Books 1977).

Young G. M.: *Early-Victorian England, 1830–65*. (OUP, Oxford 1934).

Young P. : *Alice Elgar: Enigma of a Victorian Lady*. (Dobson 1978).

———. *Elgar OM*. (White Lion Publishers 1955/73).

———. *A Future for English Music and Other Lectures by Sir Edward Elgar*. (Dobson 1968).

———. *George Grove 1820–1900: A Biography*. (Macmillan1980).

———. (ed): *Letters of Edward Elgar*. (Bles 1956).

Zon, B.: *Music & Metaphor in Nineteenth-Century Musicology*. (Ashgate, Aldershot 2000).

*Articles and Essays*

Baylen J. O.: 'The British Press, 1861–1918'. (In Griffiths D. (ed.): *Encyclopedia of the British Press*).

Bujic B.: 'Nationalist Sentiments as Factors Determining some 19th-Century Critical Standards in Music'. (*History of European Ideas* 1993, vol. xvi pp. 677–82).

Collini S.: 'Arnold'. (In Thomas K.: *Victorian Thinkers*).

Dent E. J.: 'Music in Early-Victorian England, 1830–65'. (In G.M. Young, *Early-Victorian England, 1830–65*. vol. ii).

Ehrlich C. & Russell D.: 'Victorian Music: A Perspective'. (*Journal of Victorian Culture* Spring 1998, vol. iii pp. 111–122).

Herzog P. : 'Music-Criticism and Musical Meaning'. (*Journal of Aesthetics and Art Criticism* 1995, vol. liii pp. 299–312).

Houghton W. E.: 'British Periodicals of the Victorian Age: Bibliographies and Indexes'. (*Library Trends* 7 (4) 1959).

Hughes M.: 'The Duc D'Elgar: Making a Composer Gentleman'. (In Norris C. (ed.): *Music and the Politics of Culture*).

———. 'Lucifer of Music'. (In Stradling R. A, Newton S. & Bates D. (eds): *Conflict & Coexistence*).

Hurd M.: 'The Immortal Hour' (Liner-Note Hyperion CDA 66101/2).

Jeffries S.: 'Beyond Jerusalem'. (*The Guardian* 7 August 1997).

Jones S.: 'Attic Attitudes'. (In Marsden G. (ed): *Victorian Values*).

Krummel D. W.: 'Searching and Sorting on the Slippery Slope: Periodical Publication of Victorian Music'. (*Notes* March 1990, pp 593–608).

Landow G. P. : 'Ruskin'. (In Thomas K. (ed.): *Victorian Thinkers*).

Langley L.: 'The Musical Press in Nineteenth-Century England'. (*Notes* March 1990, pp 583–592).

Le Quesne A. L.: 'Carlyle'. (In Thomas K. (ed.): *Victorian Thinkers*).

McVeigh S.: 'The Society of British Musicians (1834–65) and the Campaign for Native Talent'. (In Bashford & Langley (eds): *Music & British Culture, 1758–1914*).

Rich, P. : 'The Quest for Englishness'. (In Marsden G. (ed.): *Victorian Values*).

Weber W.: 'Miscellany vs Homogeneity: Concert Programmes at the Royal Academy and the Royal College of Music in the 1880s'. (In Bashford & Langley (eds): *Music & British Culture, 1785–1914*).

*BBC Radio 3 Programmes*

(Writer, title, date)

Hughes M.: 'Elgar and the English Class System'. (26 Jul. 1990).

———. 'Elgar and Academe'. (21 Jul. 1991).

———. 'Elgar and his Patrons'. (3 Jul. 1992).

———. 'Elgar and the Press'. (20 Jan. 1995).

# Index

Chapter and chapter-section references are given in bold type